MR. CAPOTE'S DANCE

PLEASE PRESENT THIS CARD FOR ADMITTANCE

PARTY OF THE CENTURY

THE FABULOUS STORY OF TRUMAN CAPOTE
AND HIS BLACK AND WHITE BALL

Deborah Davis

TRADE PAPER
PRESS

Trade Paper Press
An imprint of Turner Publishing Company
Nashville, Tennessee
www.turnerpublishing.com

Party of the Century : The Fabulous Story of Truman Capote and His Black and White Ball

Design and composition by Navta Associates, Inc.

Library of Congress Cataloging-in-Publication Data:

Davis, Deborah, date.
    Party of the century : the fabulous story of Truman Capote and his black and white ball / Deborah Davis.
        p. cm.
    Includes bibliographical references and index.
    ISBN 978-0-471-65966-2 (cloth : alk. paper)
    ISBN 978-0-470-09821-9 (paperback)
    1. Capote, Truman, 1924-1984. 2. Balls (Parties)—New York (State)—New York—History—20th century. 3. New York (N.Y.)—Social life and customs—20th century. 4. Capote, Truman, 1924-1984—Friends and associates. 5. Authors, American—20th century—Biography. 6. Plaza Hotel (New York, N.Y.)—History. I. Title.

PS3505.A59Z64 2006
813'.54—dc22
[B]

2005025149

Printed in the United States of America

10 9 8 7 6 5 4 3 2

For my family

Contents

Acknowledgments

When I started to research the Black and White Ball, I imagined that unearthing material from the 1960s would be easier than excavating the 1880s, as I did in my previous book. I was surprised to discover that recent history can be more elusive than the distant past. Consequently, I am extremely grateful to the many eyewitnesses whose vivid memories helped to bring this extraordinary moment in 1966 to life. Special thanks to the delightful Elizabeth Hylton and Susan Payson Burke for their invaluable assistance, sage advice, and constant good humor. Thanks as well to Adolfo Sardiña, Don Bachardy, Ann Birstein, Bill Berkson, Kenneth Paul Block, Joanne Carson, Peter Duchin, Joe Evangelista, Tom Fallon, Kitty Carlisle Hart, Ashton Hawkins, Kenneth Jay Lane, Robert Launey, Wendy Lehman, Karen Lerner, Al Maysles, Kay Meehan, Arthur Schlesinger, Jean Harvey Vanderbilt, Kay Wells, and Richard Winston.

I am indebted to biographer Gerald Clarke for his magnificent books about Truman Capote and for his generosity. My thanks to Alan U. Schwartz and the Truman Capote Literary Trust; George J. Gillespie III and the Katharine Graham Estate; William Stingone, Wayne Furman, and Tom Lisanti of the New York Public

Library; Phyllis Magidson of the Museum of the City of New York; Phyllis Collazo, Marilyn Cevino, and CJ Satterwhite of the *New York Times*; Eric Russ of Fairchild Publications; and Caroline Graham, Jay Cantor, Amy Fine Collins, Jean Palmieri, Michael Stier, Renee Zulueta, and Curt Gathje, who graciously shared his impressive knowledge of the Plaza Hotel.

At Wiley, my deepest appreciation to my extraordinary editor, Tom Miller, and his able assistant, Juliet Grames. At the Harvey Klinger Agency, my thanks to Harvey and to my dear friend Wendy Silbert. Finally, at home, where all good things happen and wishes come true every day, I am grateful to my husband, Mark Urman; my mother, Jean Gatto; and my children, Oliver and Cleo, for their love, faith, patience, and support.

Introduction

I WAS A TEENAGER IN PROVIDENCE, RHODE ISLAND, WHEN I FIRST heard of Truman Capote's Black and White Ball. On Monday, November 28, 1966, the day of the party, I listened to a radio announcer deliver an animated account of the sudden frenzy that had taken over New York City. Capote's guests were arriving from all over the world to attend his highly anticipated masked ball at the Plaza Hotel. Limousines carried socialites and celebrities to last-minute appointments, clogging the streets. Hairdressers fashioned elaborate coiffures for hundreds of clients whose heads were filled with thoughts of the festivities to come. Designers placed finishing touches on gowns and masks that had been weeks in the making. Even though the party was still hours away and the weather was wet and punishing, spectators crowded outside the Plaza to be among the first to see the guests arrive.

I wished, Cinderella-like, for one of those coveted invitations to the ball. The night came and went, along with my fantasy. Yet the memory stayed with me until one day I asked myself the questions that transformed an adolescent's reminiscence into a journalistic pursuit. How did an event hosted by a writer, as opposed to a movie star, a political leader, or a member of a royal family, command the kind of attention usually associated with premieres, inaugurations, and coronations? What compelled the guests—the most famous, talented, and sophisticated people in the world—to throw themselves into their pre-party preparations with the enthusiasm of children getting ready for their first Halloween? And why, at the age of fourteen, did I even know about a party that was miles—worlds—away, and that had not yet happened?

I learned that 1966 was the year of Truman Capote. In January, Random House had published *In Cold Blood*, Capote's revolutionary "nonfiction novel" about the murder of the Clutter family in Kansas. The extraordinary success of this book, combined with Capote's unequaled talent for self-promotion, propelled him to the front and center of the cultural scene. He was a serious writer and had been for many years, but he was also a celebrity. A *bal masqué*, Capote decided, would be the perfect way to celebrate his good fortune. He composed his guest list in a black-and-white school composition book, deliberating over who would be included and who would be denied entry, and he refused to reveal who was on the list and who was not. Prospective guests prayed that they would be among the chosen. The more exclusive the evening became, the more important it was to be there.

Movie stars, politicians, intellectuals, journalists, socialites, literary lions, millionaires, royalty, and even ordinary folks like Capote's doorman from the U.N. Plaza and his eleven *In Cold Blood* friends from Kansas were invited to rub elbows in the same place at the same time. Traditionally, Hollywood, Washington, and New York rarely intersected. Capote's party changed all that, and not just for one night.

The lucky invitees who made the cut were given seven weeks to prepare. Caught up in Capote fever, they scrambled to find appropriate outfits and perfect masks, preferably ones that were stunning or witty or made some sort of fashion statement. If they cared about making an entrance—and most of them did—their preparations had to be exhaustive.

Because of this mania, the Black and White Ball was headline news long before the first invitation went out, the first masked guest entered the Plaza, or the first photograph was snapped. Gossip columnists smelled a hot story the moment Capote announced his intention to host a masked ball for his nearest and dearest friends. In their pre-party coverage, they wrote about the guest list, the décor, the menu, and the masks, offering insider information to all those outsiders who were not among Capote's "intimates," the select 540 names on the list.

When the night finally arrived, the party was a great success. The details were reported faithfully by newspapers, magazines, and television and radio broadcasts the world over. If the Black and White Ball was famous even before it happened, it became legend in the decades that followed. Throughout the 1960s, the '70s, the '80s, and the '90s, magazines such as *Vogue*, *Esquire*, and *Vanity Fair* continued to run stories about this extraordinary night, searching for reasons why the event was a cultural and sociological benchmark. With every description and photograph, the party's significance increased. Pundits analyzed it, and fashion layouts celebrated it.

The ball was also a window into a bright and beckoning world. The 1960s, a decade often defined by images of Jackie Kennedy's sunglasses, James Bond's martinis, Andy Warhol's soup cans, and Mary Quant's miniskirt, were a time of high style and high expectations. Life seemed more glamorous then—sex was sexier, success more attainable. Even the moon, as the space program promised, was within reach for the very first time.

Yet many issues in this era were more serious than the rising and falling of hemlines or rockets. The war in Vietnam, the civil rights movement, women's liberation, and the unprecedented coming-of-age of seventy million teenagers, many of whom were eager for a revolution, created an atmosphere of discontent and instability. The night of the party, there was a great contrast between the glittering and carefully ordered world inside the ballroom and the simmering social and political revolution outside.

Every party, large or small, begins with its host, and Truman Capote was uniquely qualified to conceive and execute an event that would make social history. He called it "an act of imagination." A consummate stylist, Truman gave the ball the kind of attention and care he usually lavished on his prose. But it was the needy little boy in him, "about as tall as a shotgun and just as noisy," who wanted to throw "the most wonderful party New York has ever seen." He succeeded beyond his dreams.

1966

"I'm beside myself! Beside myself! *Beside myself!*" This chant, often accompanied by a series of agile handstands, was usually the way Truman Capote expressed excitement. He certainly had reason to be excited tonight. Truman was sitting on top of the world. Even though he owned a high-priced apartment with a spectacular view of the other side of Manhattan, he had checked into the Plaza, his favorite hotel, because he was hosting a party there that evening. Not an ordinary 1960s dress-up-and-toss-back-a-cocktail-affair. It was a fabulous *bal masqué* to celebrate the extraordinary success of his new book, *In Cold Blood*.

"Mr. Truman Capote requests the pleasure of your company at a Black and White Dance," the invitation read. The tasteful white card, bordered in yellow and orange, had an immediate effect on its recipients. With it in hand, they would spend weeks and bundles of money frantically preparing for a party that promised to be the event of the year.

Truman, thrilled to have elicited such an enthusiastic response, was even more delighted by the reactions of those who were not invited. Wounded and disgruntled supplicants called constantly, begging, demanding, and rudely offering to purchase the coveted invitation. Truman had stopped answering the telephone, left the city, and declared that he was officially incommunicado.

His hiatus from society refreshed him, and he was now eager to greet the "nearest and dearest" friends he expected to see in the ballroom: Frank and Mia, Tallulah, Andy, Swifty, Norman, Cecil, and Lynda Bird. No last names required. Jackie, Bobby, and Teddy sent regrets, but Rose and Eunice were coming. Elizabeth and Richard were out of town, working on a movie, as were Audrey and Mel. Yet there would be no shortage of celebrities in the room. Truman knew everyone who was anyone.

He was dressed in a classic black tuxedo. Truman usually added an outrageous touch or two—a flamboyant scarf or a whimsical hat—to his outfits. Not tonight. His hillbilly-turned-socialite mother had taught him to dress appropriately—conservatively—for high society. This evening, his only offbeat accessory was a small black domino mask from F.A.O. Schwarz.

The guests weren't expected until 10 p.m. Truman watched as crowds of paparazzi photographers and bystanders gathered in front of the Plaza in the misty early evening, ignoring the rain as they jockeyed for the best vantage points from which to witness the arrivals. He mentally ran through his schedule for the next few hours. He and Katharine "Kay" Graham, the president of the *Washington Post*, his friend and tonight's guest of honor, would make an appearance at a small dinner party hosted by his friends Bill and Babe Paley. After downing a quick cocktail, they would return to Kay's room at the Plaza for a light meal, then head for the ballroom to form the receiving line. So many details to remember, despite his five months of careful preparation.

Tonight, Truman was able to banish thoughts of another hotel room, one that was dark, empty, and ominous. It was the cause of a nightmare that had plagued him for most of his life. In it, his mother had locked him up in some rented room and gone out until the wee hours with her gentleman callers. Frightened and lonely, he had cried all night, but no one came to his rescue. Decades later, these memories of abandonment still had the power to trigger the "mean reds," a sudden attack of acute depression described by Holly Golightly, Truman's most appealing and most vulnerable character, in *Breakfast at Tiffany's*.

Tonight, abandonment was not an issue for the host, who was preparing to greet hundreds of friends and important members of the press in New York City's most beautiful ballroom. One final preen in the mirror, and Truman Capote was ready for his close-up.

1

A Lonely Boy

LILLIE MAE FAULK WAS A BEAUTIFUL TEENAGE ORPHAN WHO LIVED unhappily in the small, sleepy town of Monroeville, Alabama. Her cousins, the Faulks, had given her and her siblings a home after their mother died. Yet Lillie Mae was blind to the virtues of rural life—the relaxed pace and the familial atmosphere of this convivial southern community. A thrill-seeking teenager, she was eager to put the drawls and the dirt roads of Monroeville behind her. In 1923, escape came in the form of twenty-five-year-old Arch Persons, a fast-talking bachelor with a reputation as a ladies' man. His two biggest assets were his easy charm and a flashy sports car. Dazzled by both, Lillie Mae imagined driving off to the big cities of her dreams with her Prince Charming by her side. Her wish came true when she and Arch married impulsively soon after they met, and they set off on a grand honeymoon.

Before Lillie Mae could congratulate herself on her brilliant escape, she was confronted by some unpleasant realities. Arch was not wealthy, not even comfortable: his finances were so shaky that he ran out of money during their two-week honeymoon and was forced to send his petulant bride right back to her relatives in Monroeville. Lillie Mae was smart enough to know that she was worse off than before the marriage: when she was single, life still held possibilities. The only sensible course of action was to seek a divorce. Nature intervened, however, and the unhappy bride became an even unhappier expectant mother. She told her relatives she wanted an abortion but never pursued the idea. Instead, she reconciled with Arch and went to live with him in New Orleans. On September 30, 1924, Lillie Mae gave birth to Truman Streckfus Persons, a beautiful, blond, doll-like infant.

She may have hoped their beatific baby boy would transform her troubled marriage into a domestic fairy tale, but Lillie Mae and Arch were not made for each other. He was a con man, always in pursuit of a dollar and another big deal. She was a social climber, propelled by unrealistic aspirations and an uncontrollable libido. Both were far too self-absorbed to make any room in their lives for a child.

Arch and Lillie Mae lived in a series of hotel rooms across America while they pursued their latest fantasies and get-rich-quick schemes. Even as a baby, Truman had been aware of his mother's assignations with other men. He was conscious of the handsome strangers who visited their rooms when Arch was away, images that remained with him for the rest of his life. His parents thought nothing of locking their young son in a hotel room while they went out for the night. Truman suffered this upsetting itinerant life, moving constantly until the age of six. At that point Lillie Mae, replicating her own childhood, deposited him with the Faulks in Monroeville. The town she had been so desperate to leave became her son's first real home.

Monroeville was slow and hot, especially in the summer, when the temperature often shot up to over a hundred degrees. Residents rose in the darkness before dawn to take advantage of the cooler morning hours. By midday, when the heat was unbearable, women put away their aprons, bathed, dressed in freshly pressed frocks, and assumed their positions on the front porch, ready to visit and share the news of the day. The telephone switchboard was a source of up-to-the-minute information. Three operators alternated shifts, reporting the latest rumors as they connected calls.

Meals, served unfailingly three times a day, were happy occasions. Breakfast, lunch, and dinner consisted of large, varied menus of southern specialties, including fried chicken, catfish, pork chops, grits, biscuits, and pies. On Sundays, the intimate family circle expanded to include others. Relatives, friends, and even newcomers and strangers were invited to partake of steak with brown gravy, always served on the family's best china.

Gossip was everyone's favorite pastime. Gossip was not merely an exchange of information: it was a form of storytelling, a diversion, equivalent to listening to the radio or going to the picture show. The population was so closely knit that there were new dramas every day, with neighbors playing all the lead roles.

When Truman settled into the Faulks' large, wood-framed house on South Alabama Avenue, his life changed completely. He became a member of a community steeped in history and tradition. Jennie Faulk, the forceful matriarch of the family, owned a dry goods store in the town square, the center of the Monroeville universe. Her sister Callie worked in the shop as a bookkeeper, while her other sister, Sook, kept house for the family and was assisted by an outspoken black cook, Aunt Liza. Bud, their brother, was quiet and withdrawn.

Young Truman might have been lonely in this landscape filled primarily with old people, but Sook proved to be an ideal companion. Although she was a grown woman, a childhood illness had left her shy—as people said at the time, "simple." She liked to stay close to home where she felt secure, and when Truman arrived, she became his devoted playmate. She called him "Buddy" after a childhood friend and took him on excursions through the woods to find herbs for the special dropsy medicine she brewed and sold for pocket money. When the weather was fine, they flew kites in the nearby fields. On cold days, they played in the attic, where they unpacked boxes of old clothes and mementos. Sook often dressed Truman in antique finery—evening gloves, stoles, and dancing slippers—and told him, "Don't you look like an elegant lady ready for the ball?"

The other members of the family were not as kind or playful as Sook. Truman described them many years later in his story "A Christmas Memory." "Other people inhabit the house," he wrote of the Faulks, ". . . and though they have power over us, and frequently make us cry, we are not, on the whole, too much aware of them." Together, Truman and Sook created a private world where they never had to feel like misfits or outsiders.

Small, white-blond, and extremely precocious, Truman did not blend in with the children of Monroeville, who eyed him with suspicion. A teacher said he looked like "a bird of paradise in a flock of crows." Truman was always woefully overdressed, thanks to Lillie Mae's misguided idea of an appropriate summer wardrobe for a seven-year-old boy on a country vacation. She filled his suitcase with city-slicker ensembles, including linen shorts that buttoned onto tailored shirts and a Hawaiian swimsuit with a matching jacket.

He was lucky to find an accepting friend in the house next door, a tomboy his age named Nelle Harper Lee. Truman made such an impression on Lee, who grew up to write the 1960 Pulitzer Prize–winning novel, *To Kill a Mockingbird*, that she based the character Dill on him. In her book, she described him as a "curiosity" with hair "stuck to his head like duckfluff." As soon as they started spending time together and discovered their mutual passion for books and spinning fantasies, the young neighbors were inseparable. He was a "pocket Merlin," Lee wrote, "whose head teemed with eccentric plans, strange longings, and quaint fancies."

Monroeville offered many diversions during the long, lazy summers they spent together. The pharmacy in the town square had a first-rate soda fountain. Hatter's Mill, a dilapidated old building located next to a cool body of water, was a favorite swimming hole. And a giant tree in Lee's yard served as a retreat where the two friends could hide from the world and play their elaborate games of pretend. They would be Tom Sawyer and Huck Finn adrift on the Mississippi until the next book they read dictated their new roles. Spinning tales came naturally to Truman, who, even as a child, recorded his observations and ideas in a journal. He enjoyed writing and was so confident about his early literary efforts that he entered a short story contest sponsored by a local newspaper.

His story, "Mrs. Busybody," was a candid account of the meddling ways of a local gossip. He hoped it would win him a pony from Alabama's *Mobile Press Register*. Instead, the story almost landed him in hot water because it was rumored that he had based his characters on Lee's parents. Truman pretended to be contrite and told people he had given up writing. He lied—he was writing constantly, using words and ideas to explore worlds that were otherwise inaccessible to a young boy.

Far away from their son, Lillie Mae and Arch were busily pursuing their separate lives. Lillie Mae fulfilled a lifelong dream of moving to New York City, where she supported herself by working as a restaurant hostess. Hoping to advance socially and financially, she resumed the search for her real Prince Charming. Arch sought advancement, too, but his improbable schemes were usually derailed by bad luck or his penchant for larceny. He could not resist passing a bad check when he needed cash. Consequently, Arch spent considerable time in jail.

Lillie Mae's prospects improved when she met Joseph Capote, a charming and successful Cuban businessman. They enjoyed a passionate relationship that seemed to have a future; he could provide her with the means to leave her hillbilly self behind. With her new man and her new situation came a new resolve. She asked Arch for a divorce, demanding custody of Truman.

It was an unreasonable request, considering how little time she had spent with her son. But courts were predisposed to keeping children with their mothers, even if the mother in question had demonstrated little maternal instinct. In September 1931, Lillie Mae won the divorce and custody of Truman. The judge ruled that he would spend nine months a year with his mother and the remaining summer months with his father. Instead of claiming her prize, Lillie Mae deposited Truman in Monroeville while she returned to New York City. Eventually, she promised, she would send for her son.

৩৶৹

One year later, Lillie Mae summoned Truman to his new home in New York. He had fantasized about this reunion for a long time and looked forward to living with his mother. Yet the transition from one world to another was quite difficult. Truman wanted to make sure his family and friends in Monroeville would remember him, so he decided to host a farewell party. According to his cousin Jennings Faulk Carter, Truman spent weeks planning the event and had definite, highly unconventional ideas for an eight-year-old boy. He invited his guests to attend a costume party in the evening, even though children in Monroeville did not normally entertain at night. The guest list was eclectic. Nelle, Jennings, and Truman's schoolmates were obvious choices. But Sonny Boular, a young recluse who was almost a man (and who would serve as the inspiration for the character Boo Radley in *To Kill a Mockingbird*), was an unusual addition. Truman even persuaded John White, a black field worker, to dress up in a white suit and oversee the apple-bobbing.

The evening was filled with spectacle and drama. Instead of wearing a mask, Truman painted his face to look like Fu Manchu and pinned a pigtail to his hair. His guests enjoyed the elaborate party games he invented. They consumed treats prepared by Sook and Aunt Liza and listened to music on Jenny Faulk's phonograph.

The most dramatic point of the evening was a surprise raid by the Ku Klux Klan. Local Klan members mistakenly believed that John White was a guest at the party. They took exception to the notion of a black man socializing with whites and decided to teach him a lesson with a rope. They seized a costumed guest they thought was John White, but it was the wrong person. When they pulled off their prisoner's mask, they found a terrified Sonny Boular. The Klansmen were lambasted by the townspeople for their foolish behavior, and they lost whatever tenuous standing they had in the community.

Truman was delighted. His party had been a success.

Truman soon left for New York as planned. Arch was still smarting over the loss of his son, and he appealed to the courts, testifying that his ex-wife was "fast" and irresponsible. There was mudslinging on each side. Arch's attempts to discredit Lillie Mae backfired when his own sordid state of affairs—his repeated run-ins with the law and his failure to pay child support—came to light. Neither parent was particularly qualified to raise a child, nor had they ever spent much time with their son, but Lillie Mae seemed the lesser of two evils, and the judge ruled against Arch. Lillie Mae married Joe and blocked Arch from any further custody attempts by convincing her new husband to legally adopt her son. At the age of nine, Truman Streckfus Persons became Truman Garcia Capote, a boy with a new name, a new address, and a new life.

Leo Lerman had no use for the lonely-child-in-Monroeville story that had become a stock part of Truman's history and claimed that he knew the exact moment when Truman first decided to host the ball. It was 1942, Lerman said, and he and "Marge" (his pet name for Truman, who playfully called him "Myrt") were fledgling writers taking a train to the artists' colony at Yaddo. Truman was largely unknown but supremely self-confident, and he bragged that when he was rich and famous, he'd entertain all of his rich and famous friends at a fabulous party.

Truman dismissed Lerman's yarn as nonsense. But Lerman was such an entertaining raconteur and his anecdote was so colorful that it was repeated everywhere—at cocktail parties, at dinner tables, and even in newspapers—during the weeks leading up to the ball, and it, too, became a stock part of Truman's legend.

2

Small Man, Big Dreams

AFTER A FALSE START IN A HOUSE IN BROOKLYN, THE CAPOTES moved into a spacious apartment on Riverside Drive in New York City. Lillie Mae had high social ambitions for herself and her family, so the first thing she did was change her name to "Nina," hoping her southern roots would not be apparent. Truman was enrolled at Trinity, a prestigious private school for wealthy New Yorkers. Nina discovered that she could change her name, but she couldn't change Truman. His eccentricities—his high voice, feminine good looks, and flamboyant ways—were as conspicuous in New York as they had been in Monroeville.

Nina decided that drastic measures were in order. She pulled Truman out of Trinity and sent him to St. John's, a military school in upstate New York, hoping the experience would make a man out of him. But uniforms and drill exercises did not whip Truman into shape. If anything, the all-male establishment encouraged him to be more outrageous, just in different ways. A year later, Truman was back in Manhattan, unchanged.

In 1939, Nina and Joe moved to the wealthy suburb of Greenwich, Connecticut, where Truman enrolled at the public high school. He was in the tenth grade but looked much younger. Greenwich, a homogeneous world, was an unlikely place for Truman to find soulmates, but he managed to find two significant friends there. Phoebe Pierce, a schoolmate, was an exotically beautiful teenager who shared his interest in writing. Like Harper Lee before her, Phoebe became Truman's constant companion and confidante. They traveled to Manhattan—the Emerald City for culture-starved suburbanites—to visit jazz clubs, see foreign films, and do anything that wasn't available in dreary Connecticut.

Truman found another unlikely friend in his English teacher Catherine Wood. Faculty members were rarely supportive of Truman, because he made no effort to hide his indifference toward schoolteachers and assignments. But "Woody," as Truman called her, was a perceptive woman who saw beyond his inattention and poor performance. She recognized that Truman had the temperament and the talent of an artist. With unwavering loyalty, Wood encouraged Truman to pursue his interests and predicted he would have a great future.

Contrary to what Nina had expected, suburbia was not an ideal place for her, either. She felt confined in their closely knit community, which turned out to be a glossier version of Monroeville, and she compensated for her disappointment by drinking too much. Eventually, Nina convinced Joe to move the family back to New York. This time, they settled into a Park Avenue apartment.

Truman had graduated from Greenwich High School and had no plans to go to college. Nina convinced him to repeat his senior year at the Franklin School in Manhattan to give some structure to his life. He went through the motions of being a student, dropping into classes when the mood struck him, but a more alluring world than high school beckoned.

Truman had a knack for networking. A friend at Franklin introduced him to Elinor Marcus, a teenager who lived on Park Avenue with her mother, stepfather, and sister, Carol. Truman visited Elinor after school one day, and, curious about the reclusive Carol, he impulsively climbed a ladder to spy on her through a transom window. Carol, stark naked, was outraged when she noticed an imp-like face peering into her bedroom. Yet Truman charmed her by complimenting her beautiful figure and pale, luminous skin, claiming that she looked as if she had been made on the moon. They bonded immediately. Like Truman, Carol had had a difficult childhood. Her mother had been a struggling young millinery model who placed her two daughters in foster homes while she set out to find a rich husband. She landed wealthy Charles Marcus, the cofounder of Bendix Aviation. His money enabled her to reclaim Carol and Elinor and set up housekeeping in a posh eighteen-room apartment. Carol was still a little stunned by her quick transition from rags to riches.

Truman and Carol, the precocious boy and the young beauty, were an odd couple physically, but they shared high spirits and an appetite for fun. Carol's best friends were Oona O'Neill, the daughter of the playwright Eugene O'Neill, and Gloria Vanderbilt, the heiress. The girls never seemed to have much supervision while they played at being adults, dressing up at night to tour the city's most exclusive nightclubs and restaurants. They wore their hair long and draped seductively over one eye, like the actress Veronica Lake. El Morocco and the Stork Club welcomed them because they were young, fresh, attractive, and wealthy.

ᘓᑎᘖ

Truman couldn't spend all of his time clubbing, though. In 1943, he landed a job as a copy boy at the *New Yorker*, the magazine that all writers aspired to. He considered the job an entry-level position and imagined working his way up to join the ranks of talented staffers and contributors such as James Thurber, Brendan Gill, and Dorothy Parker. Yet the reality was quite different, for he spent his time sorting cartoons and running errands. The work was boring; Truman often hid cartoons rather than go through the tedious process of filing them. He may have been a copy boy, but he refused to behave like one. Truman loved to impress his coworkers by ordering lunch from fancy restaurants like "21," a remarkable extravagance for an underpaid lackey. Everything about him—from his expensive lunches, high-pitched voice, and sassy banter to his elfin appearance—was unusual and completely out of place in the quiet, tweedy hallways of the *New Yorker*. One day the magazine's publisher, Harold Ross, saw Truman racing through the office in an oversized cape and asked, "What was *that?*"

Truman capitalized on the fact that he still looked like a young boy by seeking—and usually winning—the affections and the sympathies of older women. He turned his charms on Daise Terry, the *New Yorker*'s surly office manager, who never had a good word for anyone. Before long, she was his friend and protector. Much to the amazement of less resourceful copy boys, he and Terry often socialized together, teaming up for parties and the theater. Truman's offbeat charm and terrier-like persistence won over several *New Yorker* editors, too. He showed them samples of his writing and benefited from their advice.

Truman's stint at the *New Yorker* was becoming a little stale for him, so he may have been relieved when a disagreement with the poet Robert Frost cost him his job. Frost complained that Truman had behaved disrespectfully at a reading, walking out while the poet was presenting his work. Truman insisted that a leg cramp, not displeasure, had forced him to leave the room while Frost was speaking, but the damage had been done. Truman was fired—although he always said he'd quit.

Losing his job turned out to be a blessing. Truman was itching to write a novel and saw his sudden unemployment as a sign that it was time to get to work. There was a problem—he didn't have any money—so Truman asked Joe Capote to support him while he wrote, and his stepfather came through for him. For the next few months, Truman could devote himself to his art.

Truman knew what he wanted to write. He planned to tell the

story of a Fifth Avenue debutante's coming-of-age. He was familiar with the rarefied world of New York society through Nina, Carol, and his other glamorous young friends. Nina was obsessed with climbing the social ladder. Evenings on the town were field trips for Truman, who was a keen observer of people. He noticed every detail and remembered everything he saw. He wanted to recreate that world, with its evening gowns, perfume, and beguiling, long-haired young women, in his novel, which he would call *Summer Crossing*.

Instinctively, Truman knew he had to leave New York and all of its distractions if he was to pay serious attention to his writing. The best place to find peace and quiet was in Monroeville, where there wasn't much of anything else. Truman moved in with the Faulks and attempted to write the unhappy debutante's story.

In his tiny handwriting, he filled four composition books with the summer adventure of Grady McNeil, the seventeen-year-old daughter of a wealthy and socially prominent family in New York City. Her mother, Lucy McNeil, had high hopes that Grady would mature into a proper society matron. Her career would be launched with a spectacular debut party, then Grady would follow in the footsteps of her dutiful older sister, Apple, by settling down with an appropriate husband. But Grady dreamed of a more exciting future. She convinced her parents to let her stay home for the summer while they vacationed in Europe. On her own for the first time, she had an affair with a Jewish war veteran who worked as a parking lot attendant and made several impulsive decisions that negatively affected her future.

Truman moved the plot along and tried to create interesting problems and dramatic resolutions for his troubled characters. Despite his best efforts, though, he had a feeling that *Summer Crossing* was not working. He may have convinced himself that he knew all about high society, but his novel showed that he was an observer, not an insider. There was too much distance between Truman Capote and Grady McNeil for the story to be authentic.

Truman realized that the story he should be writing had nothing to do with a rambunctious debutante in New York City, so he decided to write a semi-autobiographical tale about a young boy who embarks on a thorny voyage of self-discovery when he moves in with eccentric southern relatives.

This time, Truman couldn't stop writing. The story, the characterizations, and the dialogue flowed through his pen with such ease that there were times he felt he was taking dictation. At the center of the book was Joel Knox, a lonely, somewhat effeminate twelve-year-old boy who, like Truman, found a home with an unusual collection of relatives in a small town in the South. Skully's Landing, the ramshackle mansion that becomes Joel's new home, and Noon City, the nearby town, were familiar turf to Truman. He exaggerated the gothic qualities of his character's situation to suit his story, giving Joel a stepmother who enjoys killing birds. Joel also has a paralyzed father and an uncle who dresses in drag and mourns the loss of his boxer lover. Yet Joel's psychological journey, as he matures from an uncertain boy to a young man with a strong sense of self and acceptance of his homosexuality, paralleled Truman's southern adventures. He called his new novel *Other Voices, Other Rooms*.

Truman discovered that he worked best at night, so he slept all day and wrote until the wee hours of the morning. His unusual work habits perplexed his hosts, who still adhered to the up-with-the-chickens, down-with-the-sun lifestyle Truman had known during his childhood visits to Alabama. Their conflicting schedules created difficulties. Since Truman needed privacy and freedom more than he needed security, he headed for New Orleans.

Truman found a small room in the French Quarter. He was completely at home there, although his strained finances dictated a spartan lifestyle. He stayed through Mardi Gras and early spring, the most delightful time in New Orleans, writing and working odd jobs. As the temperature rose, Truman wisely decided to return to New York, feeling confident and hopeful. *Other Voices, Other Rooms* was going well, and he also had some short stories that he wanted to sell to magazines.

Fortunately, 1945 was an excellent year for the magazine industry. During World War II, Americans depended on magazines for both information and entertainment. Readers came out of the war with an increased appetite for periodicals of all kinds, especially those enhanced by color and illustrations. The women's magazines, including *Harper's Bazaar, Vogue, Mademoiselle*, and *Cosmopolitan*, published high-quality fiction, usually in the form of short stories, and subscribers actually enjoyed reading literature alongside fashion and beauty layouts. *Mademoiselle* retained a full-time literary editor, George Davis, who had a reputation for being snobbish and tyrannical. Truman was not at all intimidated. As soon as he moved back to New York, he boldly presented himself at *Mademoiselle's* offices and arrogantly offered to wait in the reception area while Davis read his story submission. Davis rejected "The Walls Are Cold," Truman's tale of a spoiled rich girl who was a literary cousin to the heroine of the abortive *Summer Crossing*. Yet he was intrigued by Truman's oversized personality and raw talent, and he asked to see more of Truman's work.

Truman showed Davis "Miriam," a story about a lonely woman's encounter with a menacing little girl. The child in Truman's story turns out to be a figment of the woman's imagination, a supernatural doppelganger who raises questions about the myth of childhood innocence. Davis bought "Miriam" immediately and rushed it into an upcoming issue. The lead character was an effective tiny terror who may have served as the precursor to a whole subgenre of stories about ominous children, such as William March's *The Bad Seed*.

Editors at other magazines were impressed and eager to get their hands on anything by this fresh new talent. That year, *Story* and *Harper's Bazaar* bought short fiction by Truman. By early 1946, he was proclaimed "the most remarkable new talent of the year" by Herschel Brickell, the editor of the annual anthology *O. Henry Memorial Award Prize Stories*.

As much as Truman enjoyed his overnight success, he still needed to finish his novel. Several forces were working against him. He was living at home with his mother and stepfather, a troubled domestic situation that was exacerbated by Joe Capote's escalating financial problems. Nina drank too much and picked on her son when she was inebriated. She resented him for being too effeminate, too talented, and too different. Truman, who radiated confidence with other people, withered in the face of his mother's hostility. Their apartment was often a war zone, and Truman spent as little time there as possible, preferring to be out on the town with friends.

In 1946, New York City was a splendid place to have a good time. World War II was over, spirits were high, and the city had an air of optimism and opportunity. Most artists gravitated toward Greenwich Village. With its quirky architecture and bohemian Left Bank atmosphere, the Village had become a campus for young painters, writers, and musicians much like Paris in the nineteenth century. They migrated to its colorful, cobblestoned streets because rents were cheap, bookstores were plentiful, bars catered to intellectuals, and young women were reputed to be easy. The San Remo Bar on MacDougal Street was a popular hangout for such emerging talents as William Burroughs, Tennessee Williams, James Agee, Jackson Pollock, and Miles Davis, while the Welsh poet Dylan Thomas and his cohorts preferred the White Horse Tavern on Hudson Street. Smoke-filled clubs like the Village Vanguard offered alternative jazz music, while coffeehouses promoted poets and folksingers.

Truman knew this world and had several friends, Tennessee Williams among them, who were at its center. But Truman was not a supporter of the earthy downtown scene. Visions of "21," El Morocco, and the Oak Bar at the Plaza Hotel danced through his head. The twenty-one-year-old had a taste for glamour and took pleasure in deviating from the artistic stereotype of the time. Truman headed uptown and cleverly embraced any traits that distinguished him from his peers—his flamboyant personality, his almost feminine beauty, and his blatant, completely uncloseted homosexuality. Truman enjoyed emphasizing his southernism; he infused his speech with languid cadences and colloquialisms that set him apart from abrupt New Yorkers who rushed through their sentences and never thought to call anyone "magnolia." People were charmed into believing he was the person to know.

Truman collected friends carefully. Inevitably, one introduction led to another, until he had an impressive, far-reaching network of mentors, companions, and bright young things with whom to surround himself. His magazine contacts, including George Davis at *Mademoiselle* and Mary Louise Aswell, Carmel Snow, and Diana Vreeland at *Harper's Bazaar*, were enthusiastic supporters who repeated his name until it sounded familiar in all the right places.

Literary acclaim for his short stories brought him into contact with other celebrated writers, such as Carson McCullers, the author of *The Heart Is a Lonely Hunter*. Truman and Carson bonded because they were both from the South, and she used her connections to help him find an agent, Marion Ives, and a publisher, Random House, for *Other Voices, Other Rooms*. When it became imperative that Truman find a quiet place to finish his novel where he would not be subject to his mother's drunken rages, McCullers arranged for him to join her at Yaddo, a summer retreat for writers and artists located on a secluded estate in upstate New York.

At Yaddo, founded in 1900, days were quiet, as all residents worked in solitude in their cottages. But nights were lively and communal, filled with entertainment, drinking, dancing, and, for a lucky few, debauchery. The writers and the artists in residence were subject to the same sudden attachments—and breakups—experienced by children boarding at school or summering at camp.

Truman had strong feelings about his companions during his stay at Yaddo. He spent a lot of time with McCullers, but he was cross with Katherine Anne Porter, the essayist and short story writer, because she had an inflated ego and was a bad dancer who expected him to be her partner. He was most intrigued by Newton Arvin, a literature professor, critic, and biographer who taught American literature at Smith College. They were completely different types: Truman was outrageous and extroverted, while Arvin, at forty-four, was an older, buttoned-down academic who played hide-and-seek with his sexuality and was intensely private. They became lovers within forty-eight hours of their first meeting.

With its lush rose gardens, dense forests, and hidden pools, Yaddo was an idyllic setting for a new romance. Truman's tower room in the main house was directly above Arvin's bedroom and studio, making it easy for the lovers to spend the night together. Invigorated by Truman's lively personality and forthright appreciation of sex, Arvin loosened up in the course of the summer. Truman, in turn, received something he desperately needed at this critical juncture in his career: a formal education. "Newton was my Harvard," said Truman. The professor, who Truman boasted "reads Greek at the breakfast table," knew everything about literature, history, and all the subjects Truman had assiduously ignored while he was in school. Truman was ready to be a student.

Arvin introduced Truman to the American writers who were his specialties, Herman Melville, Nathaniel Hawthorne, and Walt Whitman, to name a few. Truman admitted to being bored by *Moby Dick*. Arvin encouraged his protégé, whom he affectionately called "Spooky," to sample other nineteenth-century writers, although Truman was not always favorably impressed. "Now Spooky," Arvin wrote admonishingly in a letter, "George Eliot's not a bore."

Truman was more interested in *Remembrance of Things Past* by Marcel Proust. He felt he had a great deal in common with the French writer. Both men had the eccentric work habit of writing while reclining in their small beds, both were fascinated by the behavior of people in high society, and both, though gay, sought out women as their closest friends and confidantes. Truman said of Proust, "I always felt he was a kind of secret friend."

Proust's special understanding of the rich and the famous would be helpful to Truman in twentieth-century New York, the world he was poised to enter and conquer. Like Napoleon, another small man with large ambitions, Truman envisioned an empire composed of many different parts. His "early adopters," the first people to embrace the new and the different, were the New York literati—the editors, the writers, and the readers who appreciated his short stories. But there were other frontiers ahead. He wanted to conquer New York's upper crust, Hollywood, and, eventually, Europe.

Truman came out of his summer at Yaddo with a reputation that was growing larger by the day. *Life* gave him the media's seal of approval by featuring him in an article about up-and-coming writers. He was called "the best-known unpublished novelist in America." His unusual name may have been difficult to pronounce—the tendency was to drop the "e"—but it was impossible to avoid.

Bennett Cerf, Truman's publisher at Random House, and his wife, Phyllis, jump-started the young writer's conquest of high society by welcoming the literary scene's newest prodigy into their elite circle. They were one of New York's power couples, and an invitation to their East Side townhouse was an indication that Truman had arrived. A presentable extra man was always an asset at smart dinner parties, but an outspoken and slightly wicked one was a treasure. Everyone loved Truman. Women surrounded him, amused and enchanted by his lively stories and fresh wit. His unusual appearance always sparked a reaction: upon seeing the oddly boyish writer in his dinner jacket, the writer Edna Ferber thought the Cerfs were trying to pass off their little boy as an adult. Whether Truman was viewed as a curiosity, a court jester, or a coveted confidant, he was on his way to becoming a regular on the social circuit.

Truman turned his attention to the West Coast. *Vogue* sent him to Los Angeles to write an article about contemporary Hollywood. He was welcomed by his friend Oona O'Neil, who had moved to Los

Angeles to pursue an acting career. She had abandoned that plan in 1943, when, at the tender age of eighteen, she married fifty-four-year-old Charlie Chaplin. The press jumped on the story, hoping to expose Oona as a gold digger or, at the very least, Charlie as a dirty old man. They failed: Oona called Chaplin "the love of my life," and they settled into happy domesticity, despite the fact that he had been embroiled in a paternity suit at the time of their marriage.

Truman's visit prompted the Chaplins to host a party in his honor. Their endorsement was invaluable. As he had experienced in New York, one introduction from the right person led to another, then another. Truman was no stranger to celebrities: his New York address book already boasted entries for Tallulah Bankhead and Marlene Dietrich. He was happy to tell his friends back home that he had made conquests of significant movie stars during his two-week stay. He visited Joan Crawford at her home, lunched with Greta Garbo at a studio commissary, and claimed he had spent the night with Errol Flynn. Since Truman had a tendency to exaggerate, it was difficult to separate truth from fiction, but his Hollywood anecdotes were so entertaining that veracity didn't really matter.

Truman had a lifelong love/hate relationship with Southern California. As much as he enjoyed Hollywood's superficial charms—wealth, climate, and access—he saw it as a place that lacked style and intelligence. Truman maintained, "It's a scientific fact that if you stay in California, you lose one point of your IQ every year." He may have had mixed feelings about California, but California was falling in love with him. Twenty-three eager customers in San Francisco placed orders for *Other Voices, Other Rooms* six months before it was expected to land in bookstores.

Other Voices, Other Rooms was published in January of 1948. The back cover of the book featured a provocative photograph of Capote. Most authors, especially those who consider themselves literary, make every effort to appear serious and professorial on their book jackets. Truman had something more theatrical in mind. In the picture, he reclined on a couch, his boyish bangs framing his enormous eyes while his hand rested languorously on his hip. He looked straight at the camera in a challenging, inviting, seductive manner. It was an eye-catching image that bordered on the lewd.

Random House used the photograph in an advertisement in the *New York Times*, along with the headline "This is Truman Capote. His amazing first novel marks the debut of a powerful new talent in American literature." The combination of the erotically charged photograph with the risqué material inside the book propelled *Other Voices, Other Rooms* to the *New York Times* best-seller list. On February 15, just a few weeks after it was published, the book debuted at number nine on the list.

Usually, it is difficult for a first-time novelist to get his book reviewed, but critics had anticipated Truman's novel for so long that they were eager to express their opinions. "The most discussed writer in New York literary circles today is a young novelist with the face and figure of a schoolboy," wrote Selma Robinson in *PM's Picture News*. "The most exciting first novel by a young American in many years," proclaimed the *New York Herald Tribune*. The writer Somerset Maugham called Truman Capote "the hope of modern literature." Various critics compared him to William Faulkner, Eudora Welty, Carson McCullers, Katherine Anne Porter, and even Oscar Wilde and Edgar Allen Poe. Truman was flattered and amused, confessing to a reporter that Gustave Flaubert, the author who was really his main influence, hadn't been singled out.

There were reviewers who thought the young literary god had feet of clay and found his novel forced, false, even decadent. The critic at the *New York Times*, for example, was dismissive. Truman was vulnerable to harsh words, all the more painful to him because his short stories had won uniform praise. Yet even detractors who were underwhelmed by Truman's writing had to agree that he was a genius at self-promotion. He understood that projecting the right image—especially one that captured the imagination of the press— was crucial to his success. The *Times's* critic may have been indifferent to Truman's book, but for months running, the *New York*

Times Book Review featured a section it called "Capote Corner," implying there was always something to say about the controversial young writer. One week, Truman put a new spin on his departure from the *New Yorker*. Never alluding to his contretemps with Robert Frost, he implied that he had quit his job because an hour-long lunch break was not enough time to enjoy a meal at "21." Another week, the *Times* actually noted that there was nothing to report. In an item that ran in April, the *Times* announced that Truman Capote had been invited by an "enraptured admirer" to finish his upcoming collection of short stories in a villa outside of Paris, where he would be attended by a retinue of servants. Truman wanted to be considered an artist, of course, but it was also important to him to be perceived as an insider—a player in the upper echelons of society. The "retinue of servants" may have been a fabrication, but it was great for his image.

After having been a guest at so many dinners and receptions, Truman decided to make his debut as a host. When he looked around, he saw that there were contradictory recipes for a successful party in New York. Leo Lerman, a popular magazine editor, hosted impromptu gatherings in his townhouse on the Upper East Side, serving what he called "nasty red wine," old biscuits, and pounds of cheddar cheese. Yet despite his atrocious refreshments, the most interesting people in the city flocked to his door. William Faulkner argued with Tennessee Williams in the living room. Singers, actors, artists, writers—Truman, Maria Callas, Marlene Dietrich, Marcel Duchamp, Cathleen Nesbitt—and dozens of others engaged in heated conversations on crowded stairwells, while their host, a bemused Lerman, often held court in his bed. In later years, the dancer Rudolf Nureyev could be found sitting on the bedroom floor discussing his upcoming ballet.

The atmosphere at the moneyed Bennett Cerfs' home was more formal and upscale. Phyllis Cerf carefully observed the rule that a dinner party should have an equal number of men and women. Edna Ferber, who dined frequently at the Cerfs' house, found the notion quaint and poked fun at it by pointing out that the guests were getting together to eat, not to mate. In these circles, menus, flowers, and wine selections were taken very seriously. Unlike Leo Lerman, dedicated hostesses like Phyllis Cerf actually kept careful records of the dishes they served so that their guests would not be subjected to the same meal twice.

Truman's first party fell somewhere between the bohemian get-togethers at Lerman's and the elegant evenings chez Cerf. He chose a fashionable address, Nina and Joe's apartment at 1060 Park Avenue. For his guest list, he simply invited everyone he knew, and it seemed that he knew everyone. Phyllis Cerf recalled seeing "everybody from Marlene Dietrich to Walter Winchell." Inexperienced at being a host, Truman summoned his guests without giving any thought to numbers, space, flow, or comfort. They fought their way in only to find there was no easy way out. It may not have been the best party, but Truman proved that at the age of twenty-four, he could put together a sensational guest list.

∞

That spring Truman traveled to Europe for the first time. He visited London, Paris, and Venice without the benefit of that mythical retinue of servants he mentioned in the *New York Times*. Hip Europeans knew all about *Other Voices, Other Rooms*, which enabled Truman to carve a comfortable niche for himself in the international artistic community. The English were curious about the notorious new writer from America who had posed so provocatively on his book cover. In London, Truman spent time with the artist and designer Cecil Beaton, the writer Evelyn Waugh, and the editor Harold Nicolson. In Paris, he visited the artist Jean Cocteau; Albert Camus, who was his editor; and the writer Colette, who gave him one of her prize paperweights, inspiring him to start his own collection.

He was a frequent guest at the Ile St.-Louis salon of Jenny Bradley, who became his literary agent in France. She had firsthand recollections of "sad-eyed" Proust and other important French writers who had frequented her salon. Truman then moved on to Venice, where he was so distracted by the exhausting social life and the potent martinis at Harry's Bar that he had to remind himself he was supposed to be working. He detoured to a quiet Italian village where he could concentrate on writing a collection of short stories.

Truman returned to America refreshed. He discovered that while he'd been having a good time abroad, Newton Arvin, still his lover of record, was having an affair at home. It seemed that Arvin had some reservations about their relationship. He was used to a quiet, solitary life, and there were times when he found Truman too young, too exuberant, and too exhibitionistic in matters of sexuality. Instead of cold-bloodedly breaking off their affair, Arvin sabotaged it by sleeping with Truman's close friend the writer Andrew Lyndon and writing about their encounters in his diary. Truman found out when, as Arvin expected, he sneaked a look at the diary. He and Arvin continued to see each other, but their affair was on the wane.

Arvin's betrayal was not a tremendous blow, because Truman was ready to move on, both personally and artistically. He called *Other Voices, Other Rooms* "a satisfying conclusion to the first cycle of my development." The same could be said of his first love affair with Arvin, his first entry into society, his first tour of Europe, and the other rites of passage he experienced at the time. The lonely little boy who spent his early years living in hotels, rooming houses, and households not his own was making a place for himself at the center of the world.

Truman's Swans

Throwing a party for himself when *In Cold Blood* was at the height of its success would have been seen as shameless self-promotion on Truman's part. He needed a suitable someone to serve as his guest of honor to make the occasion seem less egotistical. The logical place to find one was within his select circle of beautiful, socially prominent female friends. Truman prided himself on his ability to woo and win the affections of the most desirable women in the world. He quickly became their confidante, fashion and social advisor, and soulmate—whether helping to select a new hairstyle, lipstick, or lover, Truman had an uncanny talent for making himself indispensable.

He called these women his "swans," an apt description because they were usually gorgeous, graceful creatures with beautiful plumage. Truman was inspired to use the word *swan* by a passage he'd read in a nineteenth-century journal by Patrick Conway, a poetic young gentleman who wrote that he had seen "a gathering of swans, an aloof armada . . . their feathers floating away over the water like the trailing hems of snowy ball-gowns" and was reminded of beautiful women. Truman quoted these words in his introduction to the photographer Richard Avedon's book *Observations* and dedicated his entire essay to defining the attributes of a modern-day "swan."

"Of first importance," he wrote, "is voice, its timbre, how and what it pronounces." Swans should, of course, be clever, although he observed that "dumbness seldom diminishes masculine respect." In other words, some men liked stupid women.

According to Truman, one of the most important attributes a swan could have was money. "Authentic swans," he said, "are almost never women nature and the world has at all deprived. God gave them good bones; some lesser personage, a father, a husband, blessed them with that best of beauty emollients, a splendid bank account. Being a great beauty, and remaining one, is, at the altitude flown here, expensive." Money alone could never produce a swan—otherwise, there would be hundreds of them. A swan also had to have great personal style, as well as the confidence to make everyone believe in her superiority.

With his discerning eye, Truman found several remarkable women who fit this exacting description: Babe Paley, Gloria Guinness, Marella Agnelli, Slim Keith, C. Z. Guest, and Pamela Harriman. They were women of a certain age, mature beauties who had spent decades turning themselves into works of art. In 1966, fifty-four-year-old Gloria Guinness was the oldest of the swans and thirty-nine-year-old Marella Agnelli was the youngest. While they differed from one another in style, the fact that they each had an individual style was one thing they all had in common. Babe was precise and elegant; Gloria, fiery and spirited. Marella, a true Italian princess, was reserved and patrician, while C. Z. was a cool, classic, Boston blonde. Slim, nicknamed for her lean figure, was a western thoroughbred, while Pamela was a soft pink English rose.

Though each swan had a look and a style that was completely original, they all had one important accessory: a wealthy husband. The road to a brilliant marriage and those "waters of liquefied lucre," as Truman lyrically described the big bank account required to support swandom, was often long and arduous. For many of these swans, the most difficult part came after their I do's. One of life's greatest ironies was that happily ever after and pots of gold rarely came at the same time.

⊙⅄⊙

3

❖

Romance and Sadness

Truman was enjoying his status as prodigy, personality, and man-about-town, but his private life was in disarray. His relationship with Arvin was beyond repair. Never the ideal mother, Nina had hit a new low: her drinking was out of hand, and her behavior was so unpredictable that Truman never knew whether she would be kind or cruel. He escaped her "hectic, nerve-wracking influences," as he called Nina's attacks, by moving into a small apartment on New York's Upper East Side. For the first time, Truman had money, acclaim, and a little home of his own. The missing ingredient was someone to love.

Romance came one November night in the form of Jack Dunphy, a thirty-four-year-old writer with an unusual past. Dunphy was one of six children born to a poor Irish family in Philadelphia. He had dreamed of becoming a writer but had to settle for the more prosaic job of factory worker to support himself. He liked to dance, so he added variety to his colorless life by taking dancing lessons. No one was more surprised than Dunphy when he turned out to have real talent. He was such a good dancer that he was able to quit his job at the factory and find work as a chorus boy. His new profession introduced him to new people, including Joan McCracken, a charismatic young performer She and Dunphy were cast in the hit musical *Oklahoma*. Though her role was small, McCracken received rave reviews for being the girl who fell down and was hailed as a performer who was on her way up. Dunphy and McCracken married but were often separated because they were dancing in different shows.

Although dancing was a good way to make a living and a much better way to spend time than working in a factory had been, Dunphy's heart was never in it. During the long, lonely nights when he was on the road with a show, he concentrated on his first love, writing. He worked diligently on *John Fury*, a novel about the poor Irish world he had left behind in Philadelphia.

Dunphy interrupted his career to go off to Europe to fight in World War II. By the time he came home, he found that his wife had fallen in love with another man. They divorced, and Dunphy nursed his broken heart by experimenting with different kinds of relationships. As much as he enjoyed being with women, he was open to the idea of an affair with the right man.

Truman and Dunphy met at the home of their mutual friend Leo Lerman. For Truman, it was love at first sight. He thought that Dunphy, with his red hair, blue eyes, and lean dancer's body, was the most beautiful man he'd ever seen. Truman was also intrigued by Dunphy's reputation for being an interesting new writer. *John Fury* had been published right after Dunphy came home from the war. The book was called "a remarkable first novel, warm and strong" by the *New York Times*, whose reviewer praised Dunphy for his "compassion and restraint." Smart and fit, Dunphy was an irresistible combination of brains and brawn, and Truman made up his mind that he had to have this man. But he was unwilling to leave their shared future to chance. Truman was a highly superstitious person who practiced rituals to ward off disappointment and disaster. He assiduously avoided the number thirteen, rejecting hotel rooms that added up to that figure, and refused to board a plane that had two nuns as passengers. In matters of the heart, when Truman wanted someone as much as he wanted Dunphy, he cast a kind of spell. He told Gerald Clarke, his biographer, "If you want something badly enough, you'll get it, whatever it is. You've got to really want it, and concentrate on it for twenty-four hours a day, but if you do, you'll get it. I have never found that to be untrue."

Truman's magic was in full force that November night. Dunphy was charmed and suggested they see each other again. Their relationship progressed so quickly that by the end of the year, they were living together and planning a trip to Europe. Truman wanted to concentrate on his writing: he thought he would finish *Summer Crossing*, and Jack was working on a new book, too. They traveled to Tangier, where Cecil Beaton maintained a house, and later to the primitive little island of Ischia, off the coast of Naples. Truman and Jack set up housekeeping in airy, sun-bleached houses, often without electricity or other modern amenities, and they lived simply and worked happily without distraction.

With Jack by his side in their new surroundings, Truman was wonderfully productive, even monastic. In New York, his flamboyant behavior led people to believe he was hedonistic and undisciplined. But the real Truman was a serious artist who understood the value of a business plan. At twenty-four, he was ambitious in his aspirations, spartan in his work habits, and in control of his life. The writer Paul Bowles, who spent time with Truman in Tangier, observed that the young man's career "was like a carefully planned military campaign." Truman told Bowles that he hoped to write a travel book along the lines of the travel pieces he had done for magazines such as *Vogue* and the *New Yorker*, and he wanted to try his hand at writing plays. "The works he described in 1949 appeared, one after the other, over the years that followed," marveled Bowles. "They were all there in his head, like baby crocodiles waiting to be hatched."

Truman fussed with *Summer Crossing* but put it aside a second time to work on *Local Color*, a collection of travel essays, and *The Grass Harp*, a new book about his Alabama childhood. It was more fanciful than the gothic *Other Voices, Other Rooms*; *The Grass Harp* tells the story of Dolly Talbo, a determined older woman much like Truman's beloved Sook, who moves into a tree house to escape her tyrannical sister. Truman himself can be found in the character of Collin, a boy who stands by his cousin even when she drops out of society to create her own world.

In Ischia and the other places where Truman and Jack lived, when they weren't working, they were entertaining. Truman celebrated Jack's thirty-fifth birthday with an unusual beach party in Tangier. Truman planned every detail, including flowers, lanterns, Arabic music, and handsome serving boys. Guests drank champagne in a seaside grotto. The evening was a feast for the senses.

Truman wrote regularly to Andrew Lyndon, who had remained his friend; Leo Lerman, his editor; Robert Linscott; Bennett and Phyllis Cerf; and many others. In one very funny letter to the Cerfs, Truman outlined a new party game he had invented to pass the time. He called it IDC, or "International Daisy Chain." Like Six Degrees of Kevin Bacon but a little racier, the object of the game was to make a chain of names, each one connected by the fact that he or she has had an affair with the person previously mentioned. Truman was such an expert on sex and gossip that he was able to establish connections between the most unlikely people. His favorite IDC improbably linked the black performer Cab Calloway to Adolf Hitler by way of Marquesa Casmaury, Carol Reed, and Unity Mitford. Truman told the Cerfs that the composer Moss Hart and his wife, Kitty Carlisle Hart, would be wonderful at the game.

Truman finished *The Grass Harp*, and Random House published it in 1951. The book caught the eye of the Broadway producer Arnold Saint-Subber, whose most recent work, *Kiss Me Kate*, was enjoying a long, lucrative run. Saint-Subber wanted to produce a stage version of *The Grass Harp* and asked Truman to write the adaptation. Truman, always confident, agreed. The Broadway veteran Robert Lewis directed the show, and Truman's friend Cecil Beaton came from England to do the sets and the costumes. With such distinguished creative talent at the helm, *The Grass Harp* was poised to be a hit. It opened on Broadway in March of 1952 and closed only one month later.

A disappointed Truman tucked the failure behind him. He was still enthusiastic about trying new forms of writing and was intrigued when the producer David O. Selznick, who was shooting a movie in Rome, asked him to rewrite the dialogue for a troubled screenplay. The project, *Stazione Terminal*, was a love story starring Montgomery Clift and Selznick's wife, the actress Jennifer Jones. Despite the filmmakers' impressive credits—Selznick had produced *Gone with the Wind*, *Rebecca*, and *Spellbound*, and the fact that the director Vittorio De Sica was one of Europe's most exciting talents—the combination of Hollywood glamour and Italian neorealism was disastrous. The movie, ultimately titled *Indiscretion of an American Wife*, failed miserably at the box office. But Truman came out of the experience with two new friends and fans, the Selznicks.

When Selznick was asked to recommend a screenwriter for John Huston's upcoming movie *Beat the Devil*, also to star Jennifer Jones, he instantly named Capote, pointing out that he was "easy to work with, needing only to be stepped on good-naturedly, like the wonderful but bad little boy he is, when he starts to whine." Huston engaged Truman for the project, which would shoot in Italy. Humphrey Bogart, *Beat the Devil*'s leading man, raised an eyebrow when he saw the diminutive writer for the first time. Truman was used to this kind of response and knew how to deal with it. Strong for his size, Truman vanquished the manly actor in a round of arm wrestling. Bogart dubbed him "Caposey" and they became friends.

Truman and Jack continued to enjoy the expatriate life in Italy, spending the summer of 1953 in the village of Portofino. Both writers had an agenda: Truman was working on a stage version of *House of Flowers* for Saint-Subber, while Jack was laboring over a new novel. Truman's favorite diversion at this time was the company of his friend Cecil Beaton. Like Truman, Beaton was a man with an insatiable appetite for good gossip who had perfected the art of collecting the right friends. Their combined address books listed everyone of note in America, Europe, and the rest of the globe. Beaton's visit to Portofino in August was a pleasant end to the summer.

The months that followed were gloomy. Truman was unhappy with his work on the play and feeling adrift.

The New Year, 1954, began in the worst possible way. Truman was in Paris when he received a devastating telephone call from his stepfather. Nina, who had become more depressed, alcoholic, and emotionally unstable over the years, had killed herself by taking an overdose of sleeping pills. Truman flew to New York immediately and stayed by Joe Capote's side for the funeral. Given the painful relationship he had with his mother, Truman experienced conflicting feelings about her death: grief, but also a sense of relief that they would no longer disappoint each other.

On her dark days, Nina was subject to self-destructive spells of melancholy and rage, but friends recalled a lighter side of this complicated southern belle. According to them, Nina *really* knew how to throw a party. The floors at the Capotes' Park Avenue apartment had been waxed to a high sheen and ready to receive the eclectic combination of writers, editors, society figures, and other personalities who were Nina's guests. Doris Lilly, Truman's friend and the author of *How to Marry a Millionaire*, fondly remembered lavish buffets of southern specialties all prepared by Nina.

Yet another one of Truman's friends recalls a story about a party of Nina's that went awry. On the day it was to take place, Joe Capote, who was walking a financial tightrope, was accused of embezzlement. None of the guests showed up.

4

Babe Paley and High Society

IN JANUARY 1955, EXACTLY ONE YEAR AFTER NINA'S SUICIDE, TRUMAN met a woman who was the goddess he had always imagined—and desperately wanted—his mother to be. Barbara "Babe" Paley was beautiful, refined, stylish, and completely at home in the rarefied worlds of money, power, and high society. The daughter of Harvey Cushing, a Boston surgeon, Babe had been brought up by her ambitious mother, Katherine, to be beautiful and gracious and to marry well. She and her two sisters, Betsy and Minnie, indeed married well, and more than once, prompting *Life* to devote an article to the Cushing brides and their excellent catches.

Betsy, the middle sister, was the first to accomplish their mother's goal. She married James Roosevelt, the son of President Franklin Roosevelt, and enjoyed and exploited the excellent Washington connections that came with the union. President Roosevelt adored her, and she often served as his hostess at White House functions. Eventually, her marriage foundered, and she divorced James. But Betsy was not single for long. She married Jock Whitney, one of the wealthiest men in the world, and set up housekeeping at Greentrees, his Westchester estate.

Minnie, the eldest and the most spirited of the sisters, "did just as well with only one try," according to the article in *Life*, by marrying the multimillionaire Vincent Astor. She tried to enjoy her good fortune, like Betsy, but found it impossible to repress her bohemian ways. Eventually, Minnie engineered an ingenious escape from her stifling marriage by finding a new wife for Vincent. She invited Brooke Marshall, an appealing young widow, to spend the weekend at the Astor estate. Minnie encouraged her husband to spend time alone with Brooke, hoping nature would take its course. After one leisurely automobile ride together, Vincent was smitten with Brooke and granted Minnie her freedom. She, in turn, married James Fosburgh, an artist who was reputed to be homosexual. There were similar rumors about Minnie, who had lived with a well-known lesbian before she married Vincent Astor.

Babe, the youngest of the remarkable Cushing sisters, was also the most beautiful. Slender, fine-boned, innately elegant, and very self-possessed, she appeared to be lit from within.

In 1939, Babe moved to New York City, where she found an editorial job at *Vogue*. Prince Charming came in the form of Stanley Mortimer, the handsome young scion of a family with superior bloodlines. They married in 1940 and set up housekeeping in a brownstone in New York City. Unlike her sisters, Babe did not have access to unlimited sums of money. What she lacked in funds, though, she made up for in taste. She was the embodiment of style—the darling of fashion designers and photographers—and she often modeled for *Vogue* because she looked dazzling in the latest fashions. The couple had two children, Amanda and Tony, and seemed to enjoy a storybook marriage until Mortimer joined the Navy. When he came home in 1945, he was not the sunny young man who had left. Like so many of his contemporaries, he was unable to forget his wartime experiences and drank to fight his depression. In 1946, Babe stopped trying to maintain the illusion of

Babe Paley at President Eisenhower's inaugural ball in 1950.

domestic bliss and divorced her husband. Though she continued to work at *Vogue*, which always employed a roster of beautiful socialites in the 1940s, money was tight. Babe had to be practical. There was only one way to improve her circumstances: she had to follow in the footsteps of her older sisters and marry a very rich man.

Babe's close relationship with Betsy and Minnie placed her in a good position to meet suitors with deep pockets. The Astors and the Whitneys socialized with the wealthiest people in the world. In fact, Betsy and Jock's estate was right next door to Kiluna, the home of William S. Paley, the millionaire president of the Columbia Broadcasting Company, and his wife, Dorothy. Paley was rich, powerful, and decisive—an inveterate collector who was determined to own the best of everything. When he saw Babe, the most elegant and aristocratic woman in the room, he wanted her for his consort. He used his considerable clout to end his marriage quickly so that he could claim his brand-new trophy wife.

Dorothy was whisked away to Reno, a fashionable destination for desperate divorcees-in-waiting, where she received an enormous financial settlement to expedite their divorce. The *New York Daily News* reported, "This rough and ready divorce capital gasped tonight when it learned that William S. Paley, president of the Columbia Broadcasting System, had given his wife a check for $1.5 million as a settlement in the divorce she obtained today." The newspaper also noted that Paley was planning to marry Mrs. Barbara (Babe) Mortimer, "a willowy socialite eyeful from Boston." The gossip columns were correct. Paley and Babe were married in July of 1947, only four days after his divorce from Dorothy was final. According to *Life*, Harvey Cushing's daughters "were married to a combined fortune of some $125 million," and Babe would be "quite able to live in the manner to which the sisters have become accustomed."

The newlyweds went to Europe on an extended honeymoon. When they returned to New York, Babe settled into the full-time and extremely challenging position of being Mrs. William S. Paley. With geishalike dedication, she managed multiple households, organized calendars, and personally attended to the countless details that went into satisfying her fastidious husband. Paley had impossibly high standards: Babe was known to go to great lengths to secure the foods he liked, even running out to Kennedy Airport to pick up game she had ordered especially for him. His meals— sometimes as many as eight a day—had to be perfect. His shirts had to be ironed in a certain way. Babe was responsible for making herself perfect, too. Paley expected her to look beautiful all the time: Babe would rise early to "put on her face," as she called it, reluctant to let her husband see her without makeup.

There were children to manage, too. The Paleys started out with four from their first marriages, Tony and Amanda Mortimer and Hilary and Jeffrey Paley, and they went on to have two children, William and Kate Paley, early on in their marriage. Their offspring were tucked away at Kiluna, while Babe and Paley moved back and forth between the "farm" and a small, exquisitely decorated pied-à-terre in the St. Regis Hotel. Paley's fortune paid for everything, but Babe was the one who did all the work, planning, overseeing, and anticipating her husband's every desire.

The Paleys' residences included a home in Round Hill, Jamaica, where they frequently vacationed with friends. David Selznick and his wife, Jennifer Jones, were invited to spend a long weekend there in January 1955. Selznick was one of Paley's closest friends, so the producer felt comfortable asking if he could bring his friend Truman along for the vacation. Paley agreed instantly, assuming the guest would be Harry Truman and delighted by the prospect of entertaining a former president. When the travelers met at the airport to board his private jet, Paley was mystified by the appearance of a short, vivacious young man. Selznick introduced him as "Truman Capote, our great American writer."

As far as Paley was concerned, the diminutive interloper was the wrong Truman, and his odd voice and eccentric appearance did not make him very likable. In the time it took for the plane to reach Jamaica, however, Truman had charmed everyone on board, including his hosts. "Babe looked at him and Truman looked at her, and they fell instantly in love," recalled Jennifer Jones, who was the tiniest bit jealous that her friends were so interested in each other.

Meeting Babe was an important moment for Truman. She was a gracious and elegant woman of style who had become social royalty, everything his mother had aspired to. Truman and Babe became inseparable. They were best friends, unafraid to tell each other their deepest secrets and confess their insecurities. For all her money and social position, Babe felt unsure about her education. Truman took over with the enthusiasm of a Henry Higgins, giving his beautiful protégé reading lists and insisting that they discuss the works of Proust and other authors he admired.

Babe taught Truman, too. She was his finishing school, they joked, and no one knew better than Babe how to navigate the treacherous waters of high society. Her expertise covered a variety of topics; always write a thank-you note immediately after—in fact, the very night of—a party or a dinner; be an attentive listener; give every room a personal touch by mixing expensive decorations with dime-store discoveries; choose gifts that have special meaning for the recipient. If Truman had any rough edges, in Babe's hands, they were polished to a smooth finish.

Mutual enhancement, however, was not the focus of their relationship. Truman and Babe genuinely loved each other. He called her "one of the two or three great obsessions of my life."

Truman's reverence for all things Paley extended to Bill. He was one of the most powerful businessmen in the country, and Truman was flattered to become a valued member of his innermost court. Truman had an open invitation to Kiluna Farm and to the Paleys' home in Jamaica, estates that Babe ran like five-star hotels. In the British tradition, guests were attended by servants who did everything for them. Truman also accompanied the Paleys abroad, vacationing in castles and on yachts, usually at their expense. At home in New York City, Truman lunched with Babe at exclusive restaurants such as Lafayette, the Colony, and Quo Vadis. These places were so popular with the rich and famous that photographers stood outside at lunchtime, snapping pictures of the beautifully dressed and coiffed guests for *Women's Wear Daily*, the bible of the fashion world.

During more private moments, Truman and Bill Paley engaged in talks that kept them up all hours of the night. Truman credited Paley with giving him marvelous advice and was happy to benefit from the older man's experience. But there was one topic that Truman knew best: women. Despite the fact that Paley was married to one of the most beautiful women in the world, he was a notorious ladies' man who was constantly on the lookout for a new conquest. Paley valued Babe the way a connoisseur treasures a prized possession; she was to be maintained and admired. But Truman understood that what Paley really wanted was "Marilyn Monroe, a sexy broad," an earthy woman he could enjoy sexually. Truman, it turned out, could be very helpful in lining up dates for Paley because he was on close terms with some of the most attractive women in New York, many of whom relied on him for advice about their love lives.

◐◑

His friend Carol Marcus, who was separated from her husband, the writer William Saroyan, often turned to Truman when she needed a shoulder to cry on. One night in 1955, she visited him at his Brooklyn apartment. During a cozy dinner for two in his colorful bohemian lair, he broached a delicate subject. The head of one of the television networks, one of the most powerful men in America, he told Carol, was an admirer and wanted to meet her. Yes, the man was married, but, Truman assured Marcus, "He'll take good care of you, honey, that's the one thing you wouldn't have to worry about." Marcus turned him down, but that didn't stop Truman from moving on to other young women who were candidates for the position of Paley's paramour.

A few years later, in 1959, Truman approached another friend on Paley's behalf. He told Gloria Vanderbilt that Paley wanted to arrange a rendezvous. Vanderbilt, recently divorced from the legendary conductor Leopold Stokowski, was interested in getting together with Paley because she was an aspiring actress and had just appeared on Art Carney's television show *Very Important People*. She thought the network head might give her some career advice. Truman explained that Paley had something else in mind, something more daring, and even suggested that Babe admired Vanderbilt and would appreciate her cooperation in this very delicate matter.

The sad reality was that Babe, the woman who appeared to have everything, was a prisoner in golden handcuffs, trapped in a marriage that gave her money and position but not love. When Babe wept about her unfortunate situation to Truman, her closest confidant, he coolly cautioned her to face up to reality. Without her husband, he said, she would not have the privileged life—the homes, the wealth, the security—she enjoyed. Being Mrs. William Paley, he advised, was a job, the best job in the world and one she was uniquely qualified to do. Most of the time, when her life was running smoothly, Babe was able to follow Truman's advice and maintain her elaborate illusion of domestic happiness.

But that meant her husband's affairs had to be discreet. The wrong kind of woman—someone who didn't understand how an upper-crust marriage of convenience worked—could be trouble. According to Vanderbilt, Truman tried to explain the complicated nature of the Paleys' relationship when making his pitch to her. "Now Babe knows that he has other girlfriends and she handles it beautifully, but sometimes it gets . . . messy; it's upsetting to her, naturally. She likes you, you know, respects you; if he was involved with you it would be fun for you, ease things up for her; it would even in a way be doing everyone a favor—so to speak."

Vanderbilt had one disastrous meeting with Paley. His attempted seduction was clumsy and unoriginal. Like a caricature of a philanderer, he chased her around the couch in the New York pied-à-terre Babe had decorated so beautifully, certain that Vanderbilt was just playing hard to get when she refused his advances.

Truman's position in this bedroom farce was delicate and a little diabolical. He hurt Babe by helping Paley to stage his infidelities, then "helped" his unhappy friend by advising her how to survive the injury. All the while, his writer's brain was processing and storing every bit of information, every anecdote, every secret.

Truman had been busy writing *The Muses Are Heard*, a journalistic account of the adventures of a black touring company of *Porgy and Bess* in Soviet Russia; various magazine pieces, such as his scathing profile of the actor Marlon Brando for the *New Yorker*; and *Breakfast at Tiffany's*, his bittersweet novel about a high-priced call girl's Huckleberry Finn–like adventures in New York City. Readers loved Holly Golightly, the book's madcap and sexually liberated heroine, partly because she was so different from the 1950's prim and proper ideal of womanhood. When the book was published, Norman Mailer called Truman "the most perfect writer of my generation" and insisted he would not have "changed two words" of the book.

Truman was happy about the reception *Breakfast at Tiffany's* received and excited about a new project he had in the works, his "magnum opus," as he called it. It was very hush-hush, he told Bennett Cerf in a letter. In fact, he didn't want a soul to know about it. "The novel is called *Answered Prayers*," wrote Truman to Cerf, "and, if all goes well, I think it will answer mine." The reason for secrecy was that Truman was using his friends in high places—the Paleys and all the others—as source material for his story. He referred to them as "sitters," an art term used to describe a person who is posing for a portrait. In this case, however, the sitters did not realize they were posing. Truman knew they would be alarmed if they thought they were being watched, and he knew this might limit his access to their world. At this point, he was better off saying nothing about his plans.

Truman generally had a firm idea of what his upcoming writing projects would be and was expert at juggling fiction and nonfiction, novels, short stories, and articles. In the upcoming months, he planned to concentrate on *Answered Prayers* and a few other ideas he had in mind. He planned to travel to Greece, Italy, and Spain with Jack Dunphy. Truman's carefully considered agenda and itinerary, however, were derailed by unanticipated events in Kansas. Suddenly, he set aside *Answered Prayers*, his roman à clef about the rich and the famous, to pursue a completely different kind of story set in a completely different world.

Gloria

Women's Wear Daily called Truman's friend Gloria Guinness "the Ultimate." A slender woman with a perfectly coiffed cloud of jet black hair, bright, expressive eyes, a knowing smile, and an air of perpetual youth and easy elegance, she was born Gloria Rubio y Alatorre in Vera Cruz, Mexico, in 1912. Her father was a journalist, her mother a seamstress. Gloria said that her family sent her to Europe when life in Mexico became dangerous, but rumors persisted that beautiful young Gloria came from nothing and supported herself by working in a Mexican dance hall, where she dazzled men with her sultry charm. Eventually, she found a more lucrative and reputable line of work: marriage. There are those who believe she snuck in an insignificant first marriage to a man named Scholtens, but if it happened, it was not a distinguished-enough union to become part of her official biography.

In addition to those whispers about the dance hall and the discarded first husband, other aspects of Gloria's history were shrouded by a veil of mystery, and she wore it well. It is known that at some point before the start of World War II, Gloria moved to Paris, where she lived simply in a walk-up apartment. She had no money to spend on designer clothing, but somehow, she always radiated style. Her uniform, a modest black sweater and skirt, looked like haute couture when she put it on. One of Gloria's favorite fashion tricks was to buy a beautiful piece of jersey, cut a hole in the top, pull it over her head, and wrap the fabric around her tiny waist with a sash. She was always amused when people asked where she had bought her unique dresses.

In 1935, at the age of twenty-three, Gloria entered a new world of privilege and luxury when she married a German count, Franz Egon von Furstenberg-Herdringen. Their marriage produced two children, Dolores and Franz, but Gloria was not happy. When Hitler came into power in Germany, she packed up her children and moved to Spain, prompting dramatic rumors that cast her in the role of international spy.

Subsequently, she succumbed to the charms of a younger man, Ahmed Fakhri Bey, a grandson of King Faud I of Egypt, and they married in 1942. Fakhri did not have much money, but Gloria claimed that she actually enjoyed the years she spent living in Cairo with her charming and impoverished Egyptian. Seven years later, the storybook marriage ended in divorce, and Gloria, now the mother of two teenagers but still remarkably beautiful, was back on the market.

Her next husband, Thomas Loel Evelyn Bulkeley Guinness, came to her courtesy of his previous wife. According to Gloria, her friend Lady Isabel Manners had been married to Guinness for fifteen years when Lady Isabel asked Gloria to accompany her husband on the family yacht because she hated being at sea. "It is such a bore to me. Please be a darling and go entertain," Lady Isabel pleaded. Gloria did as her friend asked, and her enthusiasm

Gloria Guinness (at left) and C. Z. Guest in Palm Beach in 1950.

for sailing served her well. In 1951, she became the new Mrs. Loel Guinness, and her world expanded considerably.

In addition to his 350-ton, fully staffed yacht, Guinness owned a seven-story home in Paris; a villa in Switzerland; a stud farm in Normandy; homes in Palm Beach, Florida, and Acapulco; a suite at the Waldorf Towers in New York; and a fleet of airplanes and helicopters. His latest acquisition, Gloria, happily settled into a life of arrogant elegance, traveling from residence to residence with a retinue that included a valet, multiple chefs, and assorted maids. The Guinnesses were in constant motion, a process facilitated by the fact that they had a private jet outfitted luxuriously with Louis XVI furniture. And they never had to worry about anything as troublesome as luggage (not that they would have packed it themselves): complete wardrobes awaited them at each residence.

Gemini, the Guinness retreat in Palm Beach, was the one that journalists singled out for praise. The property was unusual because a highway ran through the center. Gloria provided a beautifully appointed tunnel, complete with hand-painted screens, plants, and cozy furniture, so that guests could cross from the Lake Worth side of the estate to the ocean side in high style.

When talking to the press, Gloria enjoyed sounding like a woman who never had to think about money. In a *Time* piece, "Having a Marvelous Time," she described her high-priced lifestyle with great enthusiasm. "You can't possibly spend twelve months in any one place," she argued. As for all that real estate: "So many people think it is difficult keeping so many homes, but I believe it is easier to keep six than one." For all his fortune, though, Guinness was tight with his money. The truth was that Gloria had no money of her own and often had to find inventive ways to cut corners in order to pacify her husband, who was so parsimonious that he kept her jewels under lock and key. One of her many tricks was to buy inexpensive fabric—chintz or such—and give it to an expert seamstress for perfect tailoring. Or, she would buy dozens of Mexican paper flowers to turn the Guinness yacht into a bower. She often tied a dime-store scarf around her swan neck to complement her expensive designer dress.

In 1963, Gloria became a regular contributor to *Harper's Bazaar*, a magazine that was just as likely to feature her in a fashion layout as on the masthead. She was uniquely qualified to write her articles, which were light, punchy insider pieces about fashion, lifestyles of the rich, and popular culture. One of her first assignments was to look at the biblical book of Genesis from a fashion point of view: Gloria had highly original ideas about Adam and Eve and the infamous leaf. In another piece, she catalogued the "best" people to know, probably using her address book as her source material. She also wrote at length about new developments in fashion, such as her impassioned diatribe against the miniskirt, which she insisted looked terrible on mature women. In 1964, she even covered the Sonny Liston–Cassius Clay fight, which she watched ringside with her pal Truman.

Gloria and Babe Paley were Truman's dearest friends and closest confidantes, so he was able to observe the darker side of their seemingly amicable relationship. The two women vacationed together every year on the Guinness yacht; attended the same luncheons, parties, and balls all over the world; and dominated the style sections of newspapers everywhere. But underneath their air-kissing, Gloria and Babe were engaged in mortal combat, vying for the coveted position of first place among the "fashionable savages," as the *Women's Wear Daily* publisher John Fairchild called the social elite.

Frequently, the weapon of choice in their rivalry was the baby vegetable. Both women were celebrated hostesses who viewed the dinner party as a showcase for their talents. Serving the tiniest, most expensive vegetables at a time when they were rare was a surefire way to establish social superiority. After years of watching his extravagant hostesses in action, Truman decided that the size of a vegetable was indeed an indication of class. "The real difference between rich and regular people," he observed, "is that the rich serve such marvelous vegetables. Little fresh born things, scarcely out of the earth. Little baby corn, little baby peas."

Gloria and Babe's game of one-upmanship extended to their wardrobes. One summer, as the two couples prepared for their annual vacation on the Guinness yacht, Gloria assured Babe that the dress code was casual: no need for her to pack jewels and party dresses. But on their very first night at sea, Gloria appeared in a stunning gown and her best jewelry and announced to a seriously underdressed Babe that they were attending a formal dinner. The following year, Babe vowed to be prepared. She packed her most dazzling wardrobe, only to find that clever Gloria had bested her again: this time, the cruise was completely casual.

Babe was famous for being exceedingly polite, yet she and Gloria brought out the worst in each other. When particularly annoyed at her duplicitous friend, Babe made catty remarks about Gloria's shady past, reminding Truman that the Latin beauty had, after all, worked as a shill in a Mexican nightclub.

⊙⥁⊙

5

In Cold Blood

THERE ARE TWO VERSIONS OF HOW TRUMAN CAPOTE WAS INSPIRED to write *In Cold Blood*. The first account, the one he most enjoyed telling, described a lively moment of serendipity. Truman was reading the *New York Times* on an ordinary Monday morning in November 1959 when he noticed a small picture of a middle-aged man, along with the eye-catching headline: "Wealthy Farmer, 3 of Family Slain." The man in the photograph was Herbert Clutter. He and his wife, Bonnie, along with their two teenage children, Kenyon and Nancy, had been murdered in their own home in the small, quiet town of Holcomb, Kansas.

In the *Times* article, Sheriff Earl Robinson of Holcomb was quoted as saying, "This is apparently the case of a psychopathic killer." The term was familiar to *New York Times* readers in 1959, but they were more accustomed to seeing it in the newspaper's movie and book review sections than in the headlines. They may have read that Alan Ladd had been cast to play a psychopathic killer in *This Gun for Hire*, or that Ned Calmer's new book *Strange Land* included a psychopathic killer as one of its characters. These psychologically twisted villains were popular in the 1940s and 1950s because they were thought to be more intelligent—more cunning—than the average criminal. "A psychopathic personality," wrote Dr. Olga Knopf of the New School for Social Research, "usually has normal or superior intelligence." Actors enjoyed playing them in dramas, and writers found them endlessly fascinating. For the most part, they seemed to exist primarily in the world of fiction. When the article about the Clutter murders appeared, the *New York Times* had used the term *psychopathic killer* only once before in a news story.

Truman pounced on the article about the Clutters because he had been looking for a true-life story to use as the foundation for what he called a "nonfiction novel." The fact that this case seemed to involve psychopathic killers who could have stepped from the pages of a novel made it all the more intriguing. Truman had a theory about reportage. He believed that he could combine the art of the novelist with the technique of journalism, "fiction with the added knowledge that it was true." The idea had been in the back of his mind for several years, and he was eager to try it.

The Clutter case sparked his curiosity because there were several incongruities. The brutal murders took place in the American heartland, in a place where people felt so safe that residents seldom locked their doors. The Clutters were good people, pillars of the community, beloved by all. The most disturbing revelation was that the victims did not put up a fight. Herbert Clutter was a brave man who would have done anything to protect his family. People wondered whether the Clutters knew their assailants. Truman was curious about the circumstances surrounding the murders, but he also wanted to know how the townspeople were reacting to the crime. The *New Yorker* shared his enthusiasm for the subject, and he won himself an assignment in Kansas.

The other version of *In Cold Blood*'s genesis was more ordinary. A friend of Truman's claimed that the *New Yorker* gave Truman a choice of topics, among which was the Clutter case. The other idea was to follow a New York City cleaning woman on her daily rounds. Truman thought he was taking the easy way out when he decided to head for Kansas.

Whatever the motivation for the story, Truman set out for Holcomb in December 1959. He asked his friend Andrew Lyndon to accompany him so that he wouldn't have to face the unfamiliar people of Kansas on his own. When Lyndon declined, Truman convinced Nelle Harper Lee to go. She had just finished writing *To Kill a Mockingbird* and agreed to be Truman's companion and research assistant.

Their excitement was dampened by the chilly reception they received in Holcomb, the scene of the murders, and in nearby Garden City. As Truman suspected, the crimes had affected the locals: they were confused, suspicious, and understandably frightened by the idea of having strangers in their midst.

Even in the days before their community was traumatized by the Clutter murders, the townspeople would have been apprehensive about Truman Capote. He did not modify his appearance or his flamboyant personality when he came to conservative Kansas. Wherever he was, Truman was Truman. He dressed in odd little outfits, a large sheepskin coat, tiny moccasins, and a six-foot-long scarf. He bombarded locals with penetrating questions, delivered in his annoying high-pitched voice. They had never seen anyone like him and were not sure they liked what they saw. Famous writer or not, Truman faced a wall of silence.

Luckily, Truman was used to this kind of hostile reaction and had a tried-and-true strategy for turning a foe into a friend. When he was a child, Truman performed cartwheels to distract and disarm schoolyard bullies. Now, he exaggerated his already extreme mannerisms to distract and disarm the wary adults of Holcomb. "I do something so outrageous that all they can do is laugh and then it's okay," he confided to a friend. "I have to do that every time I walk into a room or meet somebody." Truman was patient and persistent. Eventually, several key players in the area—most important, the lead investigator, Alvin Dewey, and his wife, Marie—finally responded to his charm.

Like Truman, Marie was from New Orleans, and once this connection had been established, they found they had much in common, including a passion for the Creole dish of red beans and rice. When the Deweys accepted Truman, other families followed their lead. They stopped ostracizing Truman and Nelle and welcomed them as visiting celebrities. He was so entertaining, the locals thought, with his stories about the Kennedys, Humphrey Bogart, Jennifer Jones, and other famous friends.

Truman was good with people, and he genuinely liked and enjoyed his new acquaintances. He was as comfortable with Marie Dewey in her kitchen in Kansas as he was with Babe Paley on a yacht in the Mediterranean.

Truman's investigation intensified when Al Dewey and his team tracked down the murderers and captured them in Las Vegas. They were Perry Smith and Dick Hickock, ex-convicts who had met in prison. Just as Sheriff Robinson predicted, they were psychopathic killers, intelligent men who, for different reasons, had lost their moral compass. They had heard about Herbert Clutter in prison and mistakenly believed that he kept a quantity of cash at his farmhouse. Desperate for money, Smith and Hickock set out for Holcomb to rob him. The irony was that Clutter rarely used cash: he was a meticulous record-keeper who wrote checks for everything, even amounts under a dollar.

Smith confessed to killing Herbert Clutter and his son, Kenyon, and accused Hickock of murdering Mrs. Clutter and her daughter, Nancy. Almost immediately, he changed his testimony and confessed to killing all four victims. He told Al Dewey that he didn't want Hickock's parents to think of their son as a killer, whereas he was alone in the world, and there was no one to care about Perry Smith's reputation.

The capture of Smith and Hickock added an exciting new dimension to Truman's project. If the accused killers, who were in a position to give him firsthand information about the murders and their motivations, would cooperate, he could profile them. Although Smith and Hickock were reluctant to trust Truman at first, in time, he persuaded them to talk. After a few interviews, the lonely prisoners looked forward to his visits. Truman supplied them with cigarettes and magazines. He also made them feel important. He was a famous writer, listening to them at a time when they were reviled and shunned by everyone around them. With Truman, they could at least pretend they had a friend.

Truman's interviews with Smith and Hickock transformed his journalistic piece into what he called a "Big Work." They supplied him with all the details he needed to make the story come to life. Hickock had an extraordinary memory that was almost photographic in its accuracy. Truman was able to reconstruct entire trips, down to addresses and roadside stops, that the fugitives took while dodging the authorities in Mexico. If Hickock's total recall provided reality, Smith offered metaphor. He was a dreamer who had a boyish obsession with buried treasure (he had seen John Huston's movie *Treasure of the Sierra Madre* eight times) and imagined finding riches that would change his life. He also fantasized about being an artist, a songwriter, a painter, and a successful writer like Truman Capote. Truman, who had a talent for getting close to his subjects in the most routine of circumstances, became intimate with these men who had been cut off from every other kind of social contact.

In Perry Smith's case, there was an extraordinary emotional connection between the writer and his subject. When Truman looked closely at Smith, he saw a distorted reflection of himself. There were physical similarities. Both men were short but powerfully built—when they sat down, their feet did not touch the floor. They shared an interest in literature. Smith considered himself literary and prided himself on his vocabulary. He kept a list of words he categorized as "beautiful," "useful," or "worth memorizing"—many of them, including *thanatoid*, which meant "deathlike," and *myrtophobia*, meaning "fear of darkness," were difficult to drop into everyday conversation.

The most striking similarity between the two men, however, was their backgrounds. Like Truman, Smith had been abandoned by his mother, a drunken and promiscuous woman who entertained lovers in front of her children. Alvin Dewey, who had numerous opportunities to observe both men closely, agreed that there were strong parallels between them. "Truman saw himself in Perry Smith, not in being deadly, of course, but in their childhood. Their childhood was more or less the same; they were more or less the same height, the same build." Yet their destinies were completely different: Truman was a celebrated writer with a brilliant future, while Smith was a psychopathic killer on his way to the gallows.

Truman's identification with Smith caused him to think about the life he might have had if his unhappy childhood had led him on a different path. He believed there was a moment when he could have made a bad choice, a wrong turn. Some observers felt that Truman's fascination with Smith was more than intellectual curiosity. Harold Nye, an officer with the Kansas Bureau of Investigation, was convinced that Truman and Smith had become lovers during their long interview sessions together in Smith's cell. According to Nye, Truman repeatedly bribed Smith's guard to leave them alone when he came to the prison to visit. Smith certainly behaved like a jealous lover, enraged when Truman appeared to pay more attention to Hickock or sullen when he felt that Truman did not acknowledge the special bond between them. An impersonal dedication in *Breakfast at Tiffany's*, "For Perry. From Truman who wishes you well," sparked an angry retort from Smith, who thought he was entitled to a more impassioned sentiment.

Truman's feelings for Smith, his curiosity about the case, his need to know every single detail of the story—or possibly a combination of all three reasons—compelled him to return to Kansas over and over again. The case was on the fast track the moment Smith and Hickock were apprehended in December 1959. Armed with the killers' confessions and physical evidence against them, the authorities carefully built their prosecution. The trial began on March 22, and the accused were found guilty a little more than a week later, on March 29. Their execution was set for May 13.

At that point, Truman estimated he would spend a year writing *In Cold Blood*, then would move on to his next project. He did not anticipate that the killers would win a stay of execution from the Kansas Supreme Court. To his surprise—and dismay—Smith and Hickock remained on death row, their destinies uncertain, for the next five years. In a letter to Al Dewey, Truman worried that justice was disturbingly elusive. "Will H & S live to a ripe and happy old age?" he wondered, "—or will they swing, and make a lot of other folks very happy indeed?"

Truman lived a complicated life during this time. He partied with the Paleys and other wealthy and privileged friends, then escaped with Jack to a fishing village in Spain. They hibernated in a snow-covered chalet in Verbier, Switzerland, where it seemed to be eternal winter, and moved to less punishing climates in the Mediterranean during the spring and the summer. In both locations, Truman dedicated himself to the long and painful process of writing *In Cold Blood*. His subject was so serious that it became harder and harder for him to connect to the frothy world of cocktails and gossip. "Gregariousness is the enemy of art," he said. "When I work, I have to forcibly remove myself from other people. I'm like a prizefighter in training." Only Kansas, and the people there, seemed real and important to him.

Despite the intense connection he felt to Kansas, Truman more or less stayed in Europe for the next three years. He was conflicted about the fact that Smith and Hickock still lingered on death row. As a writer, he wanted a conclusion for his story so that he could finish his book and get on with his life. But in this case, the conclusion— a final ruling from the Kansas Supreme Court—would almost certainly mean death for his unfortunate friends.

One way to sidestep confronting this cruel paradox was to

return to New York and dive headlong into the social whirl. By March 1964, Truman was in top form, back in his seat of honor at the city's most exclusive dinner parties. He spoke obsessively about his book, whetting the appetites of the intelligentsia with descriptions of the murders, the murderers, and their motives.

In April, Truman visited San Francisco and Los Angeles with Alvin and Marie Dewey. They kindly brought along Vi Tate, recently widowed after her husband, Roland Tate, the judge who presided over Smith and Hickcock's trial, passed away. The West Coast trip was one of Truman's typical whirlwind jaunts, booked with dinner parties and reunions with the rich and the famous. Truman took great pleasure in introducing his Kansas friends to celebrities they had admired from afar, and they were thrilled to have the opportunity to experience Hollywood glamour firsthand. In Los Angeles, they stayed at the luxurious home of Truman's friends David Selznick and Jennifer Jones, who hosted a dinner party in their honor. They were feted by the power agent Irving "Swifty" Lazar and his wife, Mary, who were famous for their Hollywood bashes. The high point of their trip, however, was a very special party hosted by then producer Dominick Dunne and his beautiful wife, Lenny, to celebrate their tenth anniversary.

Guests received formal invitations to a dance at the Dunnes' Beverly Hills home. The evening commenced at 10 p.m. on April 24, 1964. The party's theme would be a black and white ball, inspired by the striking Ascot scene created by the designer Cecil Beaton for the film *My Fair Lady*. Men were instructed to wear black tie, while ladies were given a choice of dressing in white or black. The Dunnes planned the party for months, even engaging a stage designer to decorate and build sets and emptying their house of furniture.

The Dunnes' guest list could have filled an issue of *Photoplay*, with partygoers who ranged from Loretta Young and David Niven to Tuesday Weld and Natalie Wood. Truman was invited, but the Dunnes, fearing a fire department raid if they packed the house too tightly, made it clear they could not accommodate guests who wanted to bring guests. Never one to take rules too seriously, Truman pressed his hosts until they said yes to the Deweys and Vi Tate.

That night, in such star-studded company, the Deweys should have been invisible. Instead, they were the center of attention. "In a tentful of famous people," recalled Dominick Dunne, "Dewey became the most besieged. Everyone wanted to talk to him." Dewey had that effect on people wherever he went because he was handsome, reserved, and decidedly American. His relentless pursuit and prosecution of Smith and Hickock were reassuring to a nervous public who had come face-to-face with a new kind of villain. In a world where alienated psychopaths killed randomly and without motive, a dedicated lawman like Alvin Dewey was a real-life hero. In addition to being a hero, Dewey was a wonderful advance man for *In Cold Blood*. Even though the book was unfinished, Truman could count on his most sympathetic main character to attract attention and keep the material alive.

Truman had enormous fun at the party. There were two different bands that night, and no one appreciated them more than he did, as he danced and danced, with Natalie Wood, Tuesday Weld, Hope Lange, and Jennifer Jones. When the guests needed a break from all the dancing, they were treated to a late-night supper. Finally, the party ended at 4 a.m., very late for a town that was famous for retiring early.

In Manhattan a few months later, Truman was scheduled to do a public reading of passages from *Breakfast at Tiffany's*. When he walked onstage, he surprised the audience by instead delivering tantalizing excerpts from the unfinished *In Cold Blood*. The audience was riveted. In a way, the agonizing delay in completing the book worked in Truman's favor. Every day, more and more people had the opportunity to hear about the new book. The longer they had to wait, the more they wanted it.

Finally, the day Truman both dreaded and longed for arrived.

Smith and Hickock's last appeal was denied, and their execution—death by hanging—was set for April 14, 1965. The condemned men wanted Truman to be there at the end. He traveled to Kansas with his editor Joe Fox for moral support, but he made up excuses to avoid paying a last visit to Smith and Hickock in their cells. Instead, he saw them immediately before they were led to the gallows. Truman held their cigarettes and listened solemnly to their nervous chatter, just as he had listened to them for the previous six years.

Hickock was taken away first, then the guards came to collect Smith, who asked permission for one more moment with Truman. "Adios, amigo," Smith said, and kissed him good-bye. Truman joined the other observers in the warehouse where the hooded executioner waited. He said it was the most intense emotional experience of his life.

When it was over, Truman wept all the way back to New York. Yet the stronger part of him, the writer who needed to finish what he had started, went to work immediately. "For the entire three days that I was throwing up and crying and carrying on," he confessed to a journalist, "in another part of my mind I was sitting and quite coolly writing the story."

Truman's five-and-half-year vigil was over, and he had been changed by the experience. Kansas, once a distant point on the map, was a second home to him. He had close friends there, especially Al and Marie Dewey, who called him T and considered him a member of their family. But now it was time to move on. Truman ordered headstones to mark the graves of Perry Smith and Dick Hickock, a generous gesture on the part of their only friend. But the act was also a symbol of closure. He wanted to finish his book and end his self-imposed exile. Truman was ready to rejoin the living.

Marella

Marella Agnelli's face, combining the strong features on a Roman coin with the mystery of a Botticelli Madonna, always appeared cool and knowing, as if she were watching from on high, observing lesser mortals at play. She was born in 1927, a Neapolitan princess from a fine, though somewhat impoverished, Italian family. Princess Marella Caracciolo di Castagneto's father was an Italian diplomat who represented the best of the Old World. Her mother, an American from the Midwest, brought a touch of the New World into the family. Marella was familiar with the Agnellis because her home in Trastevere was near their palace. She knew all about their wild son, Gianni. While young Marella was diligently working, posing for *Vogue* and entering beauty pageants (she became Miss Florence early in her modeling career), Gianni Agnelli was making headlines as a playboy. With a hefty allowance of $1 million a year, courtesy of the family fortune amassed by his grandfather, Agnelli circled the globe in constant pursuit of pleasure. He was a handsome man's man, with swarthy skin and an air of power and prosperity that was irresistible to women.

Agnelli's relatives, especially his sisters, were unhappy when he began a long-running affair with Pamela Digby Churchill, a former English debutante who had transformed herself into a modern-day courtesan (and who would become one of Capote's second-string swans). Divorced from her husband, Randolph Churchill, the son of Winston, she used her ample physical charms to cultivate lucrative relationships with wealthy, powerful men. She was extremely well-connected in political circles, and a word whispered in the ear of an influential former lover such as Averill Harriman or Aly Kahn could be very helpful to the new man in her life. In 1948, her new man was Gianni Agnelli.

There was nothing covert about Agnelli's long-standing relationship with Pamela. She lived openly in one of his houses, served as hostess at his parties, and was the happy recipient of extravagant gifts of jewelry, designer clothing, and money. But Agnelli could not be faithful to one woman, even to his mistress. A spat with Pamela over an infidelity (she came home unexpectedly to find him kissing another woman on the terrace) provoked Agnelli to race off in his sports car. He crashed into a truck, shattering his right leg.

Concerned about their brother's self-destructive lifestyle, the Agnelli sisters conspired to depose Pamela. Princess Marella, a family friend, was persuaded to visit Agnelli at the hospital. The beautiful twenty-six-year-old was dazzled by the famous playboy, and he was equally attracted to Marella. From his point of view, she was the girl next door, fresh, familiar, and thoroughly suitable for marriage. In 1953, Marella became Mrs. Gianni Agnelli, and Pamela resumed her quest for her next rich husband.

Marella's new role as consort to Italy's most important industrialist promoted her from princess to queen. In the spirit of creating

Princess Marella Caracciolo marrying Gianni Agnelli in November 1953.

a dynasty, she gave birth to a son, Edoardo, several months after the wedding. But Marella was to discover that Agnelli was not good husband material. He enjoyed women—all kinds of women—far too much to settle down with one. Starlets, such as the blond bombshell Anita Ekberg, were plentiful in Rome, Cannes, Paris, and London, the preferred playgrounds of the very rich. Agnelli fondly called them "tarts" and partied with them, while dutiful Marella raised their children and turned their villas into showplaces. Even married, well-connected women were susceptible to Agnelli's charms: Jacqueline Kennedy seemed smitten with him during a Mediterranean vacation in 1962, prompting Jack Kennedy to send a curt telegram admonishing her "More Caroline, less Agnelli."

Marella's life with the *avvocato*, the Italian word for "lawyer" and a title conferred on Agnelli by his workers as a sign of respect, was often trying and unpredictable but never dull. She pursued her own interests while she monitored her husband's peccadilloes. Her passions were gardening (the Agnellis owned several exquisite estates, including the Villa Perosa in Torino and a palazzo in Turin), photography, and fashion.

Blessed with a tall, slender body and a neck rumored to be the longest and most graceful in Europe, Marella was a fashion designer's dream. Magazines such as *Vogue* and *Harper's Bazaar* featured her in layouts, and *Women's Wear Daily* ran sketches of her in fashion-forward outfits such as tunics and tights. No matter how often she was photographed, there was a mysterious, Sphinx-like air to her expression that distinguished her from other women who were more conventionally beautiful.

Marella's regal aloofness fascinated Truman. In comparing Marella to Babe, he said, "If they were both in Tiffany's window, Marella would be more expensive."

As much as Marella liked Truman and enjoyed his company, she often rebelled at the idea of being part of the official flock. She recalled a ladies' luncheon that Truman hosted at the Colony. He had invited all of his swans to join him at a table. Marella knew the women well and was aware of their friendships with Truman. But the reality of seeing them together was unsettling. She no longer felt like a special friend and confidante. Instead, as far as she was concerned, she was one of many—*too* many— swans.

⚮

6

Truman and Kay

THE SPELL HAD BEEN LIFTED. TRUMAN WORKED QUICKLY, FINISHING *In Cold Blood* in June, just two months after Smith and Hickock were executed. He happily handed in the book to Random House and tried to shake off the gloom that had become a constant in his life. After so many years of studying the dark side of human nature, he wanted to kick back and have a good time. "When I'm flying my flag in town, there's nobody in the world more sociable than I am," he boasted. Truman had been living in an apartment he rented in his friend Oliver Smith's Victorian mansion in Brooklyn Heights, a place he loved for its Old World charm. But he wanted a new place to hang his flag—sleeker, bigger, and closer to the action. At that moment, the center of New York City's real estate world was the United Nations Plaza, a brand new, twin-tower luxury high-rise with a prestigious address on the East River.

Described as a "luxury liner" by *Newsweek*, the thirty-eight-story glass-and-aluminum complex had been designed to make the hearts of Manhattan's power brokers beat a little faster. For $25,000 to $166,000, depending on the size of the apartment, buyers would enjoy spectacular views of the city, enormous windows draped in glass fiber cloth, bathrooms made of Carrara marble, room service from an on-site gourmet restaurant, a concierge, and a fleet of support staff, including valets and seamstresses. But the compound's real drawing card was its superstar tenants. Senator Robert F. Kennedy paid approximately $68,000 for a five-room apartment on the fourteenth floor to use as his New York residence. The philanthropist Mary Lasker bought three and a half apartments in the East Tower and then customized the space, turning twenty-two rooms into five, to house her collection of contemporary art—paintings by Georgia O'Keefe, Mark Rothko, and Franz Kline, among others—while Mrs. Lasker planned on staying in her house on nearby Beekman Place. The television host Johnny Carson, the producer David Susskind, and assorted captains of industry bought apartments, creating a micro-climate of wealth and privilege. One tenant confessed to the *New York Times* that she wanted to live in the United Nations Plaza simply "because it's so glamorous."

Truman was in the vanguard of the beautiful people who moved into the fashionable new building. By June, he had selected an airy, five-room apartment on the twenty-second floor, which he described as "very cozy" and loved for its "huge enormous view." He planned to decorate it with the help of his friend Evelyn Weil Backer, a socialite and an interior designer. Not that Truman would consider leaving the décor entirely in her hands. He had definite ideas about how to turn the spare, modernist space into a home that reflected his personality. "It's like writing a book," he told *Newsweek*. "In an apartment, an atmosphere is important, and I've worked very hard on this one."

Truman created a showplace that was simultaneously elegant, bohemian, and a little off center, just like him. He covered the living room in discreet beige silk. But the dining room was painted bright red and reminded Truman of a hot raspberry tart. A menagerie of animal statuary—a bronze giraffe, carved lions, porcelain cats, dogs, rabbits, and owls—held court around an ornate

Victorian sofa, while colorful antique paperweights (the collection started by Colette when Truman was in Paris) covered every surface. A friend observed that Truman's eclectic treasures "somehow remind you of the contents of a very astute little boy's pockets." On the wall was a portrait of Truman painted by James Fosburgh, Minnie Cushing Astor Fosburgh's husband. To top it off, Truman had purchased a $5,500 Tiffany lamp and a green Jaguar XK-E convertible, accessories that confirmed he was enjoying a new level of financial security.

Some friends were not impressed by Truman's new luxury apartment. Cecil Beaton, who had exquisite taste in all matters of style, called it "expensive without looking more than ordinary" and bemoaned the fact that the over-hyped building "is the new world, no one in sight, every hyper-gadget, a great view, but no personality."

With his newfound success, Truman's social life took off like a rocket. In July 1965, after purchasing his apartment, Truman made plans to join Marella and Gianni Agnelli on a sailing trip along the coast of Turkey. He invited Katharine Graham, the president of the *Washington Post*, to be his companion.

Everyone felt sorry for poor Kay Graham. Two years earlier, her husband, the media mogul Philip Graham, had killed himself. Their marriage had been a rocky affair. Phil Graham had been a manic-depressive whose irrational behavior had a serious effect on his wife and their children. He'd traveled in the highest political circles in Washington, numbering John Kennedy among his close friends. His very public love affair with Robin Webb, a young writer, was a source of constant humiliation to his long-suffering wife. Then, Graham killed himself with a shotgun in his own home. After twenty-three years of dedicating herself to her family, Kay Graham had reluctantly assumed control of the *Washington Post* and *Newsweek*, a media empire founded by her parents, the Meyers. She had had great difficulty adjusting to a life in the spotlight and was very selective in choosing her friends. Kay liked Truman, to whom she'd relatively recently been introduced by Babe Paley, because he was always amusing company and helped her forget her troubles. He talked her into accompanying him on the Agnellis' cruise, even though she feared she was too dowdy to hold her own in the company of international jet-setters.

Truman and Kay rendezvoused in London, then proceeded to the *Sylvia*, the yacht the Agnellis had secured for the trip. The Agnellis were delayed in Italy because of a death in the family, but Marella urged Truman and Kay to start the cruise without them. The voyage was idyllic when it was just the two of them. While they sailed, Truman proofread the galleys of *In Cold Blood* and shared them with Kay. She was enthralled by the book and paid close attention to his stories about Smith and Hickock, the Deweys, and his experiences in Kansas. The spell was broken when the Agnellis arrived with the other guests. The boat was crowded, and the absence of air conditioning in the middle of summer was a little uncomfortable. But Truman and Kay had established a bond while they drifted at sea, exchanging stories and ideas.

Truman combined business with pleasure by writing an essay about the trip that was scheduled to run in the January 1966 issue of *Vogue* magazine. He called it "The 'Sylvia' Odyssey" and illustrated his reminiscences with candid photographs of his friends at play. Kay could be seen in her bathing suit, wet and unadorned. She didn't seem to mind. Somewhere along the line, Truman had persuaded her to buy an apartment at the U.N. Plaza. A brand-new place in a new city without memories of her late husband would be good for her.

❧

After the cruise, Truman returned to New York for the official opening of the *In Cold Blood* season. Readers would finally have an opportunity to experience the long-awaited story in the *New Yorker*, which was publishing *In Cold Blood* in four parts or, as *Vogue* wrote, "in four big gulps." The first installment, "The Last to See Them Alive," appeared on September 25, followed by "Persons Unknown" on October 2, "Answer" on October 9, and "The Corner" on October 16. Each issue performed sensationally at the newsstand. Hooked on the unfolding drama of the Clutters and their killers, readers snapped up every issue and eagerly awaited the next. They already knew the facts about the case: the murders and Smith and Hickock's capture and execution had been well documented by newspapers all over the country. It was Truman's storytelling—his evocative descriptions of the characters, his uncanny insights into their personalities and motivations, and his ability to take a crime in a small town and turn it into a shocking metaphor for contemporary alienation—that made them a captive audience. A critic writing for the *Houston Post* called the *New Yorker* excerpts "a tour de force of reporting" and observed, "the series has an impact that is at times almost physically sickening."

The media frenzy surrounding *In Cold Blood* flared for several months before the hardcover edition of the book was published, and Truman kept the flame alive. He was featured in magazines and newspapers throughout the fall of 1965. The women's magazines, Truman's earliest supporters, rallied to give *In Cold Blood* strong advance publicity. In a column aptly called "People Are Talking About . . . ," the October 15th issue of *Vogue* profiled Truman, praising his new work as "the first non-fiction novel, a precise documentary, in many ways brilliantly composed, inventive in the telling, a mystery-detective story, true and factual."

The word *documentary*, a term defining a specific kind of fact-based film, was often applied to *In Cold Blood*, as critics tried to come up with a label for Truman's experimental nonfiction novel. Truman and his book attracted the attention of two young filmmakers who were making a name for themselves as revolutionary documentarians. What Truman was to literature, the Maysles brothers, Albert and David, were to nonfiction film. They challenged the establishment by trading the tripod for the hand-held camera so they could shoot their subjects more realistically. They refused to impose their own point of view on their material, preferring the objectivity—and truth—that comes with distance. Albert Maysles said that "the natural disposition of the camera is to seek out reality." The brothers called their new technique of naturalistic movie making "direct cinema," which was the American counterpart of cinema verité in France.

When National Educational Television invited the brothers to make a film about an American writer, their first choice was Norman Mailer, the celebrated bad-boy author of *The Naked and the Dead*, *The Deer Park*, *Advertisements for Myself*, and *An American Dream*. Mailer declined, explaining he had been doing "too many advertisements for myself" to consider being the subject of a documentary.

Although Truman Capote was their second choice, he turned out to be a more interesting subject and a better match for their talents. Their objective, turning reality into art, was very much in line with Truman's approach in *In Cold Blood*. Al and David recognized Truman as a kindred spirit and were excited about working with him at this pivotal moment in his career.

The Maysles brothers started filming Truman in the fall. For their first location, they chose the Oak Room of the Plaza Hotel. Anyone who knew Truman was aware of his affection for the Plaza. When he was a young writer in 1944, he set the opening scene of his first novel, *Summer Crossing*, in one of its dining rooms. The swank location was meant to telegraph the elevated social standing of seventeen-year-old Grady McNeil, her older sister, Apple, and their parents, before they set off on a cruise to Europe. Truman wrote that the family matriarch had been the guest of honor at a "distinguished dance" at the Plaza.

Truman loved all the restaurants at the hotel. He frequented Trader Vic's for Polynesian fare, the Palm Court for tea, and the Oak Room, which had the old-moneyed atmosphere of a gentleman's club, for lunch. His favorite dish was the Plaza's signature Chicken Hash, an uptown spin on a diner classic, refined by the use of chicken instead of the more traditional corned beef.

The documentary *A Visit with Truman Capote* begins at the Plaza. Seated at a table with the Maysles brothers, Truman inscribes a copy of *In Cold Blood* for them, joking that they will get a better dedication because they have been so complimentary about his writing. He is completely at home in front of the camera, relaxed, witty, and charismatic. In a subsequent scene, the setting is the editor Joe Fox's office at Random House, where Truman warmly greets Karen Gundersen, a young *Newsweek* reporter who has come to interview him for a cover story.

Gundersen, as Truman points out in the film, was young and beautiful. She was also blessed. Her job, working for *Newsweek's* culture czar Jack Kroll, was the kind of dream position that inspired countless would-be Lois Lanes to move to New York City to pursue careers in journalism. Gundersen was always knee-deep in simultaneous stories and loved every minute of it. She interviewed newsmakers—established celebrities such as Frank Sinatra and rising stars, including young Andy Warhol. While she worked on the Capote piece, she was also interviewing the lyricist/librettist Alan Jay Lerner, the musical genius responsible for *My Fair Lady* and other Broadway hits. Lerner was living in Boston, fine-tuning his new musical *On a Clear Day You Can See Forever*. There were the usual nail-biting dramas as the show prepared to move to Broadway, including the fact that the French leading man Louis Jourdan had to be replaced at the last minute by John Cullum. Gundersen discovered that Lerner and his coworkers had something else on their minds: all they wanted was the latest installment of the serialization of *In Cold Blood*. The eager readers didn't want to live in suspense a moment longer than necessary. They were so concerned about getting their hands on the *New Yorker* that they sent someone from the company down to New York City to pick up a copy and race it back to Boston.

In the documentary, Gundersen accompanies Truman to his beach house in Sagaponack, New York. The Maysles brothers film them during the drive, with Al operating the camera and David recording the sound. Continuing her interview, Gundersen asks Truman to define the term *nonfiction novel*. He answers quickly, probably because he has been asked the question so many times before, that it is his belief that a writer could produce a work of art out of factual material.

At the house, Truman slips easily into the role of host. He enjoys himself as he mixes Bloody Marys, prepares his special oyster stew for lunch, and strolls on the beach with Gundersen, seemingly unaffected by the camera's presence. There is an emotional moment when Truman speaks about his relationships with Smith and Hickock.

Back in New York, the Maysles brothers capture a lighter side of Truman. In November, he is joined by his friends from Kansas Alvin and Marie Dewey and Vi Tate. With characteristic largesse, Truman planned an exciting agenda for his Kansas friends on the occasion of their first trip to the city. The documentary follows them strolling up Fifth Avenue with Truman. He takes them to Tiffany's for a quick spin in the revolving door, commenting that the store could have been more appreciative of all the publicity and business that *Breakfast at Tiffany's* had generated. Tiffany's had sent Truman a china breakfast set as a housewarming gift for his new apartment. But he suggests that a solid gold breakfast set would have been more appropriate.

The documentary continues with the Deweys and the filmmakers touring Truman's glamorous new apartment. At all times, Truman is completely at ease with his friends. Despite the distance between their worlds, they share an affection that is almost familial.

This closeness motivated Truman to roll out his considerable red carpet for the Deweys during their stay. But on the eve of *In Cold Blood's* publication, he was also conscious of the fact that his talent was in town. As he had witnessed in Los Angeles, Alvin and Marie were celebrities. Important people wanted to meet them, and columnists were eager to write about them. Truman was happy to accommodate. After all, rarely did the name Dewey appear without a mention of *In Cold Blood*.

Princess Margaret and Lord Snowden were in New York at the same time as the Deweys, but, as Marie wrote in her ecstatic holiday letter later that year, the young dignitaries "weren't treated any more royally than we were." In New York, the Deweys stayed at the Waldorf-Astoria. They saw Ginger Rogers perform in *Hello, Dolly!* They listened to Dr. Norman Vincent Peale at the Marble Collegiate Church. And they were the guests of honor at a series of festive events hosted by Truman's friends, the details of which were widely reported by columnists all over the country. The *Topeka State Journal* headline read, "Kansas Lawman, Wife Give NY Elite Excuse for Party."

C. Z. Guest held a luncheon at her Long Island estate. Bennett and Phyllis Cerf hosted a formal dinner at their townhouse. A dramatic duplex living room belonging to Mrs. Piedy Gimbel, the former wife of the department store heir, served as the setting for a who's who cocktail party. Throughout their stay, the Deweys dined with movie stars, literary lions, and social butterflies, including John Steinbeck, John Gunther, Arlene Frances, Leonard Bernstein, Irwin Shaw, Gregory Peck, Henry Fonda, Rosalind Russell, and Kitty Carlisle Hart. They met Jackie Kennedy, widowed two years earlier in November, who sympathized with Marie Dewey about the perils of being married to a lawman. The parties were so fashionable that the writer/editor Norman Podhoretz complained he had to buy a new navy pinstripe suit because he was "put down" for wearing dowdy brown at a previous Dewey event.

New Yorkers warmed to the affable, down-to-earth Deweys. An unidentified guest at Piedy Gimbel's cocktail party told a reporter that Dewey was "the best type of American, you know, the really scrubbed, honest-looking kind." Big-city sophisticates found the couple's heartland Americanism exotic.

The Dewey love fest continued in Washington, D.C., where Truman escorted his guests to the home of Kay Graham. For an entire week, they were treated like visiting dignitaries. Graham arranged a private tour of the White House and visits to the National Gallery, Arlington Cemetery, the Lincoln Memorial, and other Washington sites. The Deweys and Vi Tate enjoyed their insider tour of the capital: Kay Graham's name, they discovered, could open any door. But the highlight of their stay in Washington was a black-tie dinner dance given in their honor by Graham herself.

Graham was a veteran hostess who planned her parties with military precision. The art and the politics of entertaining were taken very seriously in Washington, perhaps too seriously. A society writer in 1947 observed that most parties in the capital were distinguished by their lack of gaiety and the fact that guests looked pained, "as if their feet hurt them." The journalists Robert S. Allen and William V. Shannon stressed that in Washington, "Any connection between entertaining and fun is purely coincidental." Yet "receptions," as functions were called in the capital city, dominated the social scene. Whether planning a tea, a cocktail party, a dinner, or a ball, every host and hostess had to master the confounding intricacies of Washington protocol, an inflexible set of social rules observed by diplomats and heads of state.

As the president of the *Washington Post*, Katharine Graham was in the vanguard of the exciting new establishment in town. An invitation to a party at her stately Georgetown mansion was as coveted as a summons from the White House. But Graham was the first to admit that her early attempts at entertaining were disastrous. It was not enough to create a tasty menu or choose the right wines. A clever hostess had to know how to select and wrangle her guests.

In 1945, she had bravely decided to host a small dinner party while her husband was stationed in the Philippines. She invited guests—old friends and new friends who worked in government and diplomacy—thinking they would have common interests. Instead, the combination of conflicting ideologies and excessive alcohol was lethal. Graham watched helplessly as her guests drank too much and argued incessantly. Her polite dinner became a train wreck. The guests almost came to blows, and one, to his hostess's horror, relieved himself on her manicured front lawn.

By 1965, those days were long behind Graham. Years of entertaining, first as Mrs. Phillip Graham and then, more recently, as a prominent Washington businesswoman, had transformed her into an accomplished party-giver. Yet Graham was a practical woman who never entertained without a reason. She enjoyed hosting parties for visiting friends like Truman and the Deweys because the evening served a purpose: the outsiders would be welcomed into Washington society, and the Washingtonians would have an opportunity to meet interesting new people.

Typically, Graham set her parties into motion by coming up with a concept and a stellar guest list. Yet the media titan was so busy at work that there were times when she was almost a late arrival at her own events. She needed someone she could trust to bring her ideas to life. Elizabeth Hylton, Graham's secretary, was her secret weapon.

Hylton started working for Graham in the fall of 1963. She had grown up in a coal camp in West Virginia, so her new life as a career girl in glamorous Washington, D.C., was a dramatic contrast to her past. She was a quick study, turning for guidance to Graham and her socially adept friends, especially the Washington insiders Polly Fritchey, Carolyn Shaw, and Joe Alsop.

Graham invited 134 of Washington's finest to greet the *In Cold Blood* group at 8 p.m. on Saturday, November 20. Attorney General Nicholas Katzenbach; Secretary of Defense Robert McNamara; Secretary of Labor William Wirtz; Secretary of the Interior Stewart Udall; Senator Robert Kennedy; Senator Edward Kennedy; Ben Bradlee, the editor of the *Washington Post*; McGeorge Bundy, the special assistant to the president for national security; and the journalists David Brinkley, Bill Moyers, Drew Pearson, and Art Buchwald, among others, were on the list. Eighty-eight accepted and forty-six, including the senators Kennedy, sent their regrets. In addition to couples, there were equal numbers of single women and single men. Seven guests, including the actress Lauren Bacall, responded that they would join the guests after dinner.

Truman, the Deweys, and Vi Tate were wined and dined with a festive meal. A fish course was followed by loin of veal stuffed with truffles; this was served with potato balls, glazed carrots, a green vegetable, salad, and a savarin ring with fruit and accompanied by a selection of red and white wines and champagne. Graham owned enough china, cutlery, and glassware to serve her guests from her own storeroom. After dinner, there was dancing. McGeorge Bundy was one of the most popular men on the dance floor because he was so good at the waltz. According to Washington tradition, the guests of honor had to be the first to leave. Since Truman and the Kansas contingent were staying at Graham's house, the party went on longer than usual. Joe Fox, Truman's editor at Random House, said in his thank-you note to Graham that he could have stayed until 6 a.m.—but he was a hardy New Yorker. Washington society generally retired early.

The guests proved to be as courteous and proper as their hostess was. Many of them, including the guests of honor, sat down to write thank-you notes as soon as the evening ended. Their letters to Graham were warm, eloquent, and enthusiastic. For Marie Dewey, the party was the highlight of the whole week. Vi Tate said that the party was "the most beautiful and delightful one I have ever attended" and insisted, "Washington truly has the most attractive and interesting people in America." Graham was touched by their words and wrote to a friend that "I've *never* gotten such *dear* and effusive notes as from Vi and Marie."

Truman penned a short, affectionate note to Graham expressing his thanks. "Precious Kay-Kay," he wrote, "Bless you for the beautiful visit. Our Kansas friends were bedazzled and thrilled—and *so* was I. You were an angel to do that, really kind and thoughtful and generous, and I shall always remember it with great happiness and gratitude." He signed it "Love et mille tendresse [*sic*] Trubaby."

The Washington crowd was not to be outdone. They praised

Graham and had high compliments for Truman and his Kansas friends. *Washington Post* columnist Mary McGrory reported that "Marie Dewey's conversation was as good as any I have ever heard at a Washington dinner table. Modified Grant Wood, and so refreshing. And Truman C., utterly changed by his Midwestern experience, as we all are by reading what he wrote." Another guest said, "the whole party took off like a rocket," and called it "a smash hit."

Truman's visit to Washington had been a pleasant distraction. He was grateful to Graham for being so gracious to his friends and promised himself he would find a way to repay her hospitality. Like his trip to Los Angeles with the Deweys, Washington had been an out-of-town stop on the Truman tour. *In Cold Blood* was in previews, so to speak. Wherever Truman traveled, he promoted his book. The advance word generated by Truman's hard work and the *New Yorker* serialization was sensational.

The public was equally fascinated by the business side of the story, mainly because Truman was making so much money, a perquisite not normally associated with literary writing. In late December, the *New York Times* ran an article entitled "A Book in a New Form Earns $2-Million for Truman Capote." The various revenue streams generated by *In Cold Blood*—$500,000 from New American Library for the paperback rights, a hefty deal from Columbia Pictures for the movie rights, and advances from the Book-of-the-Month Club and fifteen foreign publishers—turned Truman's literary labor of love into a cash machine. The *Times* calculated that the author received $14.80 per word for his 135,000-word "nonfiction" novel.

Truman downplayed the sum, insisting that he had put so much time into researching and writing his book that averaging it out over six years, "any small time Wall Street operator gets at least that much."

There was no doubt that he was enjoying the money and the financial security that came with it. As his publication day approached, it was as if the longest overture in the history of modern literature was about to come to its coda. Yet Truman did not suffer from opening-day jitters. He was confident about his book, and he had heard early critics apply the word *masterpiece* to it enough times to suspect that praise and prosperity were around every corner. If 1965 was a year of endings—for Smith and Hickock, who were executed, and for their long-suffering scribe, who finally got to finish his book—1966 was all about beginnings. The previews of *In Cold Blood* were over: the show was about to begin.

Slim Keith in 1949 with her second husband, Leland Hayward.

Slim

Slim Keith was Truman's quintessentially American "California girl." Born in 1917 and raised as Nancy Gross in Salinas, California, Slim, unlike most beautiful young women in that part of the country, was not stage-struck and did not want to be a movie star. When she was a teenager, she met the actor William Powell at a resort in Death Valley. They became friends, and he nicknamed her "Slim" because of her lanky physique. She was young, blond, and stylish, and she radiated vitality. Slim described her beauty aesthetic as "scrubbed clean, healthy, shining, and golden." She pulled her hair back in a simple ponytail and preferred a wardrobe of denim and suede to silk and satin. And she never worried about being fashionable: Slim was more interested in being sporty and comfortable than in slavish trend following.

Her lighthearted friendship with Powell led to introductions to other celebrities. William Randolph Hearst and Marion Davies invited her to San Simeon, where she was one of the youngest guests in attendance. In her new social circle, she met Cary Grant, David Niven, and Howard Hawks, one of Hollywood's top directors and the creative force behind such movies as *Scarface* and *Bringing Up Baby*. Hawks, a married man in his forties, found the beautiful teenager irresistible and incomprehensible. He was so accustomed to being surrounded by ambitious starlets and aspiring actresses that he did not know how to categorize Slim, who was in a class by herself. Men were drawn to her because, in addition to being a stunning young woman, she was a good sport, a high-spirited buddy who enjoyed hunting, fishing, and other traditionally male pursuits.

Hawks divorced his wife and married Slim. For the next eight years, she enjoyed her own version of life on the Hollywood A list. She became the prototype for what would become known as the Howard Hawks heroine. As a counterpoint to their glamorous nightlife, the Hawkses maintained a working farm in Los Angeles, where Slim raised pigs and chickens. When they weren't at home, they were off on hunting trips with the likes of Ernest Hemingway and William Faulkner: Slim could hold her own on any expedition or adventure. Ironically, the more she retreated from fashion, boldly wearing handmade angora socks and men's jeans, the more she was pursued by fashion magazines for her unique sense of casual elegance.

In 1944, Slim made a significant contribution to the movie industry when she suggested an unknown fashion model to play opposite Humphrey Bogart in her husband's new film *To Have and Have Not*. The distinctive beauty she recommended was Lauren Bacall, a lean and long-legged young thoroughbred not unlike herself.

Hawks was great fun to be with, but he was a notorious womanizer who seized any opportunity to stray. Not surprisingly, Slim also turned her attention elsewhere. She fell in love with the agent and producer Leland Hayward, who was married to the actress

Margaret Sullavan. It took a few years for Slim and Hayward to extricate themselves from their marriages, but by 1949, they were free to be with each other. Their wedding took place at Bill and Babe Paley's estate, Kiluna.

Like Hawks, Hayward was a bon vivant who loved living extravagantly and who thought nothing of spiriting Slim off to Paris for a weekend, surprising her with jewels, or showering her with white roses. Travel was a big part of their life. Slim flew or sailed from one exotic location to another—Hawaii, Spain, the south of France, Cuba—and always in the best of company. In 1958, the producer Sam Spiegel asked Slim to join him on a trip to far-off Russia. He had been invited to show three of his films, *The Bridge on the River Kwai*, *On the Waterfront*, and *The African Queen*, and he wanted Slim, her old friend Cary Grant, and her relatively new friend Truman Capote to keep him company.

Slim and Truman became good friends during their Russian excursion. He was an enchanting companion, always armed with a quip or the latest gossip. Truman called her "Big Mama," and he was her "Trueheart." But Slim never made the mistake of confiding anything really important to her chatty friend. She wisely figured that her secrets might end up the subject of conversation with another swan.

In October of 1958, just a few months after her trip to Russia, Slim joined Lauren Bacall on a trip to Europe. She and Hayward felt she should go because Bacall was recovering from Humphrey Bogart's death and needed company. Slim went to Europe with the understanding that her husband, who stayed behind because he had pressing business in New York, would follow in a few days. It was not unusual for the couple to travel separately, and Slim was not always the most attentive wife. There were rumors of indiscretions, including a one-night stand with Frank Sinatra and a fling with a screenwriter who had worked on one of Hayward's projects. Slim's friends recognized a restlessness in her that usually signified a relationship gone stale.

While Slim was away, Babe Paley enlisted Hayward to help her entertain a guest from England. She was expecting Pamela Churchill, who, typically, would sweep into town exuding perfume and expectations. A houseguest like Pamela required a full social agenda, and most hostesses were less than thrilled about trusting flirtatious Pamela with their husbands. Babe was no exception, but with Hayward as her extra man, she found the prospect of wining and dining Pamela more tolerable.

Babe's husband may have been safe under the circumstances, but Slim's husband was fair game. While Slim and Bacall partied in Madrid, Pamela worked her magic on Hayward, using her talents to make him believe he was the only man in the world. In less than a week, he had fallen under her spell. Truman saw them together in New York and not so innocently wrote to Slim, jokingly asking if she knew her husband was "running around with the notorious Mrs. C."

Later, Slim discovered what everyone else knew: Hayward had fallen in love with Pamela. The light bulb went on when Slim walked into Pamela's home in London and saw that it was filled with white roses, the very flower Hayward had always sent to her. She hoped that her husband, like Gianni Agnelli, Averill Harriman, and the other rich and powerful men who had come before him, would have an amusing little affair without getting serious. After all, she pointed out to him during one of their fights, "nobody *marries* Pam Churchill." But Hayward was a romantic— he wanted a bride, not a mistress.

The Hayward-Churchill affair launched a scandal that had a remarkable effect on international society. In America, "tout New York is divided into warring camps," gossiped Truman in a letter to Cecil Beaton. The debacle became a lively spectator sport as socialites came out in favor of either Slim or Pamela. As for Truman, he pronounced himself "a Slimite to the death," although he cleverly managed to maintain a friendship of sorts with Pamela as well.

Slim was heartbroken. In all the years she had been romantically involved with a man, she had always been the one to leave. For the first time, she was the one who had been abandoned, an unsettling experience that left her feeling vulnerable and uncertain. While she was between marriages, Truman gave her a needed jolt of confidence by asking her to handle the movie rights to *In Cold Blood*. She agreed. Because she believed the book was a masterpiece, her hardnosed strategy was to turn down prospective buyers until they offered a million dollars.

Eventually, Slim started a relationship with a new man, Kenneth Keith, a wealthy English banker who was about to be knighted. As Keith's wife, Slim would become Lady Keith and enjoy financial security and an elevated social standing. She wasn't head over heels in love the way she had been with Hawks and Hayward, but it was time for a change. Slim married Keith and concentrated on making a success of it. She convinced Truman to let her friend Irving "Swifty" Lazar oversee the movie sale of *In Cold Blood* because she would be busy attending to the demands of her new life.

With her starchy new husband at her side and her eyes wide open to the fact that they had entered into a business arrangement rather than a love match, Slim settled in England. She discovered that she had landed in a world that was neither warm nor welcoming—the British were famous for their coolness to outsiders. But Slim was the plucky sort who managed to introduce color, passion, and joy into even the chilliest situations. She insisted on holding lively conversations at previously silent dinner tables, she decorated the country house at Christmas, and she even befriended the butler.

Lady Keith was still Truman's fun-loving "Big Mama" at heart.

7

Riding a Wave

Truman capote's new year began with a bang. On January 5, 1966, he signed a contract for a new book, scheduled for delivery in 1968. He would be working with Random House and Joe Fox again, just as he had on *In Cold Blood*. His new book, however, promised to be very different from his penetrating and disturbing investigation of the Clutter murders. Truman was ready to turn his attention to *Answered Prayers*, a project he had mentioned to Bennett Cerf in 1958. The title came from the adage "More tears are shed over answered prayers than unanswered ones," which Truman attributed to St. Teresa. The book would be a dark comedy about the very rich, "a contemporary equivalent of Proust's masterpiece *Remembrance of Things Past*," according to Fox.

Now that he was finished with Kansas and back in the company of aristocrats, celebrities, and café society, it made sense for Truman to write about this world. He could be a man about town, patronizing the hot spots while collecting anecdotes about "Charlie and Oona, Jackie, Babe, Lennie, Bobby and other such noted persons," as *Life* observed when it broke the story about his next work.

Sometimes he himself was the subject of choice anecdotes. Once when Truman was at New York's fabled "21" Club, he had the rare pleasure of witnessing two distinguished gentlemen come to blows over *In Cold Blood*. He was dining with the agent Irving "Swifty" Lazar and his wife, Mary. At the next table was the Teutonic producer Otto Preminger, along with his wife, Hope, and the Broadway columnist Louis Sobel. When Sobel innocently asked Swifty if he had any news to report, Preminger interjected that he had a story: Frank Sinatra was going to punch Lazar in the nose the next time he saw him, because Swifty had promised to sell *In Cold Blood*'s movie rights to Preminger and Sinatra, but he had pulled a fast one and sold the project to Columbia Pictures instead.

It appeared that Preminger was teasing—until he called Lazar "a liar, a cheat, and a crook" and told Mary Lazar that he felt sorry for her because she had to sleep with him. Mary slapped Preminger, who tried to strike back. Lazar stopped the angry filmmaker in his tracks by smashing a glass on his bald head. The wound required fifty stitches. Preminger pressed charges against Lazar for the assault, telling the media, "Talk about cold blood!" The story was widely reported in the *New York Times*, *Newsweek*, and other publications. The notoriety was good for Truman's ego and great for sales: people were literally fighting over *In Cold Blood* before it was even published.

January 16, 1966, was a chilly Sunday in New York City, a good day to spend a lazy morning indoors with the *New York Times*. All over America—in San Francisco, Providence, Atlanta, Miami, Des Moines, Dallas, and other cities—readers curled up with their fat Sunday newspapers. When they turned to the book section, one title stood out: *In Cold Blood*. More than twenty-four newspapers ran a review of Capote's book that Sunday, a rare occurrence in the days before electronic media made simultaneity commonplace.

Most of the critics were very enthusiastic. Those who praised *In Cold Blood* often described it in paradoxical terms: it was classic and innovative, painful to read yet impossible to put down. The *Miami Herald* compared Truman to Dostoyevsky. The *Philadelphia Inquirer* called the book "a masterpiece of storytelling." The *Charlotte Observer* praised Capote for creating "a book that claws its way into your very being and stays." And the all-important *New York Times* proclaimed that Capote had written "a modern masterpiece."

There were voices of dissent. The *San Francisco Sun Chronicle* said, "*In Cold Blood* goes down the gullet like custard" and deemed the book "as powerless and empty of significance as a dead snake," while the *New Republic* said that Capote was the "most outrageously overrated stylist of our time." One of the biggest bones of

Random House's display for its new best seller.

contention between the book's supporters and its detractors was the question of whether *In Cold Blood* should be classified as a novel. Capote, of course, called the book a nonfiction novel, a catchy expression that seemed to introduce a significant new art form. But it was a term many critics were eager to debunk. Astute readers knew that other authors had ventured into that territory before. Cornelius Ryan's *The Longest Day*, Lillian Ross's *Picture*, and John Hersey's *Hiroshima* were books that served up fact in a dramatic way, just as Capote's literary experiment did.

Reviewers also sat on opposite sides of the fence regarding Capote's journalistic detachment from his story. Some felt that his distance enhanced the inherent drama in the book. The *New York Times* called his impassive point of view "Olympian," and the *Baltimore Sun* said that the "heart and power of *In Cold Blood* is Capote's ability to objectively expose the lives of the murderers." Others found his impersonal style chilly, calculated, and even unimaginative. The *Christian Science Monitor* dismissed it as "Dragnet for Highbrows."

Conflicting opinions about *In Cold Blood* dominated the book pages for months, but people who never read books or book reviews knew all about Truman Capote and his controversial new work. Truman broke many records for media attention. In addition to its standard review, the *New York Times Book Review* published a piece on Truman that was "the longest interview in its history." *Life* devoted an unprecedented eighteen pages to the book, profiling Capote, the Clutters, and the killers. *Newsweek* featured Capote on its cover, as did the *Saturday Review*. *Vogue* published Truman's article about his cruise with Kay Graham and the Agnellis. When Marie Dewey saw the piece, illustrated with its unflattering candid shots of Graham on the beach, she observed that her Washington hostess might want to shoot Truman with something other than a camera.

When newspapers weren't printing stories about the literary merits of *In Cold Blood*, they were dedicating whole articles to analyses of the book's phenomenal publicity and marketing campaign. The

New York Times business writer William D. Smith called *In Cold Blood* "one of the greatest promotional successes in publishing history," citing the rash of magazine covers, articles, and radio and television programs that had appeared in the short weeks since the book's publication. *In Cold Blood* was considered so newsworthy that important publications such as *Life* and *Newsweek* approached Random House about covering it, instead of waiting for the publisher's publicity department to contact them. *Life* was so certain the story was momentous—and would be a big draw at the newsstand—that the magazine flashed the title *In Cold Blood* from the top of the Allied Chemical Tower in Times Square.

The *Times* was curious about the origin of the heat surrounding *In Cold Blood*. The publisher Bennett Cerf was a likely candidate. In addition to being an astute businessman and wise in the ways of book promotion, he was a popular personality, well known for his best-selling humor books and for his weekly appearances on the long-running game show *What's My Line?* Truman was his friend, and *In Cold Blood* was one of Cerf's pet projects. Cerf insisted that neither he nor Random House had done anything extraordinary to promote *In Cold Blood*. That's not how Truman's new book catapulted to the top of every best-seller list and the tip of every tongue. The book's astonishing success began and ended with Truman himself, whom Smith ultimately described as "the Svengali primarily responsible for this publishing phenomenon."

"A boy has to hustle his book," Truman told *Newsweek*. And hustle he did, whether regaling friends at posh New York dinner parties with the inside story of the Clutter investigation or talking to the lucky journalists Random House allowed to interview him. The publicity department was inundated with so many requests from the media that a good number were refused, including an invitation for Truman to be the first "professional author" to appear on the television show *Meet the Press*.

There was a downside to the publicity maelstrom surrounding *In Cold Blood*: the coverage of the book's phenomenal success threatened to overshadow its literary merits. In an article entitled "Literature-by-Consensus," Eliot Fremont-Smith of the *New York Times* protested the "vast, self-generating promotional mill in which everyone—author, publisher, magazine editor, critic, bookseller and reader—is trapped." Fremont-Smith used the word *noise* to describe the hoopla that transformed *In Cold Blood* into a commodity and called the book an inflated "Macy's Thanksgiving Day balloon . . . (that) moves gigantically along the avenue to success." He was really protesting an early manifestation of hype, a promotional tactic that was just beginning to surface in the publishing industry. Too much publicity, Fremont-Smith warned, can work against a book and its author: critics bristle at this kind of manipulation—from envy, if not from disgust—and readers develop short attention spans as they are bombarded by one promotional campaign after another.

Fremont-Smith was not alone in his negative response to the publicity blitz for *In Cold Blood*. In her monthly column in *Life*, Shana Alexander called it a "massive huckstering bacchanal" and accused Capote, one of her favorite authors, of "leading the grape-stomp." "Why," she asked, "couldn't Capote for heaven's sake just shut up?"

But Truman was enjoying himself too much to keep quiet. There was always somebody, usually a reporter, willing to listen to the best-selling author's latest bon mot, and when Truman wasn't busy with book signings and readings, he had places to go and people to see. By February 13, there were 340,000 copies of *In Cold Blood* in print, not counting additional copies earmarked for Book-of-the-Month Club subscribers. Still writing about the story, the *New York Times* called the book "the hottest property since the invention of the wheel." Booksellers may have been confused about whether to shelve *In Cold Blood* with fiction or nonfiction because they had difficulty grasping the anomalous concept of the "non-fiction novel," but they were thrilled about its sales figures and the customers it brought into the stores.

Truman Capote was good for publishing. He was also good for film, television, and the stage. Columbia Pictures was fast-tracking Richard Brooks's movie version of *In Cold Blood* in order to fully capitalize on the book's momentum. ABC announced a television dramatization of Truman's story "A Christmas Memory," to be written by the author himself, directed by Frank Perry, and starring Geraldine Page. With great fanfare, the Broadway impresario David Merrick said that he planned to bring *Breakfast at Tiffany's*, which had been made into a movie starring Audrey Hepburn in 1961, to life as a musical. Truman was hopping from one medium to another, and his talents seemed to know no boundaries.

There were indications, however, that Truman was paying a price for his great success. He was hospitalized with a virus during a trip to Switzerland in February. He confided to his friend Cecil Beaton that the only time he felt calm was when he took impromptu road trips in his beloved green Jaguar. Driving soothed him, as did motels, where he enjoyed sinking into a warm bathtub with a glass of scotch and a few sleeping pills. Beaton worried that success had changed Truman, and he wrote in his diary that "he looks like a tycoon, thickset, well-dressed, no longer the little gnome of Other Voices. . . . I secretly feel T. is in a bad state and may not last long." Harper Lee had some misgivings about her friend's condition as well. "Truman is happy," she told *Newsweek*. "But, there's only one thing worse than promises unkept, that's promises kept," she cautioned—her own version of St. Teresa's admonition about answered prayers. Success, and the good life that came with it, could be destructive.

Yet whatever Truman felt inside, he looked as if he was having the time of his life.

❧

One morning in June, while Truman was still riding the wave of adulation, he realized that he had money in his pockets and time on his hands. This was an unusual state of affairs for a writer who was generally overworked and overextended. He wanted a reward for his hard work, especially the long, difficult years he had devoted to *In Cold Blood*. To celebrate his incredible good fortune, he decided to host a party, his "great, big, all-time spectacular present" to himself. On a more practical level, such a party would be the perfect sort of high-octane finale to *In Cold Blood*'s long-running and multifaceted publicity campaign: a launch party after the fact, guaranteed to keep the author and his masterpiece in the headlines. Hosting such an event would also give him the opportunity to do some field work on *Answered Prayers*. He would invite the very people whom he intended to build that book around.

Truman thought about the party constantly and with the same concentration he'd previously reserved for his writing. He described his idea to Leo Lerman with such excitement that his friend misunderstood and asked if he was talking about a new story. Truman's answer was yes. In a sense, it *was* a story, but not one that was written. Instead, it would be written about. He envisioned the party as a kind of performance art. And art, in any form, would have to satisfy his high standards. Truman could spend days fussing over a sentence, searching for the right word, phrase, or even punctuation mark. He would be just as precise in planning this party.

The first step would be to find a clever concept, one that could capture his own imagination, dazzle his friends, and make a splash in New York, the most social of cities. It was a challenging assignment that year, when there seemed to be more parties—and parties of every sort—than ever. The winter had seen a mad rush of balls and galas. Even May, generally a quiet month reserved for weddings, European tours, and the annual opening of country houses, was packed with events.

Charity balls, the foundation of every social season, proliferated throughout the year. Regulars on the benefit circuit complained that they were boring, expensive, and time-consuming, yet fundraisers flourished. Most of these fancy events, dreaded by husbands who hated to wear tuxedos, cost anywhere from twenty-five to a hundred dollars a head and involved long evenings spent in hotel ballrooms. In one record-breaking week in May, weary guests raced from one big night to another; the Salute to Summer Ball for the Memorial Sloan-Kettering Cancer Center at the Plaza; the Safari Ball, benefiting the African Medical and Research Foundation at Tavern on the Green; a Boy Scout gala; and benefits for both the Retarded Infants Service and the Association for the Help of Retarded Children. There would have been a third fund-raiser, the Ball International for the National Association for Retarded People, but it was postponed because ticket sales fell off when key people—namely, Governor Nelson Rockefeller and his wife—could not attend. Key people were crucial components of any successful charity ball because they inspired other donors to buy tickets. "Without them," the society hostess Mrs. John R. Fell told the *New York Times*, "you're in trouble."

Balls were also popular among transplanted Europeans who wanted to express their patriotism and commemorate their traditions, if only for one night. In 1966, the Russian expatriate community rang in the New Year with a Bal Blanc. They were followed, a few weeks later, by the Viennese, who hosted their annual Opera Ball, complete with white tie, paprika schnitzel, and bowls of schlag. The Hungarians were next, with a romantic evening of rose wine and gypsy music. Guests at these festive displays of nationalism, often deposed aristocrats and their loyal followers, danced the quadrille, the czardas, and the polonaise, enjoying the opportunity to experience Europe the way it was in the old days, when there was still pomp, circumstance, and royalty. Nostalgia was in full force at the Hungarian ball, where women curtsied prettily to young Michael Hohenzollern, not because he was an up-and-coming sales representative for Pan American Airlines whose father was an assembly-line worker at Ford, but because his great-grandfather had been Kaiser Wilhelm II of Germany.

Added to the social mix was a gala at the Whitney Museum, the opening night of the Bolshoi Ballet, the April in Paris Ball, and dozens of other high-priced events. These evenings were covered dutifully by newspaper society editors, but rarely with much enthusiasm. Many of these parties were as boring to write about as they were to attend because they adhered to a dress-up, dinner, and dancing formula that raised more money than spirits.

There were even balls for the downtown crowd. Two years earlier, in 1964, the noted photographer Jerry Schatzberg hosted a Mods and Rockers Ball in honor of the Rolling Stones at his Park Avenue South loft. Resplendent in gold lamé, Goldie and the Gingerbreads, the girl group of the moment, rocked the room with their hit rendition of "Can't You Hear My Heart Beat?" Guests from the hip under-thirty set, including the super model Jean Shrimpton, danced so feverishly that the floor buckled and threatened to give way, and the rocker prince Mick Jagger was among the last to leave. The music may have been louder, the beat faster, and the clothes more youthful and daring than they were at uptown soirees, but the differences between the two types of parties were mostly cosmetic. Either way, when the evening was over, most aspects of the affair were soon forgotten.

A conventional evening, whether of the uptown or the downtown variety, would never do for a showman like Truman, an ambitious host who wanted his ball to be one of those unforgettable parties that lives in legend. For a party to become that, it had to offer some kind of engaging theme or gimmick that expressed the creativity of its host and sparked the enthusiasm of its guests. What Truman needed was a concept, one that would generate anticipation before the event and guarantee excitement long after it was over.

C. Z.

Slim, Marella, Gloria, and Babe were frequently found inside *Vogue*, *Harper's Bazaar*, and other fashion magazines, but in July of 1962, it was C. Z. Guest, dressed in riding britches and standing next to her dog, who was featured on the cover of *Time* as the icon of the "New Society." According to *Time*, the New Society had new rules and new leaders. Old money, blue blood, and even a touch of royalty simply weren't enough to keep a socially ambitious person in play. Pacesetters, as they were called, had to be larger than life in every way, and the door was open to entrepreneurs, politicians, and celebrities of all stripes. "A handful of women stand out, by virtue of their wealth, beauty and energy," pronounced *Time*, "and probably the best-known of them is Mrs. Winston Frederick Guest."

C. Z., as Lucy Douglas Cochrane was nicknamed by a sibling who could not pronounce *sister*, was born in Boston in 1920. She grew up to be a fun-loving debutante who was a breath of fresh air in stodgy Back Bay. Her high spirits and blond beauty won her a

part in the 1944 Broadway revival of the Ziegfeld Follies and a
screen test at 20th Century Fox in Hollywood. But C. Z. was more
impressive in life than on the stage or the screen, and her theatrical career was short lived.

In 1945, C. Z. returned to Boston by way of Mexico, where
she captured the eye of the artist Diego Rivera. For a society girl,
and a *Boston* one at that, C. Z. was remarkably uninhibited and
saw nothing wrong with Rivera's request to paint her, in all her
blondness, in the nude. What's more, she had no objection to the
painting hanging in a hotel bar. It wasn't there for long. Winston
Frederick Churchill Guest, a scion of the Phipps steel dynasty,
fell in love with C. Z., proposed marriage, was accepted, and
bought the Rivera for his private collection immediately before
the wedding.

The newlyweds maintained an apartment on Sutton Place in
New York City and Templeton, an estate on Long Island, where
C. Z. set the tone of casual elegance. Though she moved in the
most exclusive social circles, she was first and foremost a sports-
woman whose passion was horseback riding. When her husband
offered her jewels, she asked for more horses. She credited athletics, and especially riding, with imposing a discipline on her life
that enabled her to stay sane, healthy, and good-humored while
other, less-focused members of the social elite became fragile and
self-destructive.

Truman called her "the cool vanilla lady," and cool she was,
whether on safari with the maharaja of Jaipur or poolside with her
children, Alexander and Cornelia, in Palm Beach. Her look was
simple yet classic: outfitted by her favorite designer, Mainbocher,
she wore beautifully tailored, ladylike clothes in flattering pastel
colors. Composed but never stuffy, C. Z. made elegance seem
easy. She radiated confidence in all situations, even when financial woes threatened her cosseted world.

The Guests maintained an expensive lifestyle that required more than their sizable annual trust fund income of $600,000 to keep them afloat. They owned multiple residences in New York and Florida and expensive stables for their thoroughbreds. They routinely traveled to exotic locations and dressed in couture gowns and bespoke suits. C. Z. was a photographer's darling. Louise Dahl-Wolfe and Horst P. Horst, among others, repeatedly captured her serene beauty with their cameras.

By 1959, the Guests experienced a cash-flow problem and had to sell the Villa Artemis, the opulent family estate in Palm Beach. They held on to a comfortable living space over the garage, which served as their winter residence, but four years later, in 1962, were forced to put the Sutton Place apartment on the market to raise much-needed cash. Many society women would have been crushed by these public downsizings, but not C. Z. A true athlete, she knew how to manage her expectations, put her disappointments behind her, and get back up on the horse. In the red or in the black, C. Z. was still one of the most popular members of international society. Diana Vreeland, the editor of *Vogue* and a social arbiter herself, described C. Z.'s insider status: "For C. Z. there's no such thing as missing a party," she explained. "Either she's there, or for her it doesn't exist."

Flanked by this pantheon of remarkable women, Truman moved easily through the often impenetrable worlds of money and privilege. Yet he sensed there was a changing-of-the-guard in the works. His ladies were getting older as society was getting younger. It was time to make room for a new generation of swans.

8

Dreaming of
Masquerades

THE MOST DIRECT ROUTE TO PARTY IMMORTALITY WAS A
masquerade ball, or *bal masqué*. James Laver, the editor of the social
history *Memorable Balls*, observed that "nearly all the 'memorable
balls' of history have taken the form of some kind of masquerade."
The *Grand Larousse Encyclopedia* defines masquerade as "A diversion of Italian origin and aristocratic character, comprising allegorical, mythological, satirical, or burlesque scenes and entrances
performed by masked persons and integrated with music, dance,
and poetry."

Asking guests to dress in costumes was a way to introduce fantasy, mystery, spectacle, and romance into an otherwise routine
affair. Even the most jaded partygoers demonstrated childlike
enthusiasm at the notion of inventing disguises for themselves,
dressing up, and playing pretend.

The first *bals masqués* were elaborate entertainments hosted by
European kings who commanded their guests to attend. One of
these early masquerades, "Le Bal des Ardents," or "fiery ball," was
hosted by King Charles VI of France in 1393. The ruler's mood

swings were so extreme and unpredictable that he was known as "Charles the Well-Beloved" or "Charles the Mad," depending on his psychological condition at the time of the appellation. The unstable king's poor judgment often led to trouble, especially the night he decided to attend a masquerade ball disguised as a wild satyr.

Charles and his most trusted courtiers covered themselves with hair and wax until they were unrecognizable and then, with savage abandon, terrorized and sexually harassed several young women at court. An angry boyfriend or husband turned a torch against the hooligans, whose costumes exploded into flames when a spark came into contact with the wax. King Charles managed to escape unharmed, but several members of his court burned to death. The episode left Charles crazier than ever.

Masquerade balls flourished in London and Venice in the eighteenth century for the same reason they had become popular in Paris. Masks and costumes bestowed thrilling anonymity upon party guests, encouraging them to relax (and, in some cases, abandon) their morals and inhibitions. Held in public halls and gardens and attended by different classes of revelers, these balls were considered so decadent and debased that there was actually an anti-masquerade movement mounted by a concerned group of England's foremost artists, religious leaders, and writers, including Henry Fielding and Samuel Richardson. Many supporters of the movement believed that masquerades, which originated in "hot countries" such as Italy and France, were a plot devised by foreigners to "enslave true Englishmen by encouraging in them Licentious [sic] and Effeminacy." The government was reluctant to take an official stand against *bals masqués*, but there were occasional raids, especially when the partygoers were members of the working class, such as happened with the unhappy chambermaids, cook-maids, footmen, and apprentices whose masquerade was forcibly disrupted by the police in 1775.

The masquerade craze spread to the New World, where, in Old New York, hundreds of costume balls were held every year. The

William K. Vanderbilts, the heirs to the bulk of Commodore Vanderbilt's $100 million estate, hosted a grand *bal masqué* in 1883. William's wife, Alva, had been engaged in a long-standing competition for domination of New York society with Caroline Astor, the creator of the notorious list of the four hundred people deemed worthy to enter her ballroom. Astor had refused to include the Vanderbilts in her select group, but Vanderbilt triumphed when she excluded Astor's daughter, Carrie, from her masked ball invitation list. To appease her heartbroken teenager, Astor had to swallow her pride and pay a proper and conciliatory call on her enemy. The coveted invitation arrived at the Astor mansion immediately after the visit.

The Vanderbilt ball took place on March 26, 1883. The blocks surrounding the family's Fifth Avenue mansion were filled with bystanders who waited to watch the arrivals. Footmen greeted the elaborately costumed guests as they made their dramatic entrances into the house. One of the most outstanding costumes was worn by Alice Vanderbilt, who dressed as "Electric Light" in diamonds and a battery-operated headpiece. The Vanderbilt ball was rumored to have cost $250,000, but from Alva Vanderbilt's point of view, it was worth every penny. By the last waltz, she had become one of New York society's most celebrated hostesses.

ᄋᄿᄼ

The power of the press in matters of social standing was not to be underestimated. No one understood that better than Elsa Maxwell, the twentieth-century hostess who began her life as an ordinary girl in Keokuk, Iowa, and went on to become one of high society's most powerful arbiters. Maxwell did not achieve her elevated status because of her looks or her bank account. With her large, crude face and short, misshapen body, she was no one's idea of a beauty. Nor was she wealthy; Maxwell had to work—and depend on the financial largesse of her rich friends—to maintain a comfortable lifestyle. En route to becoming a celebrated hostess, she had been a pianist in vaudeville, a nightclub owner, a press agent, a columnist, and a radio performer, to name a few of her colorful occupations.

Maury Paul, the legendary gossip columnist who wrote under the nom de plume "Cholly Knickerbocker," gave Maxwell her start as a society reporter. She was so good at her job that her pen became her power. Maxwell's endorsement of a product, a place, or a person was an influential promotional tool. And she, in return, was rewarded for her plug. "Everything is given to me that I want," she boasted. Hotels, such as the Waldorf, supplied her with a place to live and made their ballrooms available for her famed parties, all in the name of publicity.

In his book *Who Killed Society?* the social historian Cleveland

Amory disdainfully used the word "publi-ciety," a combination of publicity and society, to explain the very existence of a figure like Maxwell. He argued that in the world of publi-ciety, the gossip columnist is king or, in Maxwell's case, queen. For better or for worse, "he, or she, and he or she alone," said Amory, "decides who, socially speaking, is who."

Maxwell's formidable promotional skills took her only so far. The real key to her success was her tremendous flair for entertaining. Maxwell knew how to make a party pop. "Serve the dinner backward," she advised. "Do anything. But for goodness' sake, do something weird." Clever at keeping guests engaged and entertained, Maxwell invented the scavenger hunt, sending socialites scrambling all over town for hard-to-find items on a list. In the 1930s, she came up with an unusual concept for a metropolitan party, a country masquerade. She hosted bucolic *bals masqués* in New York and Paris. Guests were invited to dress as country characters, milkmaids, farmers, gypsies, and such. Maxwell herself appeared as a male peasant, cradling a chicken under one arm. Animals, including scented goats, mingled with the guests, and a hog-caller led a herd of pigs through their paces. There was no danger of the Country Ball being forgotten the next morning.

In July 1965, Madame Helene Rochas hosted a *My Fair Lady* Ball in Paris. She was a friend and an admirer of Cecil Beaton, who had designed the sets and the costumes for the movie version of the award-winning Lerner and Loewe musical (and the costumes for the stage production). Rochas wanted to recreate the look of Beaton's stunning black-and-white Ascot scene and had the Grande Cascade restaurant in the Bois de Boulogne decorated accordingly. Guests dressed in costumes of the belle époque, wearing wasp-waisted gowns and plumed hats. Dominick Dunne's anniversary dance in Hollywood in 1964 had also paid homage to Beaton.

The rich history of masked balls, filled with tales of success and failure, yielded several important lessons for any would-be party-giver with ambitions as large as Truman's. From Elsa Maxwell, he learned that the successful host did not have to be beautiful or wealthy, although it helped to have guests who were both. Arrivals and entrances needed to be staged, like a form of theater. When entertaining, even on a grand scale, less was more: one tasteful menu was preferable to twenty-eight courses, yet two orchestras were always better than one. Members of the press needed to be embraced; with their help—and headlines—a party could live in legend. Every host needed that all-important gimmick, a theme to make his or her party stand out from the rest. And finally, on a cautionary note, even the most popular host had to be wary of abandonment by the very people he entertained.

ॐ

Truman decided exactly what he wanted to do. With a nod to all the hosts who had come before him, especially Dominick Dunne, he decided to throw a Black and White Ball. And he selected a gimmick that was sure to galvanize and amuse his guests and magnetize the media. He would invite the most famous people in the world—his friends—and impertinently ask them to hide their fabulous and photographed faces behind masks.

Truman trusted sharp-tongued and quick-witted Evie Backer, whom he playfully called Tiny Malice. She was not beautiful enough to be considered one of his swans, but Truman thought enough of her decorating skills to present her with a challenge. What could they do to distinguish his *bal masqué* from all the other events that had taken place at the Plaza?

Clever Evie had a solution that was good for the evening and great for Truman's budget. She recommended a less-is-more approach. No oversized floral centerpieces, no trellises, no blooming bowers, standard sights at every society party—only classic golden candelabras wrapped with graceful green vines. At Truman's ball, the gorgeous swans and all the other beautiful people would be the flowers.

9

Guest of Honor

IN 1962, A NEW WOMAN HAD JOINED TRUMAN'S FLOCK. SHE WAS LEE
Bouvier Canfield Radziwill, a young jet-setting aristocrat and a
great social catch at the time because she was the only sister of
First Lady Jacqueline Bouvier Kennedy and a prominent figure at
court in Kennedy's Camelot. Truman knew Jackie and socialized
with her, as he often bragged to the Deweys, but Lee was more fun
and infinitely more accessible. The fact that she was a princess by
virtue of her marriage to Prince Stas Radziwill of Poland made her
all the more attractive, though insiders whispered that Radziwill
was a naturalized British citizen who had no real claim to a title.

In February of 1962, Truman wrote to Cecil Beaton about his
first rendezvous with Lee. "Had lunch one day with a new friend
Princess Lee (Radziwill)," he crowed. He was delighted to serve up
his impressions in the form of gossip—"(My God, how jealous she
is of Jackie: I never knew); understand her marriage is all but finito."
With characteristic insight, Truman identified the essence of Lee.
She was locked in an intense rivalry with her sister that persisted
despite their close relationship, and she was forever restless in

affairs of the heart. To the outside world, her life seemed to be the stuff of fairy tales, including marriage to a prince. But for Lee, happiness was always elusive.

A pivotal moment in her early life had been her parents' divorce. Like Jackie, Lee adored her charismatic, reckless father, "Black Jack" Bouvier, and resented her mother, Janet, for banishing him from their lives. Lee acknowledged that Jackie was her father's favorite, reasonably pointing out that they had had four years to bond before she was born. But Lee enjoyed the freedom that came with being the baby: her father placed more pressure on his elder daughter to succeed.

At nineteen, Lee asserted her independence by marrying Michael Canfield, an amiable, impeccably groomed, not particularly ambitious young man from an eminent publishing family. Rumor has it that she proposed to him, and he accepted because she seemed to be so much in love with him. She was a glamorous young woman with a slender figure, sculpted cheekbones, and a dazzling smile. She knew how to dress, how to entertain, and how to create stunning backdrops to showcase her beauty. At Lee's urging, the Canfields moved to London in 1955 and became part of the international social scene. Good-looking, affluent, and well-connected, they seemed to be the perfect couple with the perfect lifestyle.

But there was trouble in paradise. According to Diana DuBois, who wrote an unauthorized biography of Radziwill, the couple had been trying unsuccessfully to have a baby, and there were indications that Canfield was sterile. Lee was not happy about that or about the fact that her husband was spending more time drinking than advancing his career. Searching for distractions, both Canfields strayed into the world of fashionable infidelity. It was customary at the time in English high society for husbands and wives to serve as chaperones when their spouses made public appearances with paramours. If the Canfields started spending a lot of time with another couple, it was more than likely that Lee was romantically involved with the other man. This was the case when they were seen around town with Stas Radziwell and his wife, Grace.

Prince Stanislas Radziwill was a Polish refugee who moved to England after World War II. He had been an aristocrat in his native land, but in his new home he was penniless and unknown. Fortunately, postwar London was fertile soil for a charming buccaneer who was willing to gamble on real estate. He made money and a good marriage to Grace. By the time Lee met Radziwill, he was a fixture in international society. He was drawn to her because she was young, sophisticated, and beautiful. Radziwill made no secret of his intentions. He was reputed to have told Michael Canfield, "I really think your wife is absolutely delicious, and I am pursuing her."

Lee was delighted to be pursued. She saw Radziwill as a larger-than-life figure "with an enormous heart, a particular sense of humor and a great knowledge of history." He reminded her of Black Jack, a sentiment that was echoed by her horrified mother upon meeting him for the first time. This similarity was one of the reasons Lee was attracted to him. Eventually, she left Canfield to marry her prince, and early on in their marriage, they had two children, Anthony and Christina.

The Radziwills were thrust into the international spotlight when John Kennedy became president in 1961; suddenly, Lee was the first sister-in-law. Whenever Jackie came to visit, reporters and secret servicemen followed, and every aspect of her life was under scrutiny. Imperious and composed, Lee excelled at being a public figure. She was also a fashion icon. The women's magazines—*Vogue, Harper's Bazaar*, and *Ladies Home Journal*—loved her because, with her slim figure and high cheekbones, she was the embodiment of contemporary elegance.

Lee was the subject of many articles extolling her glamorous life, but in a profile for *Good Housekeeping*, the journalist Barbara Walters suggested that Lee was searching for her place. "Unwilling to settle for simply being the First Lady's sister and unable to decide what other role—homemaker or international butterfly, career girl or society matron, princess or just plain Mrs.—will suit her best, she is currently giving them all a fling."

Walters did not write about Lee's steamy private life. As Truman had observed at their first lunch together, her marriage was already on shaky ground. There was a new man, wealthier and more worldly and powerful than Stas Radziwill: Lee was having an affair with the controversial Greek shipping magnate Aristotle Onassis. The White House was furious about this development because Onassis was not an appropriate candidate for President Kennedy's inner circle, especially if he was angling for the position of brother-in-law. It would have been unimaginable that just a few years later, Onassis would woo—and win—the former first lady herself. For the sake of appearances, Lee remained with her husband, but she was happiest on Onassis's yacht, where she was attended by a fleet of servants and surprised by extravagant gifts, including a magnificent diamond bracelet.

Lee was always busy, but she felt there was something missing from her life. As much as she enjoyed spending time with Truman and another close friend, the dancer Rudolf Nureyev, these relationships made her acutely aware of her own limitations. She wished *she* had a talent, or a métier, as she called it. "What I am seeking," she said in an interview, "is self expression." Truman, now her constant companion, closest confidante, and champion, would have to help Lee find a new outlet for her creative impulses, and they soon settled on the unlikely choice of acting.

ॐ

Who could Truman choose as his guest of honor? He didn't want to be in the position of putting one swan over another. Of course, Truman could try to be au courant and turn to one of the emerging stars of the new generation as his party muse. In 1966, the world was obsessed with youth. *Esquire* determined that half of the American population was under the age of twenty-five. That December, *Time* dubbed the "Twenty-five and Under" generation Man of the Year because the youth movement was the hottest topic in the media.

It was a good time to be young. Baby Boomers, the term used to describe people born shortly after World War II, were a privileged generation. They were likely to be better looking than their predecessors, because they were the beneficiaries of higher standards of living and superior medical care. Vitamins and solid nutrition had built them better bones, fluoride and regular dental visits endowed them with nicer teeth, and the new prosperity provided them with enough disposable income to buy cosmetics that could compensate for whatever nature had not given them The fashion world catered to the new youth market by creating designs that flattered their natural endowments, especially their trim, athletic bodies.

Older men and women who had already crossed the generation gap would emulate the young by dressing in their styles, listening to their music, embracing their ideas, and enjoying their free-and-easy sexuality. Advertisers wooed them. Pepsi positioned itself as the cola "for those who think young" and invited customers to "Come alive, you're in the Pepsi Generation." Oldsmobiles were renamed "Youngmobiles," not so much to attract younger buyers, who accounted for a very small share of the car-buying market, but to make their older customers feel young and with it. Marketing executives emphasized that youth could be a state of mind, but it was still better to actually be young.

The centerpieces of the new youth movement were generally beautiful young women who shared several identifiable characteristics. Marilyn Bender of the *New York Times* described these attributes as "money (of any vintage, quantity, and source, from recent realty venture to seasoned automobile fortune), slim figures (conscientiously honed by exercise, nervous energy and a disinterest in alcoholic beverages), girlish voices, finishing school manners, and youth." In New York City, the two most talked about young women were Baby Jane Holzer and Amanda Mortimer Burden.

The *Vogue* editor Diana Vreeland hailed Holzer as "the most contemporary girl I know," and Baby Jane (nicknamed by the *Women's Wear Daily* writer Carol Bjorkman for the Bette Davis character in the 1962 movie *What Ever Happened to Baby Jane?*) was dubbed the Girl of the Year by the journalist Tom Wolfe in a satiric essay he wrote for the *New York Herald Tribune*. Andy Warhol vowed to turn her into a superstar; the Rolling Stones played at her twenty-fourth birthday party; and women everywhere begged their hairdressers for her sexy "flip" hairstyle, which allowed her blond mane to sit sexily on her shoulders.

Though Jane lived in a Park Avenue apartment with her businessman husband, Leonard, two dogs, servants, and a valuable art collection, she was pure counterculture. Unlike Truman's swans, who had earned their celebrity the old-fashioned way with "understated clothes, dark woods, high ceilings, silver-smithery, (and) respectable nannies," Tom Wolfe wrote that Jane was all about "rock and roll, underground movies, decaying lofts, models, photographers, Living Pop Art, the twist, the frug, the mashed potatoes, stretch pants, pre-Raphaelite hair, Le Style Camp." Even her clothing, Paris couture and *le dernier cri* from interesting little boutiques on New York's Lower East Side, was a mixture of high and low, cheap and expensive, then and now. The unique marriage of uptown and downtown made Jane this season's It girl. She was a socialite revolutionary who was tearing down the walls. As she explained to the *New York Times*, "There is no class anymore. Everybody is equal."

Although Jane had not done anything particularly newsworthy, magazines and newspapers couldn't get enough of her. Her celebrity was not based on achievement. Instead, she was the epitome of the new, youth-driven society—all promise, energy, and attitude. "The press watches Jane Holzer as if she were an exquisite piece of . . . radar," observed Wolfe.

Her flamboyant charms were mostly wasted on Truman, and, had he been considering a youthful guest of honor, he would have been more likely to select the other young woman whose face was all over town. Amanda Mortimer Burden, Babe Paley's daughter and the bride of the aspiring New York City politician Carter Burden, had already made her mark on society at the age of twenty. She and Burden had had a storybook courtship and wedding in 1964 (*Vogue* assigned Cecil Beaton to photograph the festivities) and were hailed by the New York press as "the greatest pair of starring sweethearts since Mary Pickford and Douglas Fairbanks." *Women's Wear Daily* called the Burdens "locomotives" because they were a driving force in the under-twenty-five set. Carter Burden commanded attention because he was tall, fair, distinguished, and the product of some of the best bloodlines in America, including his great-great-great grandfather Commodore Cornelius Vanderbilt. But it was beautiful Amanda, affectionately called "Ba" by her family and friends, who was a magnet for reporters and photographers.

If Jane Holzer represented the wilder, antiestablishment side of the new society, Amanda Burden was the embodiment of young gentility. She did not have the smudged, Monroe-like, morning-after look cultivated by Jane. Fresh, innocent, and understated, she was described by one friend as looking like "a gazelle whose mother was a flower." Amanda Burden looked like a character from a fairy tale, and the media was quick to play up that angle by extolling her classic charms. "Switched on has had it," *Women's Wear Daily* decreed. "Amanda and Carter Burden epitomize the New Spirit— It's Right to be Proper." Being proper meant having good manners, good grooming (Amanda's hair was long but tidy), and a sense of decorum. Gossip columns reported that she demurely declined to be photographed in a St. Laurent see-through dress because, as she explained, "Carter wouldn't like it."

❧

These young girls were good at grabbing headlines, but, wild or tamed, they were ultimately too green to carry the kind of monumental evening Truman had in mind. And he wisely sidestepped the swans, anticipating that they would attack if one member of the flock were elevated above the others. Truman came up with a completely original idea for his guest of honor. His choice was a surprise to everyone, including the woman he picked, who was, arguably, more of a duckling than a swan.

"Honey, I just decided you're depressed and need cheering up, so I'm going to give you a party," Truman announced to Kay Graham while she was vacationing in Saratoga Springs. She was at a spa with her friend Polly Wisner. Kay listened, somewhat amused, and in her matter-of-fact way told him she was fine and did not need cheering up. There was no denying that she was still recovering from her husband's suicide, but on the bright side, a new Kay was emerging, one who was strong, confident, and very capable of running a media empire. That Kay did not need anyone's sympathy.

Whatever Kay said had no effect. Truman had made up his mind about his guest of honor and insisted to her that the event would be "the nicest party, darling, you ever went to." His decision was prompted by feelings of friendship and ambition. Truman was genuinely fond of Kay and wanted to do something special to show his appreciation for her hospitality. The only way to repay Kay's largesse was to host a spectacular party with her as the centerpiece.

But a case could be made that the Paleys, the Agnellis, and the Guinnesses, who had been hosting Truman at their estates and on their yachts for years, were far more deserving of a grand gesture. The problem was that fêting Babe, Marella, or Gloria would have been ho-hum—the mark of another insider party. On the other hand, Kay would be a novel, even newsworthy choice because she was an outsider and, as such, an exotic presence. More to the point, she had the power to mobilize the media. With the *Washington Post* and *Newsweek* in her pocket, she was one of the most important women in America. Kay Graham was the way to go.

Kay Graham wondered what she could possibly have in common with the sophisticated beauties who surrounded Truman. Unlike the fabled swans, Kay never wore makeup, paid little attention to designer clothing, and was rarely seen in the best places.

Eventually, she realized that this was the point. Truman did not pick Babe or Gloria or Marella or Lee precisely because he wanted an unspoiled woman, one who came from a different world and could experience the magic of the evening for the very first time.

Every ball needs a Cinderella, and Truman's Cinderella was Kay.

10

The In Crowd

Excited by the way his party plans were progressing, Truman summoned Leo Lerman to his apartment one hot summer day to reveal the latest developments. "I'm here to tell you, it's to be a black-and-white ball at the Plaza. . . . yes, THE Plaza, and every one of you will wear masks, and I'm giving it for Kay Graham. Do you know Kay? No? You will just love her, and she will love you." He was eager to share all the details—except one. His guest list.

Anyone who had ever spent time with Truman knew that keeping secrets was not his strong point. He was better known for his willingness to reveal *everything*, even the most intimate facts about his life. (One couple—mere acquaintances—had difficulty feigning nonchalance while he relayed a steamy account of his first orgasm.) Truman was equally quick to divulge other people's secrets, and the more provocative the gossip, the better. But just this once, he dug in his heels, sealed his lips, and absolutely refused to disclose his guest list to anyone.

Truman was going to enjoy the process of selecting his invitees and the incredible sense of power that came with it. He purchased a black-and-white composition book, the very kind he used for his writing. In small, neat letters, he wrote *Dance* on the cover. There were 102 pages inside, clean, white, and wide-ruled. Here, he would record the names and the addresses of the chosen.

For the next three months, the notebook was Truman's constant companion. Like a prized pet, it accompanied its owner on his rigorous summer itinerary. Wherever he vacationed—the Hamptons; Washington, D.C.; Paris; Portugal; and on a yacht in the Mediterranean—Truman dedicated himself to the monumental task of assembling the perfect guest list. He approached this project with the same energy and enthusiasm he usually applied to his writing. Notebook in hand, Truman was always in a position to jot down names as they occurred to him. Or he could just as easily cross them off if he had a change of heart.

Most hosts would have had difficulty coming up with more than five hundred names for a private party; Truman had the opposite problem. He knew so many people that his challenge was to weed, edit, and hone before committing to a final list. Truman insisted that he was throwing a party for his friends, but he used the term loosely. It was important to him that each name, whether an old buddy or a new acquaintance, be the right choice.

The year 1966 was a tricky time to engage in social engineering. As Baby Jane Holzer pointed out, "Everybody is equal." No one wanted to be perceived as stuffy or overly formal in his or her approach to entertaining. With the new equality, however, came new rules. In the previous century, Caroline Astor and other hostesses of the Gilded Age had an easy time determining guest lists because the social arbiter Ward McAllister (Ward Make-a-Lister, as he was called) carefully studied candidates' bloodlines to determine their suitability. McAllister maintained that "A ball that any one [sic] can gain admission to is never attractive, while one that is rigidly exclusive will make invitations sought for by everybody." Predictably, the families he selected for inclusion were likely to have surnames such as Morgan, Bradley-Martin, Rhinelander, or the ever-present Vanderbilt.

McAllister's list spawned several indices of society heavy-weights, including the *Social Register*. Founded by the New Jersey entrepreneur and gossip sheet publisher Louis Keller in 1887, the *Social Register* collected and published the names and the addresses of the most socially prominent people in America. Keller was a showman at heart and understood the value of shrouding his elitist directory in mystery. He refused to divulge his organization's methodology or the names of the arbiters on his "Advisory Board."

There was actually very little mystery involved in the process of compiling the register, which, first and foremost, was a money-making proposition for Keller. The names in the debut edition had been imported from an existing social directory, the *Society-List and Club-Register*. Keller sent the book to people who were listed inside, emphasizing the exclusivity and the clublike nature of the publication. These insiders were invited to subscribe to future editions, which would be published twice annually. Keller launched

Social Registers in major cities all over America, including New York, Boston, Chicago, San Francisco, and Baltimore. The only region that did not show interest in the registers was the South, where society leaders were known to say, "Down here, we know who's who without being told."

His book, designed to serve as a society bible, looked the part. The outside was black with discreet orange lettering. Inside, names were listed alphabetically, with comprehensive contact information, including addresses, telephone numbers, and abbreviations for private clubs. Subscribers were warned to "Look at Dilatory Domiciles always to insure accuracy" of listings. Changes of address that were sent in too late to be included in the main index could be found in this whimsically named appendix. A special edition noted the addresses of summer retreats and yachts. Children's names were followed by listings for their prep schools and colleges. There was a separate section called Married Maidens, where a woman's maiden name could be cross-referenced with the name she assumed in marriage. There was an inherent irony in the fact that that the very people who considered themselves part of the unapproachable social elite were willing to publish their most personal information in a glorified telephone directory.

Aspirants who wanted to be listed among the chosen had to submit an application and several letters of recommendation from existing members of the *Register*. Their fates were in the hands of Mrs. Edward C. Barry, Keller's long-standing secretary. She started working at the *Register* at the turn of the century and stayed there for more than fifty years. Even after Keller died in 1922, Barry managed the day-to-day operations of the organization for the new owners, who always had the utmost confidence in her and charged her to "use your own judgment" to keep "insignificant" people at bay.

Nervous applicants probably imagined a formidable, Brahmin-like gatekeeper standing between them and social nirvana, but Bertha Eastmond Barry was an ordinary working-class girl from

Summit, New Jersey. Her father was a railroad lineman, and the man she married was a small-town lawyer. Given the fact that she divided her time between the rural outposts of Wilmington, Vermont, and Tangerine, Florida, it is unlikely that she ever met any of the prominent families on her closely guarded list.

Barry kept abreast of the activities of *Register* regulars (and hopefuls) by corresponding with a network of former newspaper society editors who were on the company's payroll. It was their responsibility to send her clippings concerning engagements, marriages, births, deaths, graduations, and other important milestones. They were also charged with the job of reporting improprieties or scandals that could lead to a member's removal from the list. The *Register* did not approve of people from the entertainment world, and marriage to an actor or an actress was grounds for expulsion. Charles Alden Black, a San Francisco member in good standing, was dropped when he married Shirley Temple, who had been the most beloved child actress in America. The *Register* also disapproved of Jews. The form used to record information about new marriages discreetly asked for a bride's "full Christian and maiden name," a not-so-subtle way of suggesting that Jews need not apply.

The *Social Register* did not improve with age. Its archaic restrictions began to work against it when some of the more interesting and well-known members of high society, Gloria Vanderbilt and Doris Duke, for example, were nowhere to be found on its pages. Prominent men such as John Hay Whitney and Alfred Gwynne Vanderbilt declined to be listed because they thought the book was foolish. Whitney actually asked to have his name removed. He and his wife, Betsy, felt that it was anti-American, and he said, "If you willingly go along with such a travesty of democracy, you tacitly subscribe to its absurd notions of who is and who isn't socially acceptable." In the 1960s, the up-and-coming social elite, the young people known as the "locomotives," were openly disdainful of the *Register* and the people who took it seriously. Carter Burden scornfully called it "the greatest anachronism"—his father had been dropped when he married his mother, an actress—and even Mrs. Barry herself, after decades of dedicating herself to the *Register's* preservation, admitted, "I don't think anyone has any real interest in it anymore."

Social observers realized there was a need for a new kind of classification: one that could accommodate achievement and celebrity, instead of being a high-class "stud book," as *Time* once called the *Register*. Cleveland Amory, who exposed the inner workings of the *Register* in his 1960 book *Who Killed Society?* came up with a clever alternative. Joining forces with Earl Blackwell, who owned Celebrity Service, a company that monitored the comings and goings of the famous for publicity purposes, Amory published the *International Celebrity Register*.

Subtitled "An Irreverent Compendium of American Quotable Notables," the large, encyclopedia-like volume offered mini-biographies of a highly subjective list of 2,240 contemporary celebrities. Instead of using bloodlines or bank accounts to determine the Select, a panel of five judges, including the advertising and magazine dynamo Fleur Cowles, assessed "the decibel ring of the name" of the candidates. Their biographies were light, punchy, anecdotal, and often highly irreverent and included photographs and addresses. Truman, one of New York's loudest noisemakers, was, of course, among those chosen. He was described as being "quick on the drawl" and having "a foliage of blond and somehow defensive bangs." In the first edition, published in 1959, entries could also be found for people as disparate as the humanitarian Dr. Albert Schweitzer and the transsexual Christine Jorgensen, who would never before have been a candidate for any conventional blue book.

The very existence of the *Celebrity Register* signaled a growing interest in publi-ciety, the enticing world of celebrities who, in Amory's words, enjoyed "fame recognized beyond one's own field." Some, such as the contraception advocate Margaret Sanger, were included because of their accomplishments. The *Celebrity Register* prided itself on being a Do book rather than a Blue book. It also embraced scandal instead of running away from it. The retired madam Polly Adler, for example, was considered notable precisely because she added a welcome dash of infamy to the directory. And the actors and the actresses whose dubious profession excluded them from the *Social Register* were the bedrock of this popular new society field guide. As Amory explained, "Nobody looks at Mrs. Vanderbilt's pearls any more; they just want to see what Marlene Dietrich is wearing."

Movie stars were not the only women whose wardrobes inspired widespread curiosity. Fashionable women could become celebrities in their own right simply because they were well-dressed. Their names and beautifully groomed images appeared in newspapers and magazines, along with detailed and often rapturous descriptions of their head-to-toe attire. The International Best Dressed List was devised to pay homage to these fashion icons: women who succeeded at being beautifully dressed and adorned (and sometimes succeeded at nothing else) were elected to the fashionable inner circle, where they were rated in order, building to the coveted top spot of "best in show." Publications all over the world, including serious newspapers such as the *New York Times*, printed the list every year.

The Best Dressed List originated in Europe, but the French abandoned it during World War II because it was considered a frivolous pursuit at such a serious time. In 1940, the New York City fashion publicist and entrepreneur Eleanor Lambert breathed new life into the European institution by importing it to America. At the time, she was working for the New York Dress Institute, a trade group organized to promote dress sales. The best way to generate excitement for fashion, Lambert decided, was to create fashion celebrities. Her International Best Dressed List would spotlight well-dressed women who spent freely on their clothing and who could inspire imitators to do the same.

Lambert sent letters to two thousand observers, a select group consisting of fashion editors, designers, columnists, socialites, and even restaurateurs, asking them to vote for the women they would like to see on the list in a given year. The letter was accompanied by a ballot that contained the names of former winners, along with Lambert's suggestions for likely candidates, usually women in major metropolises such as New York.

But the list's impact was by no means restricted to the fashion business. Like the *Social Register* and the *Celebrity Register* before it, it became another way to catalogue "publi-ciety," since most of the women whose names appeared on the list were from the world of money and privilege. There was some controversy as to exactly how much money a woman had to spend on clothing to achieve the kind of visibility that would make her a candidate for the list. Fashion editors suggested that the range was from $10,000 to $40,000 annually, although Parisian dressmakers estimated that an aspirant had to part with about $50,000 (in today's money, more than $600,000) to get the job done. Mrs. Harrison Williams, a celebrated beauty and a list leader, sniffed at the high-end figures, claiming that she never spent more than $20,000 per year on her wardrobe. The amount spent was ultimately immaterial, for money alone rarely propelled a woman to one of the list's coveted positions. In the end, style was the deciding factor, and a woman who made the list could take pride in the fact that her signature way of dressing was a quantifiable achievement.

Not surprisingly, each of Truman's swans had been named to the International Best Dressed List. In fact, it seemed to be a prerequisite for swanhood. In 1941, Babe tied with the Duchess of Windsor for first place and became a regular until she was elevated to the Hall of Fame in 1957. Slim Hawks was elected in 1944, C. Z. Guest in 1952, Marella Agnelli and Gloria Guinness in 1960, and Lee Radziwill in 1961. Even the daughters of swans found a place on the list. Dolores Guinness was elected in 1960, the same year her mother's name appeared for the first time. Amanda Burden, at the age of twenty-two, won first place on the 1965 list and was called "the most beautiful girl going" by the designer Halston.

∽

When Truman started to compose his all-important roster of guests, he was disdainful of all the old lists that segregated people according to bloodlines and bank books. There was an intriguing new concept in social taxonomy, one that surveyed people of all stripes—writers, socialites, musicians, artists, businessmen, politicians, and others—then emphatically decreed who among them was in and who was out. The in and out list was democratic in the sense that it encompassed disparate social groups: anyone could be a candidate. Yet, typically, it was absolutely dictatorial in keeping outsiders at bay. Only a select few made the final cut.

"I'm in with the In crowd," sang Dobie Gray in 1965. "I go where the In crowd goes." Gray's words became a mantra for the socially ambitious in 1966. Everyone wanted to be in, sought after and accepted by the glamorous people who were members of the social elite. The term was everywhere. A real estate advertisement promised "the 'In' Crowd would love a 'way out' contemporary estate" with "LSD type views of Long Island Sound." Employment agencies invited applicants to "Join the 'in crowd'" by applying for entry-level positions in the media business. Macy's promised that its chic new crepe ensemble was "for the 'In' crowd," suggesting that any woman who put it on would magically become a fashion insider. The Jamaica Playboy Club-Hotel assured vacationers, "You could be living it up with the in crowd at the Caribbean's most glamorous resort."

In July of 1965, the confusing and often contradictory concept of In and Out was deconstructed by the journalist Sherman L. Morrow in a lengthy article in the *New York Times*. Morrow understood that the in crowd was the newest development in a long tradition of classifications and pointed out that it "emphatically replaced the Four Hundred, café society, and the Jet Set as New York's most envied social group." But he was puzzled by the qualifications that a person had to have to become one of the new elite. Some of the first names that came to mind were Adlai Stevenson, Leonard Bernstein, Babe Paley, and, of course, Truman Capote. What did they have in common? They were wealthy, successful, charming, and, more to the point, visible. In an earlier time, they might have been called tastemakers or fashion setters. In another place, they might have been considered merely popular. But in New York City in 1966, they were the consummate insiders, the ins as opposed to the outs.

Morrow pointed out that there was a simple test to determine if a person was in or out. Anyone who attended Princess Lee Radziwill's little gathering in April for one hundred of her closest friends was definitely a member of the in crowd. She called it "a teeny tiny dance . . . just a little thing we're giving before we go back to London." But the party was neither as small nor as casual as her offhand description suggested. Her Fifth Avenue duplex was decorated with masses of spring flowers flown in from France, and imported champagne flowed all night. The one hundred select guests, including Jacqueline Kennedy, Sammy Davis Jr., and Maurice Chevalier, danced to the music of Lester Lanin until 5 a.m.

Inspired by the number, Morrow created his own list of the lucky one hundred and illustrated it with photographs. The choreographer Jerome Robbins, the actress Lauren Bacall, the socialite Gloria Guinness, the agent Leland Hayward, the politician Jacob Javits, the photographer Richard Avedon, and the historian Arthur Schlesinger Jr. rubbed elbows with the conductor Thomas Schippers, the writer William Styron, the actor Henry Fonda, and the fashion designer Oscar de la Renta.

As for the outs, Morrow argued persuasively that fame and wealth did not automatically confer insider status on everyone. He cited Baby Jane Holzer, the ubiquitous "This Year's Girl," as an example of an outsider. She looked as if she belonged, but she was actually "a part of a horde of perhaps 5000 would-be Ins who doggedly follow in the tracks of the In Crowd." Her problem was that she was famous for being famous instead of for being *accomplished*, which seemed to be another of the unifying characteristics of the ins.

That same month, Gloria Guinness, whom Morrow would consider an "automatic in," tackled the subject in an article she wrote for *Harper's Bazaar*. Because she was writing for a women's magazine, she discussed the concept in fashion terms. "Who's chic?" she asked. "Who's with it?" In her opinion, members of the new social elite were distinctive and very much a product of the modern, rule-bending world of the Sixties. She saw them as "original without being beginners, exhibitionists without being pompous, insolent without being patronizing. Immodest but never vulgar, observant but not inquisitive, immoral but not obscene and notorious but not infamous." Many of the names on Guinness's list could be found on Morrow's list as well, including Truman Capote, Leonard Bernstein, Margot Fonteyn, Mike Nichols, and Jacqueline Kennedy. And since she was based in Europe and traveled extensively, Guinness added some international figures, such as Gianni Agnelli, Karim Aga Khan, and the newest arrivals on the scene, the Beatles.

Count Lanfranco Rasponi, a journalist and a public relations expert who was intimately acquainted with high society, blamed the airplane for this new "rootless, bouillabaisse society." He called jet-setters "international nomads" and complained that "these people are on the move so much they even neglect their sex lives," hence the high divorce rate among the rich and the restless.

☙

As one of society's most visible insiders, Truman had to engineer a guest list befitting his elevated position. He would take into account his feelings for an individual, of course, but he was also concerned with how that person would fit into the larger landscape of guests. As he did when he was writing, Truman followed his heart and his head simultaneously. No matter how many times he told people he was throwing together an evening for his closest friends, he was imagining an event that was bigger, better, and more momentous than the typical society ball. His guest list would be a tour de force of social engineering.

Truman couldn't help himself. It was so much fun teasing friends about their invitations that he tortured them with his feigned indecisiveness. "Honey, maybe I'll invite you to my party and maybe I won't," he would threaten playfully, pleased to be wielding so much power. Tired of listening to Truman carry on about whether or not he would include the "Princess of this," the "Maharanee of that," Leo Lerman, who had hosted some star-studded parties of his own, complained that Truman's guest list resembled "an international list for the guillotine." Truman paid him no mind. He was taking his party planning very seriously, perhaps too seriously, he acknowledged. But he was having the time of his life.

11

Making the List

TRUMAN WAS SITTING IN HIS FAVORITE CHAIR AT HIS HOUSE IN Sagaponack. First, he stared into the fireplace. Then, he looked out at the nearby sand dunes, hoping for inspiration. The first word he wrote was "Party," followed by the subheading "Kay's Friends." They were the political journalist Joseph Alsop and his wife, Susan Mary. The Alsops were followed by Secretary of Defense Robert McNamara and his wife; the chairman of the board of the *Washington Post* Company, Frederick S. Beebe, and his wife; the *Washington Post* managing editor Benjamin Bradlee and his wife, Antoinette; the *Newsweek* editor Osborn Elliott and his wife; Polly Wisner, the widow of CIA operations chief Frank Wisner; and Elizabeth Hylton, Kay's amanuensis and one of Truman's favorite lunchtime companions whenever he was in Washington. It was a start, but there were many, many names to go, and the only way Truman could accomplish the job was to work on his list throughout the summer. "I had that list with me day and night—never out of my hands until I gave it to my secretary October 1," he said.

In July, Truman sunbathed with his friend Eleanor Friede at her pool in Bridgehampton. Friede, a publisher who had been close to Truman's mother, was a recent widow. She welcomed Truman as a pleasant distraction and listened while he chattered away during the long, hot days they spent together. All the talk was of the upcoming party, as Truman fretted about his guests, the dress code, and other essential details. Instead of being annoyed that Truman was so self-absorbed, Friede thought he was playing Scheherazade, spinning stories about some mythical party to take her mind off her grief. "I thought he was inventing the ball to keep me going. He came every single day to the pool with a guest list he was working on," she recalled.

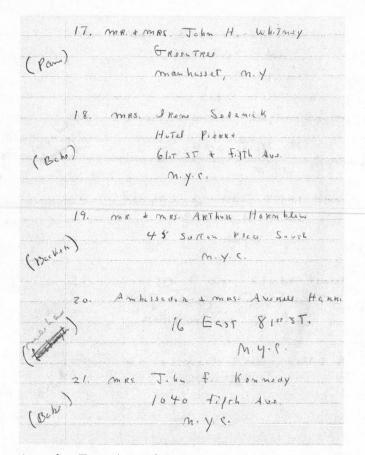

A page from Truman's guest list.

The compilation of the list was poolside entertainment at Bennett Cerf's Mount Kisco estate as well. One day, when the Cerfs were hosting their famous friends Frank Sinatra, Mia Farrow, and George Plimpton, Truman regaled everyone with a running account of his up-to-the-minute entries in the notebook. An idyllic moment—a beautiful butterfly had just landed on Farrow's décolletage as she lay by the pool—was shattered by the sound of Truman's high-pitched voice calling for attention. He wanted to know if he should invite some couple he had just remembered.

Later in the summer, Truman and Al Dewey traveled to Washington, D.C., to appear before a Senate judiciary subcommittee. They were concerned about a new Supreme Court ruling that gave suspects the right to demand the presence of an attorney at all stages of a criminal investigation. Both Truman and Dewey felt that the law would handicap police officers and prosecutors because, as Dewey pointed out, "in 90% of the cases an attorney would advise 'tell them nothing.'" They believed their *In Cold Blood* insights were important. If Perry and Dick's confessions had been inadmissible, the killers would have gone unpunished.

During that visit, Kay Graham treated the visitors to another of her "informal dinners," where Senator Robert Kennedy, Averill Harriman, Alice Longworth, and other Washington insiders reunited with the returning *In Cold Blood* folk. While they drank champagne and feasted on saddle of lamb and peach melba, Truman looked at the people around him and added more names to his guest list.

He was inspired to invite Alice Longworth, Teddy Roosevelt's daughter and a witty and acerbic Washington hostess who was famous for displaying a pillow that bore the gossip lover's adage "If you don't have anything nice to say, come sit by me." Senator and Mrs. John Sherman Cooper, Republicans from Kentucky, made it onto the list, as did Mr. and Mrs. George C. Stevens Jr.—the son of the director George Stevens and the head of the United States Information Agency's motion picture division—and J.F.K.'s speechwriter Ted Sorensen. Truman took the trouble to add the

Washington Post columnist Art Buchwald and the broadcast journalist David Brinkley, important guests of Kay's at the dinner, but had second thoughts and crossed off their names before the final list was compiled.

After his brief stay in Washington, Truman jetted to Paris to publicize the French edition of *In Cold Blood*. Overseas audiences were well aware of the hoopla surrounding the book in America and greeted the visiting author as the celebrity he had become. Truman boasted that he felt like Lindbergh at the airport because he received such a wildly enthusiastic reception. Even television crews were there to film his arrival. His time in Paris was short, however, because he had arranged to visit the Radziwills at their summer place in Portugal. In true jet-setting style, he would stay with his hosts, Lee and Stas, for one week, at which point they all would move to another luxurious venue, the Agnelli yacht.

As was their custom, Marella and Gianni had borrowed a yacht for their summer cruise. The *Tritona* was an impressive vessel, complete with a masterwork by Rubens hanging in its living room. Truman had arranged to write about the glamorous trip for *Vogue*, as he had done the previous summer when he traveled with Kay Graham. But all traces of glamour went out the window during the first few days of the voyage, when the guests, including Truman, endured rough seas and a nasty bout of seasickness. Once the seas cooperated and became calm, the vacationers settled into a state of happy camaraderie.

Truman was amused by the antics of Princess Luciana Pignatelli, a slim, aristocratic blonde on a quest for a new husband. She exercised regularly, was perfectly groomed at all times, and maintained a healthy appetite even when other seasick guests were writhing in pain at the very sight of food. She spent a lot of her time reading, engrossed by Lucius Beebe's book *The Big Spenders*, a catalogue of the wealthiest men in America. One day, when Marella asked where the melons had come from, referring to the fruit they were eating at lunch, Pignatelli quickly answered,

"Pittsburgh." The only Mellon on her mind was an American millionaire.

Truman dutifully inscribed the names of his sailing companions, the Agnellis, the Radziwills, Prince Carlo Caracciolo (Marella's brother), and the socialite Eric Nielson, on his master list. Curiously, he wrote down Princess Pignatelli's name, only to cross her off with a broad slash of his pen. The notebook was his domain, and he had absolute power over every entry. One slight, a social gaffe, or an insult, and a person could be out just as quickly as he was in.

Truman often demonstrated a pattern of free association as he entered names in his notebook. When he wrote down one name in a family or a category, he would immediately think of another one. Entries for the three Cushing sisters, Minnie Fosburgh, Babe Paley, and Betsy Whitney, followed one right after the other. The Kennedys were recorded en masse, as well. Truman jotted down Mrs. John F. Kennedy's name first, then Mrs. Peter Lawford, Mr. and Mrs. Stephen Smith, and Senator and Mrs. Robert Kennedy. Matriarch Rose Kennedy, a name from a different generation, was listed much later.

There were other interesting pairings. Truman must have been thinking about money, yachts, and jet-setting Europeans when he wrote the name Agnelli and followed it with Guinness. When Cecil Beaton came to mind, Truman immediately thought of the style diva Diana Vreeland. The photographers Richard Avedon and Gordon Parks turned up on the same page. And as Truman added the name Greta Garbo, he remembered the Hollywood siren Marlene Dietrich. An entry for the actor Jack Lemmon was followed by one for Gregory Peck.

Truman's list was broad and reflected the patchwork quilt of friends, acquaintances, and business associates he had accumulated over the years. There were the swans and their rich and powerful husbands, along with such tycoons and titans as the auto czar Henry Ford II and his new wife, Cristina; the banking heir Paul Mellon;

Dr. Jules Stein of the Music Corporation of America; Henry Heinz II; Robert Sarnoff of RCA; Stanley Marcus of Neiman Marcus; the oil magnate Charles Wrightsman; Sears Roebuck's Armand Deutsch; and Baron Guy de Rothschild of the banking empire.

Along with the Washington insiders who were friends of Kay's, there were politicians, statesmen, and ambassadors. Truman invited New York political brass, including Senator Jacob Javits, Governor Nelson Rockefeller, and Mayor John Lindsay. From the diplomatic front, he selected David K. E. Bruce, the U.S. ambassador to England; William Attwood, the U.S. ambassador to Kenya; and Llewellyn E. Thompson Jr., the U.S. ambassador to the Soviet Union.

Diverse as his list was, however, most of his prospective guests hailed from the arts. Writers were at the top of the ever-growing list. The authors of the moment—the ones celebrated on contemporary best-seller lists—were James Michener (*The Source*), Arthur Schlesinger Jr. (*A Thousand Days*), and Louis Auchincloss (*The Embezzler*). Truman invited his friends Nelle Harper Lee, Katherine Anne Porter, John Malcolm Brinnan, Christopher Isherwood, and Anita Loos. He also added the colorful, sometimes angry, and always iconoclastic young writers who had made names for themselves after the war, including Norman Mailer, Philip Roth, William Styron, Ralph Ellison, Nelson Aldrich, and James Baldwin. Finally, there were the old standbys—John Steinbeck, Irwin Shaw, Robert Penn Warren, and John O'Hara.

One noticeable omission from the literary section of the guest list was the author Jacqueline Susann, who, like Truman, was an expert marketeer and whose novel *Valley of the Dolls* was a runaway bestseller. Truman and Susann, who both entertained their fans by being irrepressible and unpredictable, had personalities too large to occupy the same room and were then in the early stages of what was to become a legendary feud.

With the writers came the literary critics. From New York's ruling intellectuals, Truman invited Columbia University's esteemed man of letters Lionel Trilling and his wife, the writer and critic Diana Trilling. He also invited the critic and writer Alfred Kazin, who was enjoying success with his book *A Walker in the City*, a memoir of life in New York in the 1930s. Ann Birstein, Kazin's beautiful young wife and a novelist and film critic, had dazzled Truman with her new book *The Sweet Birds of Gorham*. He called her a "seriously gifted writer with a freshly minted flavor all her own."

Any writer would have been overwhelmed by the publishers Truman included on his list. His own publisher, Random House, was represented by Bennett Cerf, the CEO Robert Bernstein, and Truman's longtime editor Joe Fox. Truman also invited Henry Luce of Time Inc., S. I. Newhouse of Condé Nast, Thomas Guinzberg of Viking, Cass Canfield of Harper and Row, Arthur Ochs Sulzberger of the *New York Times*, William Randolph Hearst Jr., Alfred Knopf, and Hamish Hamilton, a leading English publisher.

Truman's forays into theater had left him with many friends in that world. Among the chosen were the director Garson Kanin; Arnold Saint-Subber, the producer of *House of Flowers* and *The Grass Harp*; the composers Richard Rogers, Irving Berlin, and Harold Arlen; the lyricists Alan Jay Lerner and Betty Comden; the dramatists Tennessee Williams and Arthur Miller; Noel Coward; Thornton Wilder; Lillian Hellman; Jean Kerr; and Harold Prince, the conductor and composer Leonard Bernstein, the lyricist Stephen Sondheim, the choreographer Jerome Robbins, and the set designer Oliver Smith (Truman's friend and former landlord in Brooklyn), the team responsible for the Tony Award–winning *West Side Story*.

But the producer who was foremost in Truman's thoughts (and the third M on his list) was the the Broadway impresario David Merrick, the force behind the upcoming stage version of *Breakfast at Tiffany's*, the most eagerly anticipated musical of the 1966–1967 season. Based on Truman's beloved book about the bittersweet adventures of the enchanting Holly Golightly, the musical starred Mary Tyler Moore and Richard Chamberlain as the party girl and her writer friend. Merrick invited Truman to adapt his novella for the stage, but he refused. The veteran writer Nunnally Johnson, best known for screenwriting credits such as *The Grapes of Wrath* and *How to Marry a Millionaire*, tried but failed. Abe Burrows, fresh off his successful stint as the writer and director of *Cactus Flower* and the leading play doctor of his time, moved in to cure the show's ills. When his version, called *Holly Golightly*, bombed in Boston, Merrick asked Edward Albee to whip the musical into shape.

Albee was an unusual choice to repair a broken musical. His recent play *Tiny Alice* was ambiguous, allegorical, and so confounding that even the actor John Gielgud, one of its stars, claimed he had no idea what it was about. Albee was best known for *Who's Afraid of Virginia Woolf?*—hardly the kind of theatrical experience that had audiences singing in the aisles. But Merrick seemed to know what he was doing. Advance sales were very strong, surpassing other eagerly anticipated shows such as *Cabaret* and Merrick's own *I Do! I Do!* Despite the fact that Truman had told *Women's Wear Daily*, "I don't like the score or the leading lady," he diplomatically invited Merrick, Burrows, and Albee to come to his party.

Truman's show business contacts included movie producers, directors, and agents. The notebook listed Samuel Goldwyn, Sam Spiegel, Walter Wanger, Vincente Minnelli, Billy Wilder, Joseph Mankiewicz, Mike Nichols, and Frank Perry. As for agents, Truman invited the top two in the business, Irving "Swifty" Lazar and Leland Hayward, now married to the former Pamela Churchill.

Truman loved to talk about his actor friends in Hollywood, and he was depending on them to add wattage to his big night. He invited old acquaintances, such as Jennifer Jones and Carol Marcus Saroyan, now Matthau, following her marriage to the actor Walter. He also asked the couple of the hour, Elizabeth Taylor and Richard Burton. Then, in a mix of in and out, Truman listed Audrey Hepburn and her husband, Mel Ferrer, Sammy Davis Jr., Shirley MacLaine, Henry Fonda, Lauren Bacall, Douglas Fairbanks, Joan Fontaine, Vivien Leigh, Claudette Colbert, Roddy McDowell,

Leslie Caron, and the young and ravishing Candice Bergen, who was in the spotlight for her controversial lesbian role in the movie version of Mary McCarthy's best-selling novel *The Group*.

What would it accomplish to invite all these celebrities if there were no one to record their presence? Truman insisted that his ball was going to be a private affair just for his friends. Yet he was careful to invite journalists, especially ones who had written favorable coverage of him and his books. On the second page of his notebook, right after the list of Kay Graham's guests, the first name he entered was Miss Karen Gundersen, the charming young reporter who had interviewed him for *Newsweek's In Cold Blood* cover story. Her name was followed by Miss Jane Howard of *Life*. Gloria Steinem, another young reporter Truman was courting, appeared on the list, and she would end up writing a feature article about the party for *Vogue*.

But perhaps the most important members of the press to grace Truman's notebook were the women who covered New York's society beat: Charlotte Curtis of the *New York Times*, Aileen Mehle and Eugenia Sheppard of the newly formed *World Journal Tribune*; and Carol Bjorkman of *Women's Wear Daily*. With proper invitations, they would have the opportunity to experience the party as guests instead of as observers. Their insider status was bound to make a difference in the way they felt and ultimately in the way they wrote about Truman's evening.

There was a smattering of artists on his list: Paul Cadmus, Larry Rivers, Charles Baskerville, Don Bachardy (a portraitist who lived with Christopher Isherwood in California), Andy Warhol, and James Fosburgh, who had painted Truman's portrait. From the fashion world he summoned the designers Norman Norrell, Donald Brooks, Oscar de la Renta, and the edgy and mysterious Valentina. There were jewelry designers, too: Tiffany's Jean Schlumberger, the legendary Duke Fulci di Verdura, David Webb, and the creator of fabulous fakes, Kenneth Jay Lane.

As he inscribed the names of well-known guests who were used to being famous and to being in the company of other famous people, Truman took special pleasure in listing his friends from Kansas. More than anyone, they would appreciate the impressive cast he was assembling. Not that Truman considered Al and Marie Dewey and the other folks he befriended provincial. They were cosmopolitan, well-traveled individuals who knew how to fit in, whether they were in Kansas, New York City, or any point in between.

The Kansans had not been exposed to many private balls in their part of the world, so it was unlikely that they would be blasé about the evening. Truman invited Vi Tate; the radio station general manager Robert Wells and his wife, Kay; Dr. Russell Maxfield and his wife, Lee; the businessman Odd Williams (his real name was Edgar, but he had mispronounced "Ed" as "Odd" when he was a child and the nickname stayed with him) and his wife, Jonell; and the banker Paul Masoner and his wife, Margaret, to accompany the Deweys to New York. The Black and White Ball would be the centerpiece of their visit.

Truman wanted young people at his party to offset the older and more established guests on his list, but he had high standards and preferred youths with a pedigree. Young Mary "Minnie" Cushing and Catherine Milinaire offered exactly the right combination of bloodline and celebrity. At twenty-four, Cushing was an oft-photographed "locomotive" who wore her dark hair very long and her skirts very short. Fresh from the innermost social circles of Newport, Rhode Island, where she summered at her family's magnificent cliffside estate, Cushing quickly established herself as one of New York's most interesting and independent-minded young women. She was hired as a girl Friday by the up-and-coming fashion designer Oscar de la Renta because he was impressed by her original sense of style and her young point of view.

Cushing did not disappoint de la Renta. Her very first week on the job was chronicled by a *New York Times* reporter who wrote about Cushing's attention-getting form of transportation: she rode her bicycle to her Seventh Avenue office every day, dodging traffic and smiling at cab drivers as her long hair streamed behind her. At home, she doted on a pet snake. According to the *Times*, her free-spirited ways inspired de la Renta to make clothing that was young and "kicky, not stuffy," including jeweled pants and midriff-baring tops for evening.

Catherine Milinaire, a writer for *Vogue*, was another young locomotive whose name turned up on all the in lists. She was the stepdaughter of England's duke of Bedford and shared the colorful royal's talent for making a splash. Better known as the "groovy" duke, John Robert Russell bucked convention by turning his estate, Woburn Abbey, into an English theme park to pay a hefty thirteen-million-pound estate tax. Visitors could stroll through the grounds, purchase souvenirs, and even dine with the duke himself for a hefty fee of $150. Milinaire made headlines of her own by nonchalantly wearing a daring dress to the premiere of the movie *My Fair Lady*. The *New York Times* described it as "a gauzy black gown with a see-through top that looked as if there were nothing but Miss Milinaire underneath."

As Truman was inscribing the names of Cushing and Milinaire in his book, he was not thinking of Baby Jane Holzer. "This year's girl" of 1965 had been replaced by newer models, although it was doubtful that Holzer, even in her youthful prime, would have been a candidate for the list. She was dreadfully overexposed and, as the *New York Times* had pointed out, not quite in. Truman was more likely to include young people who were the offspring of important friends, junior achievers who were on their way to becoming some-bodies by virtue of the privilege and the access that came with a really good name.

He invited Christopher Cerf, the clever, Harvard-educated son of Bennett and Phyllis; Wendy Vanderbilt, the artistic daughter of Alfred Gwynne Vanderbilt; Kitty Hawks, the daughter of Slim Hawks Keith; Benedetta Barzini, the daughter of the Italian writer Luigi Barzini; Gillian Walker, the daughter of John Walker III, the director of the National Gallery, and his wife, Lady Margaret Drum-mond; Marcia Meehan, the daughter of the Wall Street financier

Joseph Meehan and his wife, Kay; the aspiring poet Bill Berkson, the son of the fashion guru Eleanor Lambert; Frances Fitzgerald and Penelope Tree, the daughters of the Democratic Party muse Marietta Tree; and Amanda and Carter Burden.

Truman had decided against inviting President and Mrs. Lyndon Johnson—he claimed he didn't want to deal with the fleet of Secret Service men who accompanied the first family everywhere, and he knew the Johnsons were busy on November 28—but he was delighted to include young Lynda Bird Johnson, the country's first daughter. "I asked Mrs. Longworth, Margaret Truman and Lynda Bird. I guess that's enough of the White House," Truman quipped. Johnson was moving to New York City to work as a part-time consultant and writer at *McCall's*. Journalists were enthralled with the story of the young career girl, whose first day at the office included a press conference and newspaper coverage detailing her lunch (lamb chops and asparagus), her outfit (a light green wool suit), and the décor of her cubbyhole office (windowless with slate blue walls). Johnson was dating the handsome actor George Hamilton, who, with the help of Hollywood stylists such as the makeup artist George Masters, had transformed the drab Texas ingénue into a big-city sensation. The press applauded her new image, dubbed her "lovely Lynda," and kept a close watch on her.

Truman was very definite about not wanting random people to show up at his ball and found an autocratic way to prevent that from happening: in most cases, he refused to allow single friends to bring escorts or dates. Even Andy Warhol, who never went any-where without an entourage, had to come alone. For him, his friend Bob Colacello observed, that would have been a "major agony."

When Eleanor Friede pointed out that the party was a dance and unescorted ladies would not have partners, Truman came up with an ingenious solution. At every ball, there were men who were invited simply because they were wonderful dancers: when the music started, they would jump up and immediately ask a woman to dance, compensating for less energetic husbands who had two left feet. Truman announced that he would invite one hundred of these extra men. He discovered that it was easier said than done. "Finding one hundred presentable and unattached men is no easy chore," complained Truman as he compiled his list of bachelors. At the top of the list was Drew Dudley, a dapper bachelor with an uncanny memory for faces and names, who was a prized extra man in international social circles. He was a graceful and enthusiastic dancer who endeared himself to his partners (including his young nieces and grand-nieces, who recalled dancing on the tops of his shoes at family parties). Other well-turned-out extras were Ashton Hawkins, a lawyer at the Metropolitan Museum; Andrew Lyndon, one of Capote's oldest friends, and the filmmakers and Capote chroniclers Albert and David Maysles.

"You can keep your hundred extra men," complained Friede, who was still not happy with the arrangement. It was reassuring to know she would have a dance partner once she arrived at the ball, but how could she be expected to put on a gown and a mask and walk into the Plaza all by herself? Again, Truman had a ready solution. He would ask twenty or so of his friends to host pre-ball dinner parties for a select three hundred of his guests, essentially creating a VIP section within his own list. At the end of the dinners, the guests could continue on to the Plaza together.

Truman scribbled the first, and sometimes the last, names of prospective hosts on the inside cover of his notebook: Babe, Burden, Cowles, Piedy, Meehan, Heinz, Hayward, Westcott, Backer, vanden Heuval, and Ford. Later, he added Schiff, Fosburgh, Friede, Epstein, and Berkson. He took charge of the dinner party assignments and tried to match the guests to hosts they knew or with whom they had something in common. No matter how many times Truman reworked the lists, moving a guest from one dinner party to another, some of his hostesses accused him of playing favorites. "Apparently, many of these ladies felt I could have given them more interesting lists, although I'd tried to spread the stellar names as evenly as possible," he argued.

Despite Truman's protests about parity, there was no question that Babe and Bill Paley were awarded the top-tier guests—including the Agnellis, the Radziwills, the Deweys, Cecil Beaton, Diana Vreeland, and Truman and Kay. The Burdens would take care of the locomotives, Candice Bergen, Penelope Tree, Marisa Berenson, the Eberstadts, Wendy Vanderbilt, and the rest of the younger set. The novelist Glenway Westcott was given an assortment of writers and artists such as Paul Cadmus, Anita Loos, and Don Bachardy. And Eleanor Friede was recruited to entertain her fellow publishers and editors. The dinner parties would ensure that guests arrived at the ball in good spirits.

Amid Truman's vast assortment of somebodies and nobodies, writers and intellectuals, politicians and diplomats, artists and financiers, socialites and actors, friends and idols, there were wild-card guests who could not be pigeonholed in conventional categories. The most unusual person on Truman's list was Benjamin Kean, a doctor who traveled to exotic locations all over the world treating tropical diseases. Other intriguing choices were Jack Valenti, a Lyndon Johnson supporter and the head of the Motion Picture Association of America, and a businessman named Henry Golightly, who had no connection to Truman's fabulous Holly.

If being on the list conferred a degree of insider status and celebrity to Truman's guests, being crossed off the list was noteworthy, too. Sometimes Truman simply changed his mind. A name that seemed like a good idea one day would be cut the next, as Truman edited and rewrote his choices. In addition to crossing out David Brinkley and Art Buchwald, Truman considered, then removed, Clay Felker, the editor of *Esquire*; the actors Yul Brynner and Danny Kaye; the poet Stephen Spender; the composer Aaron Copland; the heiress Doris Duke; Winston Churchill; and about ten other souls who probably never guessed how close they came to attending the big night. The formerly exiled Luciana Pignatelli, on the other hand, was very lucky. Truman reinstated her on his final list, only two names before the cutoff point. The princess was blissfully unaware that there was any suspense surrounding her invitation.

When Truman came to the final page of the notebook, he flipped it over and continued writing on the other side. In his words, "I filled all the right-hand pages and when it was full I turned it upside down and went through it again." The very last name he wrote, number 382, was Herman Levin, the producer of the Broadway musical *My Fair Lady*.

The first draft of his list was completed. Truman was ready to give it a polish and send it out into the world.

Cecil Beaton was appalled when he heard that Truman was planning a big party and candidly expressed his misgivings in his tell-all diary. "What is Truman trying to prove?" he wrote. "The foolishness of spending so much time organizing the party is something for a younger man, or a worthless woman to indulge in, if they have social ambitions."

Truman insisted this was not the case—his party had nothing to do with publicizing his book or self-aggrandizement. But Beaton, who knew his friend *very* well, suspected otherwise.

A Little Boy and His Father . . .
the Fond Memory which lingers still, . .
—and always will . . . . . .

Truman posing with his father, Arch Persons. When Truman
became an acclaimed writer, his father printed the postcard
shown above and handed out copies to his clients at the Dixie
Scale Company.

Truman (at far left) and his friends in Monroeville, Alabama, proudly displaying their festive costumes.

Truman's mother, Nina (who had changed her name from Lillie Mae), with her second husband, Truman's stepfather Joe Capote, at a nightclub.

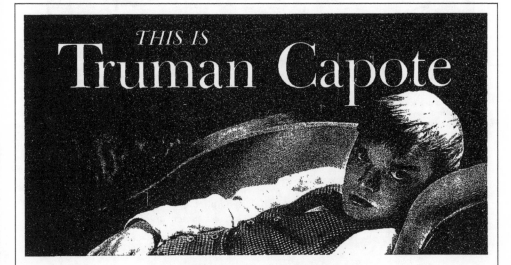

Random House's full-page ad in the New York Times Book Review for Other Voices, Other Rooms. *The unusually seductive author photo helped make Truman's first novel a sensation.*

Truman Capote, beloved only son of Arch Persons, owner of the Dixie Scale Co., on a recent visit to his father at Shreveport, La., in his new 1963 Jaguar Special. Author of "breakfast at Tiffany's", "Other Voices Other Rooms", "The Grass Harp", "House of Flowers", and many other famous books, he is ranked among the first three of his profession throughout the nation. He was recently a guest at both The White House and at Buckingham Palace. He was born in New Orleans and named for his father's close boyhood friend, Truman P. Moore, of Denver, Colorado.

Arch Persons was so proud of his son's success that in addition to circulating the picture of Truman as a child, he passed out copies of the postcard shown here of the famous author posing with his brand-new Jaguar.

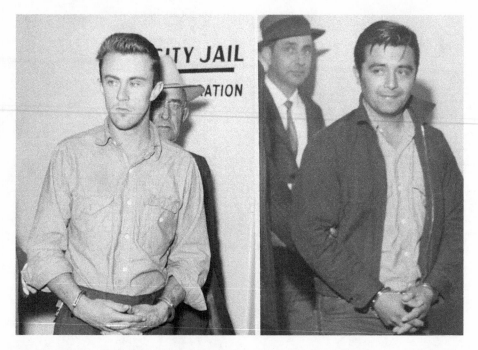

Perry Smith and Dick Hickock, whose murder of the Clutter family in Kansas was explored by Truman in his best-selling In Cold Blood.

Katherine Graham, the publisher of the Washington Post, in whose honor the Black and White Ball was held.

JOHN

(mueLan) 112. DR. & MRS. ~~Robert~~ Converse

R. 86775

700 Park Avenue

(Heinz) 113. Miss Greta Garbo
450 East 52nd St
N.Y.C.

114. Miss Marlene Dietrich
993 Park Ave.

12 Ave. Montaigne
Paris

(Cowles) 115. Mrs. Aileen Mehle
~~555 Park Ave.~~
625 Park Ave

(Cowles) 116. Mr. Walter Wanger
345 East 57th St.

John
(Cowles) 117 Mr. Emmett Hughes
1 West 67th St.

Truman optimistically penciled in Greta Garbo;
the notoriously reclusive film legend did not
attend. Her name appears immediately before
that of her fellow movie star Marlene Dietrich.
Truman made sure to correct the address of the
all-important columnist Aileen Mehle, known to
her readers as "Suzy Knickerbocker."

SCHOOLTIME
Compositions
Name
School
Grade

Truman recorded the names of his
guests as they occurred to him in an
ordinary black-and-white composition
book, which he carried everywhere.

Truman selected the celebrated Plaza Hotel, a society destination from the moment it opened its doors in 1907, as the setting for his grand party.

A sketch by the fashion designer Adolfo for the elegant, long, thin box to hold the masks and headdresses he made for the ball.

Truman's Kansas friends Margaret Masoner, Marie Dewey, Kay Wells, and Vi Tate having their hair done at the Plaza Hotel beauty salon on the morning of the ball.

Truman boasted that he paid thirty-nine cents at F.A.O. Schwarz for his black Halloween mask.

Tallulah Bankhead walking past dozens of photographers on her way up the staircase at the Plaza. She was one of the people who had begged Truman for an invitation.

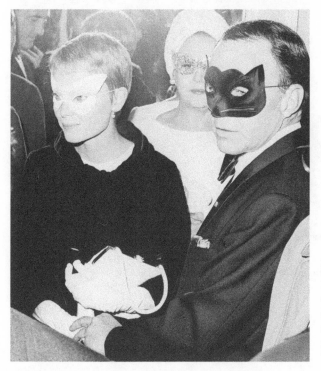

The newlyweds Mia Farrow and Frank Sinatra, who had flown to New York on a private jet and good-naturedly donned white and black masks for Truman's ball.

Jacqueline Kennedy's sister, Lee Radziwill, taking one last look in the mirror and adjusting her mask before beginning her red carpet walk at the Plaza.

Seventeen-year-old Penelope Tree, here with Ashton Hawkins; she wore a daring outfit designed by Betsey Johnson. Her unusual look and winsome beauty attracted so much attention from such fashion arbiters as Diana Vreeland and Cecil Beaton that her career as a supermodel was launched that night.

One of Truman's favorite "swans," the elegant Gloria Guinness.

The interior designer
Billy Baldwin wearing
a dramatic unicorn
mask and headdress
by Gene Moore.

Candice Bergen, dressed in a gown and with a mask Halston designed for Marisa Berenson,
dancing with a partner before making a hasty retreat from the party.

Princess Luciana Pignatelli wowed the ballroom with the sixty-carat diamond she had borrowed from the jeweler Harry Winston to wear on her forehead.

Babe Paley was so serious about her ball preparations that she commissioned four masks—three from Halston and one from Adolfo—to complement her bejeweled white gown. Always the height of chic, she wore a heavy paste necklace, though she could easily have afforded rubies.

*Truman called elegant
Marella Agnelli, the wife
of Fiat magnate Gianni
Agnelli, "the European
swan numero uno."*

*The fashion illustrator Maning's drawing of
Marietta Tree's coq feather mask.*

*A fashion illustration of Henry
Ford's Adolfo mask.*

Truman said the people were the only flowers needed at the Black and White Ball.

12

The Place to Be

"THEY'RE BACK!" PROCLAIMED A HEADLINE IN *WOMEN'S WEAR DAILY*, referring to the postsummer return of New York's beautiful people. On September 7, the Wednesday after Labor Day, vacationers dusted the sand off their feet and bade good-bye to their homes in the Hamptons, their compounds in the Adirondacks, and their villas in Europe. It was time to put away the cotton, break out the wool, and prepare for the upcoming social season.

Photographers loitered outside the city's most popular restaurants, La Côte Basque, La Grenouille, Lafayette, and the Colony, cameras poised to shoot celebrities and socialites as they hurried to their lunch dates. One shutterbug snapped Truman on his way into the Colony accompanied by Evie Backer, his friend and decorator. Truman looked rested, prosperous, and purposeful. In his left hand, he clutched his black and white notebook, signaling that he and Evie had serious business to discuss over lunch. They retired to one of the three coveted back tables at the restaurant, where they were flanked by the Cushing sisters on one side and the agent Leland Hayward and the actor James Stewart on the other. There were warm greetings all around, then Truman and Evie turned their attention to the subject that would dominate their conversations for the next two and a half months—Truman's party.

Lunch was always serious business for the fashionable set, but eating was rarely the raison d'être of the meal. The gossip columnist Maury Paul, better known as Cholly Knickerbocker, observed, "Nobody gives a damn who you sleep with. In this world, it's who you're seen dining with that counts." Though they were reluctant to admit it, one of the chief motivations for the ladies who lunch was to see and be seen by the other members of their set. Several times a week, if not every day, they patronized chic, exclusive East Side restaurants where it was almost impossible for outsiders to obtain reservations. The best maître d's cultivated a clublike atmosphere to make patrons feel both privileged and at home. Men and women who came repeatedly for lunch and dinner were known as regulars. It was not unusual for Pamela and Leland Hayward to occupy their special table at the Colony for lunch, then to return that night for dinner.

Lunch was a perfect time to show off a new wardrobe or launch a new look. It was whispered that ambitious women who wanted to make the Best Dressed List should make a point of being seated at the first red velvet banquette on the left at La Caravelle. News of trendsetters traveled quickly. One day, while dashing to or from a lunch date, Babe Paley impulsively tied her Hermès scarf around the handle of her pocketbook. Photographers captured her image for their newspapers, and a new style was born, as women all over America copied Babe's look. Fashion-conscious women who had invested time and money in their appearances chose their restaurants carefully so that the setting would be a fitting backdrop for their beauty. The right lighting was crucial, preferably a warm pink glow that would be flattering to faces of any age.

Lunch was also a good time to exchange information, or gossip, especially if Truman was at the table. The writer John Knowles recalled that Truman always came to lunch prepared. "He'd lined up things to tell you. . . . Always had stories about who had had the latest shots at that clinic in Switzerland: he was an entertainer, he rehearsed." But the latest gossip was not all that was on Truman's mind that September day. He had a full agenda to discuss with Evie. They would go through the notebook together to determine whether anyone important had been left out—Truman had room for 158 additional people before he reached his grand total of 540 guests. He also wanted to hear Evie's ideas about the décor.

During the summer, she had written him a note suggesting a few names for the list. President Harry Truman was one of them, but Truman did not follow her advice in that instance. There would be only one Truman at the Black and White Ball. He did think about including Margaret, the duchess of Argyll, especially after

Truman, guest list in hand, heading for a dishy lunch with Evie Backer.

Evie advised that a few duchesses never hurt a ball. Truman added the royal's name to the notebook, only to cross it out after having second thoughts.

Evie and Truman got along famously and were looking forward to collaborating on a look for the ball. The Grand Ballroom at the Plaza Hotel was their stage. Truman said that he selected the Plaza because "it's the only beautiful ballroom left in the United States." But his longtime friend Phyllis Cerf believed that his motivation was more complicated than simply wanting the room for its beauty. Hosting his party at the Plaza, with its history, traditions, and atmosphere of prosperity and power, represented something to Truman. Just as F. Scott Fitzgerald used the Plaza to signify status in novels such as *The Great Gatsby*, Truman's choice of the Plaza would mean that he had arrived.

The Plaza Hotel had been casting its spell on visitors ever since it opened its doors in 1890. The eight-story, four-hundred-room, Italian Renaissance edifice had been erected on the site of a skating pond located at Fifth Avenue and 59th Street. The hotel was beautifully appointed with marble and mahogany and featured works of art and expensive furnishings. As the city around it grew, the Plaza started to seem small. In 1902, real estate developers decided to take full advantage of the building's magnificent site by demolishing the old hotel and erecting a brand-new one that would be larger and even more impressive.

The new Plaza Hotel was designed by the architect Henry Hardenbergh, whose previous works included the Waldorf-Astoria Hotel on Park Avenue and the Dakota apartment building on Central Park West. Hardenbergh paid homage to majestic buildings in Europe when he conceived the massive hotel as a French château, complete with turrets, gables, dormers, and a mansard roof to give it character. The inside of the hotel was equally European in atmosphere. One hundred thousand dollars' worth of Irish linen was ordered from Belfast for the Plaza's luxurious bedding. The curtains were of a special design imported from Switzerland. The delicate stemware was crafted by Baccarat. And the china was custom-made and lavishly encrusted with gold. There were 1,650 crystal chandeliers throughout the hotel, several of them hanging over valuable Aubusson rugs.

When the Plaza opened in October of 1907, it was the tallest building in the neighborhood, a virtual skyscraper at eighteen stories. There were eight hundred bedrooms, five hundred baths, and lavish private suites with as many as seventeen rooms. Advertisements boasted that the Plaza was "the world's most luxurious hotel," and millionaires such as Alfred Gwynne Vanderbilt and Jay Gould secured rooms on a permanent basis, preferring the lavish, full-service hotel to a private residence. In fact, ninety percent of the hotel was reserved for people who lived there all the time, while a small fraction of the remaining rooms were held for transient hotel guests.

Because of its reputation for being splendid and accommodating, the Plaza was a popular destination for celebrities visiting New York City. The tenor Enrico Caruso inaugurated the tradition by checking into the hotel soon after it opened and living there during his annual season at the Metropolitan Opera. Several famous guests, including Cecil Beaton, Christian Dior, and Frank Lloyd Wright, were invited to decorate suites in their signature styles. Over the years, the Plaza hosted many generations of the rich and famous, including Bette Davis, Cary Grant, Judy Garland, Marilyn Monroe (who dominated headlines all over the world when she dropped her shoulder strap at a Plaza press conference), and the Beatles.

Hardenbergh's design included a ballroom with an elaborate white and gold décor. The most impressive feature of the room was a balcony that served more than one purpose. Built by the Otis Elevator Company, it could be raised or lowered at the push of a button to create a large stage for musical and theatrical entertainments. This mechanical wonder had been destroyed in 1921 when a larger ballroom was built on the new 58th Street side of the hotel. The new ballroom, designed in the popular beaux arts style, featured twin chandeliers, gilt appointments, a proper stage, and ten arched seating areas fashioned to look like royal boxes that lined the dance floor on two sides of the room.

The Grand Ballroom, which was eighty-three feet long and forty-five feet wide and had twenty-five-foot ceilings, seemed massive at the time it was built. But as party-givers became more accustomed to hosting debutante balls and weddings in public spaces and charity balls proliferated, larger rooms were needed to accomodate expanding guest lists. By 1963, New York City hotels were embroiled in what Charlotte Curtis of the *New York Times* called "the battle of the ballrooms," a competition to win bookings of big ticket galas. The newly opened New York Hilton offered two ballrooms to potential hosts: the Trianon, which could hold eight hundred dinner dancers, and the Grand Ballroom, with an impressive capacity of four thousand. The Hilton and the Americana, the other new hotel in town, courted the convention trade. The Plaza and the St. Regis, however, specialized in smaller events that seemed private even when they weren't. The Plaza ballroom evoked an era when people still entertained on a grand scale in their own houses.

Truman loved the intimacy of the space. Even though it could accommodate 540 people, the room would never feel empty or cavernous. Moreover, the approach had been designed perfectly for grand entrances. Guests could enter the hotel via the main door that faced Augustus Saint-Gauden's statue of the Civil War hero General William Tecumseh Sherman. From there, they would walk past the Palm Court atrium, ascend the short staircase to the mezzanine, and proceed to the long staircase leading to the ballroom. This route would guarantee partygoers plenty of time to see and be seen.

Truman discussed his plan for the décor of the ballroom with Evie Backer. His concern was that he did not want his guests to be overshadowed by the room. He envisioned the evening as a contemporary version of Cecil Beaton's Ascot scene in *My Fair Lady*, with men and women dressed in black and white, standing out like figures on a chessboard. To make the background more dramatic, he was thinking about lining the walls of the white and gold ballroom with heavy red drapes. Evie and Babe talked him out of that over-the-top idea because they thought it would make the room dark and garish. Instead, there would be red tablecloths (the Plaza did not charge extra for this color), white tapers everywhere, and, as Evie said, "miles of smilax," a slender vine with glossy foliage, entwined around the candelabra.

Truman consulted Babe, an expert hostess, about the menu, although, as with every detail concerning the party, he had several ideas of his own. The buffet would be served at midnight. There would be the traditional eggs, sausages, and biscuits that seemed to turn up at every late-night affair. But Truman insisted on serving two dishes that were not likely to be found on the menus at most fancy-dress balls: chicken hash and spaghetti and meatballs. The Plaza's Chicken Hash, an upscale version of the corned beef classic, was made with cream and sherry and was one of his favorite dishes. Truman ordered it regularly when he ate at the Oak Room and wanted to share it with his friends on this special night. As for spaghetti and meatballs, adding the casual Italian American specialty was a way of introducing a playful element to a formal evening, although it was doubtful that a woman dressed in an expensive white evening gown would hazard an encounter with tomato sauce. Pastries and coffee completed the meal. The beverage of the evening would be 450 bottles of Taittinger champagne, dispensed from four bars, placed at strategic locations in the ballroom.

More important than the décor or the menu was the choice of music. Truman had been to enough parties to know that the band-leader held the fate of the evening in his hands. The right music could make a party soar, while the wrong music (which could mean too loud, too soft, too stuffy, or a dozen other miscalculations) con-demned even the most extravagant event to failure. Refusing to take chances, Truman asked Peter Duchin, society's favorite young bandleader, to play at his Black and White Ball.

Duchin was handsome, charismatic, and hotter than hot. The son of the legendary bandleader Eddy Duchin, Peter first made a name for himself when he and his orchestra debuted at the St. Regis Hotel in 1962. Audiences flocked to the Maisonette room to hear the new talent in town and were delighted by his versatile repertoire and signature style of piano playing, which was elegant, witty, and expressive.

Duchin was an unusual combination of show business and high society. His father was a celebrity and his mother, Marjorie Oelrichs, had been a famous beauty who came from a prominent family with roots in Newport and New York. She died soon after he was born (a tragedy depicted in the 1956 movie *The Eddy Duchin Story*). While his father toured with his band, young Duchin was raised by close family friends Averill Harriman and his wife, Marie. The Harrimans were in in every circle—society, politics, business, and the arts. Duchin grew up at the center of the very world that he would eventually entertain, and his colorful background, including his adventures living on a houseboat while studying music in Paris in the 1950s, contributed to his appeal. He knew many, if not most, of the people on Truman's guest list and would have no problem orchestrating their evening as gracefully and successfully as he played his piano.

Every party was different. A bandleader had to be a keen observer of human nature to understand the subtle differences among audiences. Duchin found that he rarely looked at his keyboard while he was working. Instead, he studied the crowd. Duchin was so attuned to his audience that sometimes he could tell what kind of music he should play simply by looking at the women's shoes. That's the kind of expertise Truman wanted at his ball.

When Truman called Duchin to book him for the night, he tried to talk his way into getting a discount. "Peter," he said, "I'm going to give a party for your old buddy Kay Graham. Will you give me a deal?" Duchin agreed to the date and to the deal. Truman asked Duchin to keep the job a secret and made it clear that he wanted to be the one to tell the press. Duchin promised there would be no leaks, but almost immediately, he started getting calls from people who had heard he would be playing at the party.

Truman knew from experience that a great party had to have uninterrupted music; ideally, while one band was taking a break, another would take its place to keep the crowd dancing. Duchin could be counted on to supply the sophisticated sound that would be the mainstay of the evening, especially classics and show tunes. But for rock and roll, Truman turned to the Soul Brothers. Led by the soul performer Benny Gordon, the group, comprising of Benny's brothers, featured a vocalist and band members on electric piano, guitar, trumpet, and bass. Duchin's music would inspire social dancing, while the Soul Brothers' beat would have the crowd twisting and frugging. Together, they would keep the guests on their toes for the entire evening.

It was safe for Truman to assume that his guests would know how to dance, an essential skill for anyone attending a ball. In fact, it was more than likely that most of them had attended dancing school to learn the intricacies of the fox trot, the waltz, the Lindy, the rumba, and other popular social dances. The children of New York society folk—Rockefellers, Whitneys, Vanderbilts, and other moneyed families—were always enrolled in private classes to learn dancing and manners. These schools, run by the autocratic aristocrat William de Rham and the very proper Miss Claire Bloss, never advertised, yet they had waiting lists filled with the names of eager parents who hoped their child would be invited to participate. The best dancing schools—the ones that held classes at the Plaza Hotel, the Colony Club, and the Piping Rock Club on Long Island—had special admissions committees consisting of the dancing teacher and a few key parents to keep the right children in and the wrong children out. Exclusivity was important because, as the children matured, their dancing partners would become their friends, their companions at debutante balls, their escorts, and, ultimately, their mates.

People who were unable to enroll in a dancing school could take advantage of instruction books and home courses, some of which came with diagrams and footprints. One book, *Dancing for All Occasions*, combined detailed descriptions of dance steps with etiquette lessons in the society tradition. "Be cheerful, be a good conversationalist," the book advised guests at a dance. "If you find yourself accidentally apart from your friend or friends, introduce yourself to the nearest person or persons. Introduce yourself by saying something to the effect that 'I am John Peck,' or 'I am Martha Peach,' and you will find yourself making new friends."

Formal introductions were out of the question when the dance was the twist, the frug, the hully gully, the swim, or the go-go. The music was so loud at Manhattan's exciting new discotheques that it could "just force you to dance" and "knock you right out of your seat," according to the dance aficionado Killer Joe Piro. Social dancing used to involve synchronous, horizontal movement across a sweep of dance floor, but in 1966, dancing was a chaotic free-for-all. The popular new dances required couples to stay rooted in one place while they gyrated frantically. These dances were considered indecent in conservative circles because they seemed so primitive, wild, and uninhibited, and many Americans were shocked by reports that Jacqueline Kennedy could twist and frug with the best of them.

Truman's choice of music suggested that his evening would be a combination of the old and the new, the hip and the square. He had selected his guest of honor and finalized the party's theme, date, location, décor, and menu. The guest list was still a work in progress, but Truman was resigned to the fact that he would be amending it until the very last minute. His next task was to design an invitation.

Truman had a rudimentary format in mind and sketched it on a sheet of paper. In his tiny handwriting, he listed all the pertinent information, including the location—"in the Grand Ballroom of the Hotel Plaza, New York, N.Y." Under the letters R.S.V.P. on the left, he indicated there would be a telephone number. And in the opposite corner, after the word *Dress*, he wrote "Gentlemen: Black Tie Black Mask Ladies: Black or White Dress, White Mask, fan. Jewelry—only diamonds and pearls and jet."

Eleanor Friede, the voice of reason, balked when Truman mentioned that he intended to control the jewelry worn by the women he invited. Truman was assuming they owned diamonds, pearls, and jet. Eleanor, for one, had pawned her diamonds years earlier and was certain other guests were in the same position. Truman relented and dropped any mention of jewelry, but he stood firm on his instructions for dress, mask, and fan.

He made other changes before the invitation was printed. Truman must have been advised that it was incorrect to place a telephone number on a formal invitation. In her classic book *Etiquette in Society, in Business, in Politics, and at Home*, Emily Post decreed that when answering this kind of invitation, acceptances or regrets are always written. He took out the line for a telephone number and replaced it with a name—Miss Elizabeth Davies—along with an address, 465 Park Avenue. Elizabeth Davies was the agent Swifty Lazar's New York secretary. Truman had retained her to oversee the hundreds of invitations that had to be sent in the ensuing few weeks, as well as the hundreds of responses that would follow. The Park Avenue address belonged to the Lazars, who maintained an office as well as an apartment there.

In preparing the invitation for the printer, Truman edited his entry for the Plaza Hotel. The address line was shortened to "Grand Ballroom, The Plaza"—no city, no state, no explanation that it was the hotel. This was not arrogance on Truman's part—the guests on his list knew exactly where they could find the Plaza. The white card was simple, elegant, and exactly as mandated by Emily Post, with one exception. Truman ordered a bright border of yellow and orange to make the classic invitation seem less stuffy and more contemporary.

The invitation went off to Tiffany's, and Truman was not pleased when it came back from the printer with glaring errors. On the invitation card, Davies's name was misspelled as "Davis" and the R.S.V.P. line read "485 Park Avenue" instead of "465 Park Avenue." There was no time to make corrections, so Truman decided to cross out the wrong address and write the correct number on each invitation. His final touch was to write in blue ink "in honor of Mrs. Katharine Graham" at the top of the card.

Truman gave the notebook to Elizabeth Davies so she could get to work. First, she studied the entries and typed a master list of the names and the addresses in the order in which they appeared in the book. Even Truman acknowledged that his penmanship was difficult to read, and, as a result, some names were altered. Monroe Wheeler, a friend from the Museum of Modern Art, became "Morris Wheelan." Davies's next step was to alphabetize the names, at which point Truman started adding guests by hand. This is the stage when many of the extra men appeared, including the tropical disease specialist Dr. Benjamin Kean, who had recently become an extra when he and his wife, the philanthropist Rebekkah Harkness, divorced.

Truman's lunch with Evie—and the sight of the notebook—set tongues wagging. "The Eye hears Truman Capote is giving a party. A big party," *Women's Wear Daily* reported. The gossip columnist who wrote "Eye" was unveiling insider information that could have come only from Truman. *WWD* knew the party would be held in the Grand Ballroom of the Plaza and that Truman was inviting "everyone from Doris Duke to the Kennedys." Actually, Truman had crossed Doris Duke off the list before he gave it to Elizabeth Davies to transcribe. A *big* party meant lots of invitations, so many eyes brightened at the sight of the announcement. But the item ended with a serious warning for *WWD* readers. "If you haven't received your invitation by the time they are sent out in October, sweetie, you are out."

❧

Recipe for Plaza Chicken Hash

4 cups finely diced cooked chicken (white meat only)
1½ cups heavy cream
1 cup cream sauce
2 teaspoons salt
⅛ teaspoon white pepper
¼ cup dry Sherry
½ cup Hollandaise Sauce

Mix chicken, cream, Cream Sauce and seasonings in a heavy skillet. Cook over moderate heat, stirring often, for about 10 minutes.

When moisture is slightly reduced, place skillet in a moderate oven, 350°, and bake 30 minutes.

Stir in Sherry and return to oven for 10 minutes. Lightly fold in Hollandaise Sauce and serve at once.

Makes 4–5 servings.

❧

13

❧

"Have You Heard?"

With the announcement in *Women's Wear Daily*, the black and White Ball exploded into newsprint. What had been a writer's private obsession was now the hottest topic in the city. Columnists were on the lookout for the big story of the 1966 social season, and Truman's ball had all the right ingredients: mystery (who would be invited?), glamour (the masquerade theme), drama (the frenzied preparations), and, finally, spectacle (the evening itself). The newspapers that instantly embraced the story were *Women's Wear Daily* and the newly formed *World Journal Tribune*.

Women's Wear Daily, better known as *WWD*, had been founded in 1910 by Edmund and Louis Fairchild, brothers who recognized that there was a sizable audience for nuts-and-bolts news of the rag trade. Typical articles were aimed at retailers and probed trends in zippers, the ups and downs of hemlines, and holiday sales figures.

John Fairchild, a descendant of the Fairchild brothers, was running the Paris bureau of Fairchild Publications, Inc., when he was summoned home to New York to revitalize *WWD*. It was 1960, and there was an opportunity for *WWD* to become the paper of choice for anyone interested in news of the fashionable, as well as the fashion news. Gradually, the trade paper expanded its scope, and the trendsetters—the beautiful people, known in WWD lingo as the BP—became as newsworthy as the garments they wore. WWD transcended its mundane origins to become a red-hot read. Fairchild recruited William Cunningham (later known for his photography in the *New York Times*) to write a fashion and gossip column three times a week. His descriptions of behavior and fashion—both good and bad—were insightful and entertaining. Cunningham wasn't afraid to express himself, and a columnist with personality and attitude was exactly what WWD needed to thrive and draw in a broader audience. Reporting on a society ball, he called the party doyenne Elsa Maxwell and her friends the "elderly crowd" and said that they were "dripping phoniness." After a few months on the beat, Cunningham departed for a new job as a fashion columnist at the *Chicago Tribune*.

He was replaced by Carol Bjorkman, a beautiful young woman Fairchild had met in Paris. Bjorkman had begun her career as an aspiring actress, and she had the looks, if not the talent, to succeed. At the age of eighteen, she had been cast in a small role in Max Ophuls's 1948 movie *Letter from an Unknown Woman*. "Carol Yorke," as she called herself, was mentioned frequently in Hollywood gossip columns, usually for being on the arm of a handsome man at a popular nightclub, but she did not find fame and fortune as an actress. She abandoned her dreams of stardom and moved to New York City, where she modeled and found a job working for the avant-garde fashion designer Valentina.

Valentina's customers and her famous salon—she regularly entertained artists and intellectuals in her sprawling apartment—provided Bjorkman with introductions to the most stylish women in the city. Bjorkman, who was chic in her own right, enjoyed working in fashion and used her newfound skills to become a dress buyer at Saks Fifth Avenue. From New York, she went to Paris, where she joined the house of the revolutionary new designer Yves Saint Laurent as a liaison for his American clients.

At WWD, Bjorkman wrote the popular column "Carol," which quickly became mandatory reading for anyone who wanted to be in the know. The charismatic young writer had contacts everywhere (Hollywood, New York, and Europe), was invited to all the best places, and penned lively reports of what she saw. She wrote about Broadway openings, society dinners, movie premieres, and lunchtime tête-à-têtes, always offering an insider's point of view.

Bjorkman had presence: the frustrated actress inside her enjoyed being the center of attention, and she was famous for her grand entrances. "She would arrive at a fashion show, usually a little late, sweeping in with her white poodle, Sheba, daintily throwing back her coat so the Balenciaga label was clearly visible and making the press photographers forget to focus on the models," one observer wrote. She was so appealing that other columnists wrote about Bjorkman, and when her name appeared, it was usually preceded by the words *lovely*, *beautiful*, and *chic*.

She was also called *smart*. Bjorkman was credited with being one of the first fashion insiders to discover the exciting new designer Halston—she became his champion when he was a young milliner at Bergdorf Goodman. Many people had admired his hats, especially the pillbox designs he created for First Lady Jacqueline Kennedy, but Bjorkman recognized that Halston had the talent to produce a whole collection, and she wrote about his work and his aspirations in her column.

Eugenia Sheppard, Bjorkman's counterpart at the *Herald Tribune*, was one of the first columnists to combine gossip with fashion reporting. She began her career in Columbus, Ohio, as the society editor of the *Columbus Dispatch*. But Ohio was nowhere near the center of the fashion universe, which is where Sheppard wanted to be. She set her sights on New York City and moved there in 1937 to work briefly at *Women's Wear Daily*.

In 1940, Sheppard joined the *Herald Tribune* and, after covering home furnishings, found her real métier in writing about beauty and fashion. Initially, her column "Inside Fashion" ran twice a week. It became so popular that the *Tribune* asked her to write it every day. The column's success was fueled by Sheppard's understanding that stories about the people who made clothes and the famous people who wore them were even more interesting than the clothes themselves: designers and society women enjoyed reading their names in the newspaper and were willing partners in generating material. Geraldine Stutz, the president of the New York department store Henri Bendel, called Sheppard's lively and informative column "the beginning of modern fashion reportage."

Sheppard won many awards for her articles, which were varied in subject. In 1952, the Newspaper Women's Club named "Inside Fashion" the Best Criticism in Any Field. In 1955, they recognized her for her excellent coverage of the Dior collection in Paris. And in 1962, Sheppard won first place for "Everybody's Whispering," a story about the trend among women to imitate Jacqueline Kennedy, who sounded like "a dear little girl who has been running and doesn't want to be late."

Sheppard had a keen intelligence, a sharp eye for spotting trends before they happened, and strong opinions. She told women to wear leather boots with their couture outfits and to trade pantsuits for dresses. She used her column to wage war against that most unbecoming of garments, the baby-doll maternity smock, advising pregnant women to stick to slim sheaths if they wanted to remain fashionable while expecting.

For all her insights, Sheppard did not have good eyesight. She preferred to see the world on the blurry side, rather than spoil her carefully composed look with unsightly glasses. Sometimes, she had to depend on her companions for descriptions of what was strutting down fashion show runways.

In 1966, the New York branch of the *Herald Tribune*, the *World-Telegram*, and the *Journal-American* all died, and there rose from the ashes a combined newspaper called the *New York World Journal Tribune*. The marriage of the three dailies created a glut of columnists in the city, and unemployed journalists scrambled to find new jobs. But Sheppard, the *Herald Tribune*'s star fashion writer and editor, and the *Journal-American*'s saucy society columnist "Suzy Knickerbocker" had nothing to worry about. There was a home for both of them at the newly formed *World Journal Tribune*.

The woman behind Suzy Knickerbocker was Aileen Mehle. She was a beautiful young Texan who had used the nom de plume "Suzy" at the beginning of her career when she wrote a gossip column in Miami. Several jobs later, she moved to New York City. Mehle joined the *Journal-American* in 1963, and the paper found itself with dueling society reporters. Her rival was Igor Cassini, the brother of the fashion designer Oleg Cassini, who wrote as "Cholly Knickerbocker," a gossip column byline used by the Hearst Corporation that had been created by the society reporter and bon vivant Maury Paul. After Paul died in 1942, the column was kept alive by other writers—most recently, Cassini. But Cassini was caught up in a bad political situation that proved poisonous to his career. Cassini incurred the wrath of Attorney General Robert Kennedy because he had used his insider position—he was a close friend of Joseph Kennedy—to write indiscreet items about President Kennedy and his marriage. Cassini was threatened with jail, and it appeared that he would be ostracized from society, a serious problem for a society reporter. Mehle won the battle of the columns, and the name "Suzy Knickerbocker" was born. The *Journal-American* wisely wanted her column to suggest she was carrying on the successful Knicker-bocker tradition.

Three years later, the *World Journal Tribune* was confident its readers would support multiple society columnists, suggesting that New Yorkers had developed a heartier appetite for the inside scoop. Sheppard and Mehle appeared side by side on the front page of the women's section. Sometimes, their stories overlapped, as Sheppard reported on what the fashionable people were wearing and Mehle gave readers a peek into their complicated, gold-plated lives.

Mehle's effervescent combination of wit and irony in her column "Society by Suzy Knickerbocker" won coverage in national magazines. In *Life*, which called her "the brightest and most widely read society columnist in the country," she said that an editor had told her she wouldn't be a success until she could "walk into a room full of people who whisper 'Here comes that bitch Suzy.'" *Time* described her as the "Society Snippet" and praised her for demon-strating "refreshing irreverence" in her stories about the jet set. When talking to the magazine *Flare*, Frank Sinatra said, "I adore Aileen Mehle," and insisted that she was one of the few gossip columnists who had a sense of humor. Mehle was often singled out for her lush beauty. Even *Time* mentioned her "small hands and feet" and "widely admired bosom." On an episode of the popular quiz show *What's My Line?*, the host John Daly brought down the house when he inadvertently referred to Mehle as Miss "Knocker-bocker" instead of Miss "Knickerbocker." A good sport, Mehle had trouble keeping a straight face.

Mehle's work required her to spend her days on the telephone and her nights at parties, sometimes as many as six in one evening.

Like Truman, Mehle prided herself on her powers of total recall. She never took notes, yet rarely missed a detail. "I have the fastest eye in the house," she boasted in an interview. She also relied on a network of trusted individuals to supply her with information about the events she couldn't attend. Consequently, Suzy seemed omnipresent and omniscient.

Mehle also had a talent for making the names in her column come to life. When the beautiful young widow Dolores Guinness fell in love with her brother-in-law, Karim Aga Khan, Mehle turned the story into a romantic drama of Shakespearian proportions. "Karim Aga Khan, at 28 one of the world's most eligible bachelors, and Dolores Furstenberg Guinness, one of the world's most romantically beautiful young women, are in love and inseparable in Switzerland, Paris and any place else they happen to be," Mehle announced to her enthralled readers. Would the financier Loel Guinness give his blessing to his daughter-in-law (who was also his stepdaughter) to marry his deceased son's half-brother, they wondered? Would Gloria Guinness, Dolores's mother and Loel's wife, approve of the union? Mehle answered their questions—Loel and Gloria were supportive of the couple but cautious about their future—in a personal way that made the lovers seem like the couple next door. By reading her column, people who would never glimpse the Aga Khan or anyone like him could feel as if they were part of his circle.

Charlotte Curtis, who covered the society beat for the *New York Times*, took a different approach. Unlike Mehle, whose writing enabled her readers to feel like social insiders, Curtis promoted an attitude of bemused, and sometimes disapproving, detachment. She preferred to keep her distance in order to maintain her objectivity. Not that Curtis was an outsider—she came from a well-to-do family in Columbus, Ohio, and had attended Vassar College at the same time as Jacqueline Kennedy before she moved to New York to pursue a career in journalism.

Curtis wanted to cover serious news and was appalled when she was tapped by the *Times* to write for the women's section, in her opinion the least interesting part of the newspaper because it traditionally covered food, family, and shelter. As she plotted her escape from this writer's graveyard, Curtis was offered a new assignment that was even more offensive: society writer. At first, she wanted nothing to do with a beat that consisted of reporting on the activities of self-absorbed rich people. Then the *Times* editor Clifton Daniel, who was married to Margaret Truman, suggested that she bring a fresh perspective to the subject. Curtis had majored in sociology at Vassar. Why not observe society with the cool and clinical eye of a sociologist? If she hated the assignment, Daniel promised, he would move her to the feature desk.

Curtis was excited by this idea. Daniel opened her eyes to the fact that a society story could be as strong and provocative as any other. It was all in the telling. "Something has happened—a wedding has happened, a charity ball has happened, a murder has happened. . . . You answer all the who, what, why, when and where and how and so on. . . . And if you can, you try and tell them what it means, if anything."

Impeccably dressed in simple but stylish clothing and armed with her small notepad and pencil, Curtis set forth into society, a writer on a mission to find the story behind the story. She pointed out that sweat could be seen on the brows of Boston Brahmins when they danced, that aristocrats often had to lick their own stamps when they sent out invitations, and that certain ladies in society could be counted on to snub each other at parties. Her approach was fresh, and her stories were always original and irreverent.

When Curtis wrote about the *Social Register* in 1963, it was to show that the organization was biased, inconsistent, and anachronistic, and she did so simply by naming who was included and who was excluded in the new edition. She observed, for example, that the *Register* dropped subscribers who married Asians. The debutante Hope Cooke, despite her Mayflower connections, was removed from the *Register* when she wed the crown prince of Sikkim. Curtis also noted that Governor Nelson Rockefeller maintained his standing in the

Register even after he married his wife, Happy, a divorcée, while his cousin William Avery Rockefeller, twice divorced, was dropped when he married a "nobody."

Curtis approached each story as a scientist. Whenever she found herself writing a piece about a place that was unfamiliar, she researched its local history, financial data, and genealogy. "I bone up as if I were going to have to take an exam," she explained. She used the information to make larger points that went beyond the borders of traditional society reportage. In an article about Miami, for example, Curtis established the fact that the city had the "third largest Jewish population in the world," then went on to list the exclusive clubs that did not have any Jewish members.

Marilyn S. Greenwald, a journalist who knew Curtis and wrote a biography of her in 1999, suggested that her writing was distinctive because her stories incorporated "caustic asides" and "quotations to let her subjects hang themselves." In one instance, Curtis used a handful of well-chosen lines to expose Mr. John, a successful milliner, as an arrogant diva. "He admits he is a genius and the greatest couturier-milliner in the world, and he has tried to forget that he was once a boy from New Rochelle named Hans Harburger. . . . 'I am Mr. John,' he says over and over again. Mr. John is the dean of the industry," she wrote. People may have been afraid of Curtis's barbed wit, but they acknowledged that it was better to be the subject of her attention than to be ignored. Every host and hostess hoped to say, "Charlotte's coming," when they talked about their parties.

Bjorkman, Mehle, Sheppard, Curtis, and other society reporters (including Joseph X. Dever, who wrote a column cleverly called the "Almanach de Gotham," after the European royalty bluebook, the *Almanach de Gotha*), covered the scene in such detail that readers had up-to-the-minute news of their favorite socialites and celebrities. These journalists were assisted by a group of quick-eyed and agile-fingered artists who created images to accompany the boldface names. Newspapers such as *Women's Wear Daily*, the *World Journal Tribune*, and the *New York Times* hired illustrators to draw personalities and socialites such as Truman, Babe Paley, and Gloria Guinness.

Like photographers, illustrators created impressionistic images of the beautiful people and chronicled clothing and scenes from the fashionable life, but they used drawing implements instead of cameras. Department stores routinely hired illustrators to provide artwork for their newspaper and magazine advertisements. These artists had distinctive styles, and sharp-eyed viewers could tell at a glance which illustrator had created a particular work. The illustrations were signed by the artists, promoting the idea that they were works of art, even if they were used commercially.

One of the most familiar names in illustration in the 1950s and 1960s was Kenneth Paul Block, a gifted artist who could capture a woman's essence with a few graceful strokes of his pen. Just as the artist Charles Dana Gibson made a name for himself at the turn of the century with his romantic drawings of large-eyed, elaborately coiffed Gibson Girls, Block was famous for capturing the elegance of the modern woman. He drew Babe Paley sitting gracefully on a couch, her position suggesting motion and repose at the same time. By showing her impeccably groomed outfit, her carefully tousled coiffure, and her perfectly positioned legs, Block emphasized her legendary composure. He was equally adept at drawing clothing. Designers were delighted to find that Block had been assigned to their collections because he was certain to bring their fashions to life in stunning detail.

Block's work added wit, beauty, and personality to what had often been a lackluster trade publication. He filled WWD's pages with splendid images of women at play in the world of fashion. His drawings were so striking—and identifiable—that the WWD publisher John Fairchild said the artist was instrumental in the transformation of the character of his family's stodgy-looking newspaper in the 1950s into the jet-set and fashion bible it had become by the 1960s.

Block was a familiar figure in society. He could be found dining in chic restaurants such as Lafayette, his sketch pad poised to capture the image of a beautiful woman, a famous man, or a luncheon rendezvous. In the evening, Block attended social events, where he rapidly sketched the arrivals of celebrities and socialites. Speed was important because he had to submit his work to the press by 8 p.m., or he would miss his deadline.

As popular as Block was, he found himself in the unenviable position of being at the top of a profession that was becoming obsolete. "I started doing something at the end of its history," he said. Block, Saks Fifth Avenue's preferred illustrator, Fred Greenhill, and popular freelancer Maning Obregon consistently turned out inspired images that were beautifully crafted. The problem was that their work was reminiscent of old-fashioned portraiture at a time when realism had become the prevailing concept. Photographs, photographers, and their sexy young models—figures right out of Antonioni's hot new film *Blow-Up*—were more provocative than were line drawings of Babe Paley, Truman, and their friends. Yet Block and his drawings still had a devoted audience at WWD. Truman's Black and White Ball, with its emphasis on fashion, fantasy, and celebrity, would inspire him to do his best work.

This battalion of gossip columnists, illustrators, and photographers calculated that they could keep the story of the Black and White Ball alive for the entire two months leading up to the evening of November 28. The mailing of the invitations would have the same effect as a gunshot at the start of a race. Truman instructed Elizabeth Davies to send them out the first week in October. Several hundred cream-colored envelopes were addressed in blue ink (Davies handwrote her correct return address on each envelope's flap) and were pressed with an eight-cent stamp. Off they went around the globe, from New York to Washington, California, Kansas, France, Italy, and a dozen other locales. When they reached their destinations, the lucky recipients and the unfortunates who had been rejected, overlooked, or ignored would know once and for all who was in and who was out.

Carson McCullers was shocked and incredulous when she found out that Truman flat-out refused to invite her to his party, and no one could persuade him to change his mind. Truman Capote was a nobody when they had met, she fumed, a *nobody*. But now that he was rich and famous, Truman thought he could turn his back on the people who helped him get that way.

McCullers found satisfaction in coolly plotting her revenge. She knew she was a better writer than Truman was, and she was certain she could host a better party if she put her mind to it. The first name on her guest list was going to be Jacqueline Kennedy, and there would be no invitation for Mr. Truman Capote.

14

How to Be Lovely

As soon as the invitations were delivered, Truman made five hundred friends and fifteen thousand enemies, or so he said. According to his calculations, for every person who breathed a sigh of relief at the sight of the coveted envelope, there were three hundred others who were profoundly disappointed because it never came. "People are practically committing *suicide* because they didn't get invitations," Truman crowed.

Elizabeth Davies was bombarded with responses, most of them acceptances from happy recipients. Truman had timed his evening wisely. It was early in the social season—the night before its official start, in fact—so guests were still enthusiastic about the prospect of a formal event. By January, even the hardiest partygoer would recoil at the thought of ballrooms and receiving lines.

There were regrets, of course. Jacqueline Kennedy was not accepting invitations in November (the anniversary of her husband's assassination), and her in-laws, Robert and Edward Kennedy, made their excuses as well. Secretary of State Robert McNamara declined because he thought it unseemly to "frug at Kay's party" while the

En honor of Mrs. Katharine Graham

MR. TRUMAN CAPOTE

REQUESTS THE PLEASURE OF YOUR COMPANY

AT A BLACK AND WHITE DANCE

ON MONDAY, THE TWENTY-EIGHTH OF NOVEMBER

AT TEN O'CLOCK

GRAND BALLROOM, THE PLAZA

R.S.V.P.
MISS ELIZABETH DAVIS
485 PARK AVENUE
NEW YORK

DRESS
GENTLEMEN: BLACK TIE; BLACK MASK
LADIES: BLACK OR WHITE DRESS
WHITE MASK; FAN

country was in the throes of political unrest. Mayor John Lindsay wanted to come but had a previous engagement.

Elizabeth Taylor was filming *Reflections in a Golden Eye in Rome*, so she and Richard Burton had to decline, and Audrey Hepburn and her husband, Mel Ferrer, were otherwise engaged in Switzerland. Shirley MacLaine, Jack Lemmon, and Walter Matthau were unavailable because of work commitments. Marlene Dietrich was in Paris. Ginger Rogers sent her regrets, saying, "I don't go to parties." The director Mike Nichols was working on a new show. Lena Horne didn't want to go alone. And Mr. and Mrs. Ralph Bunche, who were mourning the death of their daughter, Janet Bunche Pierce, did not accept "because of our sorrow."

Katherine Anne Porter was ill in Washington. The writers Peter Matthiessen and William Styron decided not to go because they were wrapped up in their work and were afraid a night out would break their concentration. Walter Cronkite was on assignment in

Europe. Twenty-year-old Kitty Hawks, the daughter of Slim Keith and Howard Hawks, found it difficult to travel from Smith College. The *New York Times* drama critic Walter Kerr responded with refreshing honesty that if he didn't have to cover an opening, he preferred to spend his free time with his family. Other invited guests who were unable to attend were Samuel Goldwyn, Leonard Bernstein, Mary Martin, Harry Belafonte, John Hersey, Paul Mellon, James Michener, Governor Nelson Rockefeller, Robert Penn Warren, Thornton Wilder, and Tennessee Williams.

In addition to the customary assortment of acceptances and regrets, there were several unusual responses to the mailing. They fell into two general categories: "Are you sure I can't bring a date?" and "I'll do anything to get an invitation." Some of Truman's extra men were becoming rambunctious. "Almost all those I invited accepted; but about forty of them called or wrote me a note, indicating they were not as single as I presumed—they wanted to bring their girlfriends, fiancées, or simply ladies they were living with." But Truman was insistent: an extra man had to remain an extra man. Thirty-nine of the supplicants backed down and agreed to come alone. According to Truman, there was only one extra man who stood by his principles. In telling the story about the lone holdout, Truman always referred to him as "a television tycoon" without mentioning his name. The guest list suggests that it was Mark Goodson, the producer/creator of *What's My Line?*, *I've Got a Secret*, *To Tell the Truth*, *Password*, and other landmark television game shows, who ultimately declined his invitation because Truman refused to let him bring his girlfriend.

Several of the people who had hoped to be invited or thought they should be on the list by virtue of their standing in society sent pleading letters to Capote. "I feel like I fell into a whole mess of piranha fish," he complained to a reporter. Other would-be guests hatched harebrained schemes to secure an invitation. The most common and transparent ploy was for a person to feign ignorance of the ball and call Truman to invite *him* to an event on the evening of the twenty-eighth. But Truman was unresponsive to maneuvers that demonstrated so little imagination or finesse. As the *Life* magazine writer Shana Alexander found out, he was more likely to yield to a direct hit.

Alexander, who had written about Truman and *In Cold Blood* the year before, found herself sitting next to him at a restaurant during a visit to New York. She scribbled on her business card, "Have black-and-white dress in suitcase, just hit town," and surreptitiously tried to press it into his suit pocket. The problem was that his dandified suit had no pockets. Truman looked at her as if she were a lunatic and asked, "What the hell are you doing to me?" When Alexander confessed her plan, Truman glanced at the card and surprised her by saying, "I'd love to have you come to my party."

He was not as gracious to some of his old friends. Tallulah Bankhead, with whom he had spent many an evening at Leo Lerman's apartment, had to ask repeatedly for an invitation before Truman decided she would be a worthy addition to the five hundred. He flatly turned down the actress Ina Claire and the writer Carson McCullers, both of whom had befriended him when he was still the boy with bangs. Family members were excluded as well. Truman's aunt, Marie Rudisall, waited in vain for her invitation to the ball, and there was no mention of Arch Persons on the list.

Another story Truman loved to tell may have been designed to show his warmer, more sentimental side. He was contacted by a gentleman—an acquaintance, not a close friend—who confided that his wife was unable to stop crying or to get out of bed because she had not received an invitation. Truman listened, impressed by the husband's dignity and apparent concern for his wife. Perhaps he was thinking of Nina, his socially ambitious mother, and her unfortunate end. Whatever the motivation, he kindly told his caller that there had been a mistake: their invitation had gotten lost in the mail, and another would be sent immediately.

A few misguided individuals tried to buy invitations—after all, a private ball was a rare occurrence in New York in 1966—but they learned that their money had no value. Truman prided himself on the fact that his party was "the only ball in 25 years that people could attend *without* having to pay $200 a ticket for charity." Some petitioners refused to believe he could not be bought. Truman claimed he was approached by a representative of Charles Revson, the owner of Revlon. The beauty magnate offered to provide "door prizes and table favors" in exchange for an invitation. Truman's punctilious southern manners kicked in when he responded that he did not know Mr. Revson and therefore could not possibly invite him.

One person who was amused by the fact that no invitation came to his door was Dominick Dunne. Only two years earlier, Truman had danced the night away at the Dunnes' highly successful black and white party in Los Angeles. But when Truman had the opportunity to reciprocate, he neglected to put the Dunnes on his guest list. He wanted to believe his evening was original, and that would have been difficult with the Dunnes in the room.

When all machinations to secure an invitation failed, there was one final way to save face. The uninvited could sidestep the issue by fabricating important reasons they had to be out of town on the night of the party, implying that they *would* have attended had they been free. In order for the ruse to work, however, they actually had to go away (or stay home with the lights off).

The novelist Grace Stone placed herself in that very position when she wrote a nasty letter to her old friend Truman. She told him she was on her way to Europe, so attending the ball was out of the question, but she chastised him for not inviting her. Truman called her bluff by answering that he had sent an invitation and was expecting her to come. (He was playing his own game because Stone's name was not in his notebook or on any of his subsequent lists.) As much as she wanted to attend the party, Stone had to exit town on her proverbial high horse so that she wouldn't look foolish.

The chosen were relieved that they did not have to beg for invitations, hide their heads in shame, or invent excuses to leave New York. The word *ball* worked its magic on Truman's crowd, prompting thoughts of fairy tales and fantasies, of beautiful women and handsome princes, and, most important, of gowns and glass slippers. But for many of the guests, exhilaration turned into panic when they realized the hardest part was ahead of them. Written between the lines of Truman's elegant invitation was a challenge. Are you *really* one of the beautiful people? Will your outfit— especially your mask—live up to the occasion? How will you stand out in such distinguished company? While a few indifferent guests would pull something out of the closet at the last minute and grab the nearest mask (if there could be such a thing as a nearest mask), most partygoers would devote serious time—and money—to their appearance.

As any of Truman's swans could testify, being stylish was a full-time occupation. Fashion bibles such as *Vogue* and *Harper's Bazaar* issued bimonthly edicts about the best clothes, accessories, hair-styles, makeup, and beauty rituals. Readers who turned to these magazines for advice in the fall of 1966 knew that the hottest trends among fashion insiders were diet and exercise regimes, tans, hairpieces, short skirts, boots, and oversized costume jewelry—the ingredients that would help any woman look more youthful and with it.

The beauty icons of the moment were the tall, thin models who dominated the pages of every fashion magazine. Jean Shrimpton was a stunning young woman from England who seemed to be all hair and legs. Seventeen-year-old Twiggy, also British, had very lit-tle hair and weighed only ninety pounds but was blessed with the angelic face and eyes of a "teen-age Garbo." Although their looks were very different, both models were the embodiment of young, hip, swingin' London, the center of the mod universe. Fashion photographers such as David Bailey, the inspiration for the lead character in *Blow-Up*, and Richard Avedon were obsessed with them because they were fresh and striking. Their images were everywhere, on magazine covers, in fashion layouts, and in adver-tisements for beauty products. Women who were not young, thin,

British, or even remotely cool aspired to their lean and leggy look and would do anything to get it.

Since the average woman in 1966 weighed 140 pounds and was appreciably larger than the coltish models she admired, diet was the first step toward achieving the new look. The latest fad in Paris was the Swiss cheese diet, based on the theory that eating Swiss cheese could take the place of exercise in maintaining muscle tone. This regime did not sound as bearable as the diet that promised "Eat, Eat, Eat Your Pounds Away: The More You Eat, the More You Lose." According to *Vogue*, Dr. Heinz Humplik of Vienna spent fourteen years developing the theory that calories are not as important as the form in which they are consumed. Dr. Humplik claimed that a hard-boiled egg, which represents eighty calories, burns ninety-two calories when it is digested. Humplik recommended eating eggs, lean meats, green vegetables, and fruit, which he called "minus-calorie" foods. Presumably, eating a lot of minus-calorie foods would result in consuming no calories at all. The logic was a little fuzzy, but a diet that encouraged eating was always appreciated.

For dieters who wanted a simpler way to reduce, the nutritionally balanced drink Metrecal was the answer. The name *Metrecal* came from the term *metered calories*. Dieters who substituted the 225-calorie drink for meals lost weight without having to fuss over what they ate. Because Metrecal promoted easy, rapid weight loss—and was heavily advertised—it became a popular product that generated over ten million dollars in sales in its first two years.

Even the most dedicated dieters needed exercise, advised *Vogue*. When polled about their workouts, several socialites, such as Pamela Hayward and Brooke Astor, praised Miss Craig at Elizabeth Arden, the salon's domineering mistress of weights and dumbbells, for keeping them in shape. "Craigie," as she was called, was Marjorie Craig Cowley, a fitness expert who had been the director of exercise at Arden for thirty years and who wrote several fitness books. "Craigie tones me up and makes me feel better," said Hayward. Babe Paley swore by Joseph Pilates, the exercise guru who had developed his muscle resistance program while working as a nurse in England after the First World War. The actress Merle Oberon, Henry Ford's beautiful wife, Cristina, and Luciana Pignatelli were disciples of the exotic-sounding Sbarra, a Roman who attached weights to their feet when they exercised.

For women who did not have personal trainers, there were machines that could be used at home. Advertisements boasted that fifteen-minute daily "fun sessions" on the Exercycle helped flatten bulges and left you feeling younger. The Relax-A-Cizor promised something even better. "You rest, read, or watch TV while Relax-A-Cizor does your exercising for you." The machine, which came in four sizes, including the portable Verve model, used electrodes to tighten muscles. It was claimed that daily exercise sessions would reduce hips, waist, tummy, and thighs. One young woman swore that she left her unsightly bumps mid-Atlantic when she circled the globe on a business trip with her trusty Verve as her companion. "Can't travel without the machine," she concluded.

Women who had whipped themselves into shape (and some who hadn't) were willing to expose more of their flesh, but they did not want to look naked. The solution was a tan body, which would appear firmer, healthier, and more toned. *Vogue* recommended that fashionable women should be "tan all over for the dinner dresses that have crazy openings; bare arms, bare backs, even bare stomachs."

In the summer, tanning lotions transformed pale skin into the perfect shade of tawny. "Have a love affair with the sun," Bain de Soleil's advertisement urged. In the winter, when a trip to a sunny climate was not always possible, clever women turned to sunlamps to maintain their year-round tan. Solariums in Paris beauty institutes were overrun with women—as many as forty at a time—fighting for an inch of electrical sun. Safe sun-lamping was a delicate science because the light was so powerful: every time a tanner moved three inches closer to the lamp, she received nine times as much "sun," so burning was always a possibility. If maintaining a tan became too difficult, Estée Lauder's new waterproof leg makeup (complete with knee rouge for contouring) was available to simulate sun-kissed limbs.

Sculpted figures and bronzed skin were topped by the pièce de résistance, dramatic hair. Whether long or short, hair was a form of theater, and hairdressers were considered artists who could transform any head into spectacle with a wave of the scissors. The utilitarian, once-a-week visit to the beauty salon practiced by previous generations had been replaced by a different kind of relationship. A top-level stylist was expected to be part cutter, part confessor, and part magician. Designing a particular look for a client, one that would enhance strong features and obscure weak ones, was only part of the job. A hairstylist also had to have the imagination to create fantasy hairdos for parties and other dress-up occasions. The whole time he was creating, he had to provide a ready ear for any intimacies the woman might want to share. Hairdressers had become so important to women that when Aristotle Onassis wanted to impress Jacqueline Kennedy and Lee Radziwill during a cruise on the *Cristina*, he turned a room into a beauty salon and staffed it with two full-time hair stylists.

Women who wanted their hairstyles to make an edgy statement patronized Vidal Sassoon, a British stylist who was famous for his boyish, geometric cuts—a daring look best worn by waif-like young girls with large expressive eyes. Women who were interested in more classic looks turned to New York's Kenneth, a hairdresser who understood the importance of looking pretty.

Kenneth Battalle was eighteen and fresh out of the Navy when he enrolled in beauty school in 1945. It was an arbitrary career choice—he thought he might become a psychiatrist, but he could not afford college and medical school. His decision was fortuitous, because Kenneth proved to have a unique talent for designing hairstyles that made his clients look and feel beautiful. He could study a woman, Jacqueline Kennedy, for example, and see that her hair should be longer, fuller, and straighter around the face to offset her wonderful bones. Like a master framer, Kenneth fashioned his hairstyles to enhance a woman's features, not to eclipse them.

His salon, a five-story mansion on New York's East 54th Street, was opulently outfitted in Indian jungle flower carpeting and red-and-yellow paisley fabric. Women reveled in the luxurious atmosphere, the seraglio-like ambiance of the place. Uniformed maids served tea and tiny sandwiches to clients who awaited their turn with the maestro. When the moment came, the woman was ushered to a comfortable brown leather chair, where her feet rested on a footstool monogrammed with the letter K. Always impeccably dressed in a suit and a tie, Kenneth stepped in to give her his complete attention. "Are there things you love or hate about your hair?" he asked, inviting the client to share her hair fantasies. Rarely would a woman presume to tell him what to do. Marilyn Monroe, Lauren Bacall, Babe Paley, Slim Keith, and Lee Radziwill trusted Kenneth, dubbed the "Mr. Cool of the haute coiffure," to make them look fashionable without looking extreme.

Wigs and hairpieces in the form of falls, braids, curls, and pigtails enabled Kenneth and other hairdressers to bring hair fantasies to life. Kenneth had a special room that housed fake tresses for every occasion. Fashion-forward women who had surrendered their hair to the boy look could use these accessories to restore their lost locks. Conservative women who were afraid of the shears—or change—could try on a mod cut without submitting to scissors. Magazines featured elaborately built coiffures in fashion layouts and articles extolling the versatility of wigs and hairpieces. Alexandre, a popular French hairdresser, maintained a wig vault where he housed pop-on coiffures for fashion shows and celebrity clients.

The finest wigs were made of real hair from Italy, where women from poor villages sold their tresses for cash. Yet some of the most interesting and fashionable hairpieces were created with new synthetic materials. Women responded enthusiastically to Dynel, a fiber that was molded and cut to look like hair. Dynel never pretended to be the real thing. "It's not fake anything, its real Dynel," boasted its slogan.

When polled by *Vogue* in an issue that featured a model in an unabashedly fake wig on its cover, fashionable women claimed they could not live without their fanciful hairpieces, which were often inexpensive and easy to maintain. Luciana Pignatelli admitted to traveling with an entire wardrobe of wigs and pieces, which she must have put to good use on the Agnelli cruise she took with Truman. The empress Farah Diba owned forty. One socialite confessed that she had piled five or six on her head at a time until her husband told her, "That's *enough!*" An Italian noblewoman commissioned hairpiece flowers to cascade down her back, and several young French princesses cut off lengths of their Alice-in-Wonderland locks to make matching chignon hairpieces. Apparently, 1966 was a very good year for the wig business, as evidenced by the thirty million hairpieces sold during that time in the United States alone.

❧

While Kenneth Battale was at the forefront of the hair revolution, another Kenneth, a bright and flamboyant young artist named Kenneth Jay Lane, was pioneering an exciting new movement in jewelry. "The most important men in a fashionable woman's life," according to the *New York Times* writer Marilyn Bender, "were her hairdresser, her make-up artist, and Kenneth J. Lane." He was the king of the "faux masterpiece," costume jewelry that was so beautiful and unusual that it transcended its humble origins. Lane made his fabulous creations out of odd materials such as glass, copper, seashells, branch coral, and carved plastic. Aileen Mehle called him a sorcerer, capable of turning "rhinestones to diamonds and the blue, green, and red crystals and German-made glass he works with into sapphires, emeralds, and rubies that look plucked from an ancient idol's eye." Women who could easily afford the real thing flocked to his Park Avenue showroom for shoulder-duster earrings that were eight inches long and animal bracelets that looked like ancient treasures. Models in fashion magazines were draped with his designs because his bold earrings, bracelets, and necklaces worked well with big hair, short skirts, and caftans, all popular at the time.

In addition to being society's favorite young jeweler, Lane was also the perfect extra man, which was one of the reasons Truman added Lane to his guest list. Handsome, amusing, slightly wicked, and always beautifully dressed, Lane was said to pop up at in-set parties as often as his jewelry. He joked that waiters at functions always brought lost jewelry to him, and that his friends often asked him to perform on-the-spot repairs.

ᏸᎧ

The women invited to Truman's party may have fussed over their figures, their hair, and their accessories, but the big question they faced was the same one that confounded Katharine Graham— What will I wear to the ball?

Of his beautiful friend, Truman wrote, "Mrs. P. had only one fault: she was perfect; otherwise, she was perfect." Babe Paley made perfection look easy, but achieving it was actually a full-time job. Her preparations for the ball were so extensive that she ordered not one but *four* masks. Babe commissioned the first three from Halston, supplying him with fabric and fake jewels to match her gown. When he presented her with his designs, though, she was not happy. The problem was that Halston's masks covered her best feature—her eyes.

Babe feigned enthusiasm in her inimitably gracious way and quickly turned to Adolfo, Halston's chief rival, for a solution. He cleverly came up with oversized glasses that would frame her eyes instead of hiding them. *This* crisis averted, Babe steeled herself for the inevitable next one.

15

Plumage

IN 1920, PROUST OBSERVED, "IN MOST WOMEN'S LIVES, EVERYTHING, even the greatest sorrow, comes down to a question of 'I haven't got a thing to wear.'" His insight into the female psyche was still valid in 1966. The pursuit of the perfect dress was foremost in the minds of most of Truman's guests. Eugenia Sheppard suspected that very few old party dresses would turn up on the dance floor the night of November 28. Some women would buy European, others would turn to American designers, and many would take their chances with ready-to-wear gowns in their favorite stores. Wherever they shopped, their concern was the same. "I've never seen women putting so much serious effort into what they're going to wear," Halston remarked.

The swans took special care in choosing their dresses for the evening. Gloria Guinness selected a beautifully cut white coat dress, lavishly embroidered with white crystal tubes, created by Antonio Castillo, a Spanish designer who had taken over the house of Lanvin in Paris. In the event that the crystal tubes failed to generate enough glitter, Gloria decided to wrap her neck with not one, but two impressive necklaces, one ruby and one diamond.

Lee Radziwill also decided on a high-wattage look. She turned to the Italian designer Mila Schön (who also dressed Marella Agnelli) for a body-hugging column of silver pailletes. The more demure C. Z. Guest depended on her favorite designer, Mainbocher, to dress her in one of his signature easy-to-wear styles; she chose a simple lace gown with a white bodice and a black skirt. Pamela Hayward, who always teetered on the cusp of the swan list, planned on making a big statement in a real ball gown, an inky black tulle by Dior with a full skirt bolstered by five stiff white petticoats.

When Babe Paley was ready to select her gown for the evening, she went to Bergdorf Goodman, New York's most prestigious department store, which had been outfitting women for almost seventy years. The store's founders, Herman Bergdorf and Edwin Goodman, began their partnership in 1899 in a small custom dress shop in New York City. They were talented tailors who created chic, European-styled garments for women. Several years and a couple of moves later, Goodman opened a department store on Fifth Avenue near the Plaza Hotel. With its marble rotunda and myriad of beautifully appointed rooms, the store was reminiscent of the homes of Goodman's well-to-do patrons. Goodman designed the store as a warren of interconnecting rooms with the idea that they could be closed off or rented to outside vendors if Bergdorf's failed. The storekeepers slept above the shop, as it were: on the top floor there was the "Apartment," a sixteen-room residence for the Goodmans, with spectacular views of Central Park. Mr. and Mrs. Goodman had to list themselves as janitors rather than residents to comply with city regulations. Visitors to the store became used to the sight of the Bergdorf children and their nannies commandeering the elevators to go in and out of the "house."

Most of the floors in the store did not have open stock. Instead, customers consulted carefully trained salespeople, who retrieved merchandise from the back. Only Bigi, a brand-new boutique-like department catering to young women, displayed mod clothing on racks and shelves. In addition to offering an extraordinary sales force, Bergdorf's housed a custom department on its seventh floor that rivaled any fashion atelier in Paris. Headed by the fashion director Ethel Frankau, Bergdorf's custom workshop employed 60 tailors, 85 custom dressmakers, 75 alterations experts, 11 pressers, and 3 hemstichers, ready to turn the most complicated design into a beautifully executed garment. Babe Paley chose a Castillo original (her rival Gloria's choice of designer, though it was impossible to determine which swan had arrived at the decision first) that would be reproduced by the store's able fleet of American craftsmen.

Many women, including Jacqueline Kennedy, relied on Bergdorf's to replicate the couture clothing they admired in Paris. The first lady's 1961 inaugural gown had been created by Frankau and her team. The custom department copied garments so faithfully

Mask by Bill Cunningham.

that they were executed in the same fabrics, threads, buttons, and trimmings as their Paris originals. While it was a mark of distinction for a department store to make these authorized versions instead of the cheaper and inauthentic knockoffs turned out by Seventh Avenue manufacturers, the process was both complicated and costly.

Bergdorf paid a fee known as a *caution* for the right to attend a European designer's fashion show. The store's buyers marked their selections and purchased the garments, which arrived in New York with a *reference*, a document that specified the exact fabrics and trimmings (including zippers, bones, and buttons) needed to make the item. These prototypes were kept under lock and key and could not be sold. Sometimes, such expensive materials and costly workmanship went into custom imports that Bergdorf's lost money on the finished garment, even though the price was high.

When a woman ordered a garment, it was made on a special dress form that was built for her and padded to match her measurements. The factory, as the custom floor was called, had thousands of forms labeled with names like Paley, Whitney, and Vanderbilt. When a young woman matured and her figure changed and expanded, little pads were added in strategic places, silent witnesses to the passage of time. The custom department enabled busy women like Babe to sidestep the inconvenient practice of shuttling to Paris and Rome for fittings.

Babe's Castillo gown was a sleeveless pillar of white zibeline (a lustrous soft fabric with a silky nap), faced in cardinal red. A dramatic slit in the front created petal-like panels on either side. The neckline was decorated with an ornate ruby and diamond necklace made out of paste, a whimsical touch considering that Babe could easily afford real jewels.

The dress forms in the custom department were put to good use as other clients came to Bergdorf's to order their ball gowns. The art collector Jayne Wrightsman ordered a white crepe Jean Patou with bows offsetting the bodice. Mrs. Thomas Schippers, the wife of the conductor, chose a winter look—a black velvet gown with white mink sleeves—by Fabiani. Brooke Astor, who had decided she wanted to look like a figure in a painting by Goya, chose a romantic ball gown of white lace with a fitted bodice and a full skirt.

Fashionable women also patronized Chez Ninon, a jewel-like dress salon on Park Avenue run by two society women, Nona Park and Sophie Shonnard. Jacqueline Kennedy had been one of their best customers when she was the first lady because she could buy clothing that was designed in Paris but legitimately made in America.

Karen Gundersen, Truman's friend at *Newsweek*, headed for Chez Ninon when she received her invitation. She was preoccupied with other thoughts at the time because she and Alan Jay Lerner, the charming, successful, and oft-wed lyricist/librettist, had fallen in love and were getting married in late November, only three days before Truman's ball. The beautiful bride-to-be selected a white satin Givenchy gown that resembled the one Leslie Caron wore in the 1958 film version of the Lerner and Loewe musical *Gigi*.

With so many women shopping for gowns at the same time, there were bound to be duplications. Anne Ford and Rosie Chisholm unknowingly planned on wearing the same black Christian Dior gown and came close to a fashion disaster. But Lydia Katzenbach, the wife of the former attorney general and the new under secretary of state Nicholas Katzenbach, did not have to give a moment's thought to someone showing up in her dress—it was an original that she had designed and sewn herself.

Several of the women decided to be daring by rejecting ball gowns in favor of one of the season's most controversial new garments, the pantsuit. "They are walking out of the store . . . as fast as we can get them in," said Geraldine Stutz, the president of Henri Bendel. Women were quick to buy them because they were chic and comfortable, but pantsuits, no matter how fashionable, were not welcome everywhere. Some restaurants, the Colony and "21" in New York and Simpsons on the Strand in London, for example, denied entry to women wearing pants—the would-be diners had to remove the offending garments and hope that their tunic tops covered the essentials or run home to change into a more socially acceptable dress.

The philanthropist Dru Heinz planned on wearing billowy palazzo pajamas created by Princess Irene Galitzine, while the trendsetter Mrs. Watson Blair turned to the French designer Guy Laroche for a jet-encrusted pants-and-blouse ensemble.

Truman's younger guests were risk-takers as well. Amanda Burden sidestepped the tricky issue of selecting one designer over another by borrowing a black-and-white, Cecil Beaton–designed striped gown that had been used as a costume in the movie *My Fair Lady*. Marisa Berenson, a young model omnipresent in the fashion magazines and the granddaughter of the legendary Elsa Schiapparelli, was fitted for a sleek, black, strapless, ermine-trimmed gown by Halston, the popular milliner who had just presented his first ready-to-wear clothing line at Bergdorf Goodman.

But seventeen-year-old Penelope Tree, the daughter of the society doyenne Marietta Tree, insisted on preparing for the ball in the manner of a true youthquaker. Tree liked to shop at New York's trendy new boutiques such as Paraphernalia and the flashy retailer Tiger Morse's flea market–themed emporium, Kaleidoscope. The merchandise was on display, and the latest styles, usually the last word in mod, came in every day. These boutiques offered society's young locomotives an exciting, offhand way to dress. Couture copies, coveted by the establishment, were meaningless to them. They wanted their own fashions—in suede, in vinyl, in corduroy, and even in paper—and lusted after the revolutionary up-to-the-minute imports from Carnaby Street in London. Tiger Morse reported that lines had formed outside her door and customers were spending a hundred dollars a day on novelty buttons with irreverent sayings such as *Mary Poppins is a Junkie* and *Marcel Proust is a Yenta*.

The outfit Penelope Tree selected was designed especially for her by Betsey Johnson of Paraphernalia, and it looked nothing like any other garment that was likely to turn up at the ball. Johnson said that she had collaborated with Tree and was inspired by her "long, slim 'far-out' mysterious cool self" to create something new, outrageous, and sexy in clingy Jasco jersey. The top was a revealing black tunic, sleeveless, V-necked, and slashed under the bra-like bodice to create floating panels. The bottom consisted of black tights and black hip-hugger briefs that looked very much like underwear. It was more street urchin than socialite, exactly the look young Tree wanted to project.

On Manhattan's Upper West Side, the writer Ann Birstein was thrilled to receive her invitation, which put, as she said, "a prodigiously large dollop of joy into my already full cup." Most people assumed she and her husband, the critic Alfred Kazin, had been invited because of his literary connection to Truman, but Ann knew that Truman was *her* fan. He loved her book *The Sweet Birds of Gorham* and constantly recommended it to his socialite friends.

As much as she looked forward to attending the ball, Ann was concerned about finding a dress: there was no room for custom copies in her budget. She decided to start by visiting Shapiro's, a store on nearby Broadway. Miraculously, hanging on the rack reserved for formal wear was her dream dress, an old-fashioned ball gown with a fitted black velvet bodice and a full black-and-white-striped satin skirt. As soon as she pulled it over her head, Ann felt transformed, rich, regal, beautiful. Worries about deadlines—she was writing movie reviews for *Vogue* when she wasn't working on her own projects—her young daughter, and other day-to-day concerns evaporated. With her invitation and her gown, she could legitimately claim to be one of the beautiful people.

In Washington, Liz Hylton harbored similar expectations for her dress. In her efficient way, she was already contemplating her own choices for an outfit. She was pleased that Truman had thoughtfully provided her with an escort for the evening, his friend Andrew Lyndon.

Liz received two exceedingly polite letters from Lyndon. The first one, dated October 31, 1966, served as an introduction.

"Truman tells me he's looking forward to seeing you at his ball on the twenty-eighth of November, and I am hoping I might look forward to escorting you. . . . Just let me know when and where, if—as I hope—you aren't already spoken for," he wrote.

Two weeks later, after receiving a positive response from Liz, Lyndon replied, "You cannot believe how very glad I was to receive your letter. Like you, I was regarding the prospect of facing alone that glamorous crowd with certain trepidation. Now—if you'll forgive the metaphor—we can be the two frogs who set out to see the world, and, assuredly, we shall see some of the great world, if not the great society."

Eager to put her best foot forward in this great world, Liz spent weeks searching in all of her favorite stores before she found the gown she wanted. The dress that caught her eye was simple but classic—sleeveless white brocade with buttons and a low back. Her accessories, she decided, would be elbow-length white kid gloves and pearl earrings.

In Kansas, the Deweys, the Wellses, Vi Tate, the Maxfields, the Masoners, and the Williamses were eagerly anticipating the ball and started making plans right away. Odd and Jonell Williams lived four hundred miles away from Garden City in Lawrence, Kansas. They would join the others in New York for a week of festivities, which meant that some of the couples had to make arrangements for the children they would leave behind. The Williamses had five children, but it was not difficult for them to get away, because they could rely on a young couple who lived in a cottage on their property for babysitting help.

Foremost on their minds was the all-important question of the dress. The Kansas ladies, Marie Dewey, Kay Wells, Vi Tate, Lee Maxfield, Margaret Masoner, and Jonell Williams, put as much effort into their appearances as their big-city sisters did. Vi, Margaret, Lee, and Kay planned on wearing white. Lee bought her beaded satin gown at Irene Williams' Vogue Shop in Garden City, while Kay found her white-and-silver brocade dress at Harzfeld's in

Kansas City. Marie decided to wear a black crepe gown with a marquisette yoke, and Jonell would shop for her gown in New York.

When Kay Graham finally found the time to think about her dress, she went to the custom department at Bergdorf Goodman to make her selection. A busy executive like Kay did not have the time to park herself in Paris while a couture gown was sewn from scratch, especially when the factory could whip up a perfect, line-for-line copy. She chose a classic design by Balmain, a white wool crepe monk's robe with long sleeves. The neckline was high and embroidered with dark gray hematites, which also encircled the cuffs, like bracelets. Though conservative, the gown was striking in its simplicity and added a touch of glamour to Kay's normally sensible appearance. She was thrilled with her choice and said it would be her "best dress this winter." Like a debutante, Kay was outfitted by her mother, Agnes Meyer, who bought the gown as a present for her daughter's big night.

While Truman's female guests exhausted themselves with their preparations, it occurred to them that their male counterparts had a much easier time getting ready. A man's best friend on the eve of a formal event was his tuxedo. In *Esquire's Fashions for Men*, a 1966 style guide edited by the fledgling journalist John Berendt (who would go on to write *Midnight in the Garden of Good and Evil*), the tuxedo was hailed as the workhorse of formal wear. According to the experts at *Esquire*, it rarely changed design from year to year, and a gentleman need only decide which kind of lapel—the popular shawl, the conservative notched, or the more formal peaked—best suited his personal sense of style. A choice also had to be made between a cummerbund, a wide fabric belt worn at the waist, and a waistcoat, which was essentially a dressy vest. The finishing touch was the bow tie, an easy accessory now that the clip-on version had been deemed socially acceptable. Best of all, a man could wear the same tuxedo to every event.

❦

Men may have escaped the tyranny of the dress, but they were subject to the same pressure as women in the pursuit of the mask. Truman was fascinated by masks. He wrote about them in *Breakfast at Tiffany's*, depicting Holly Golightly and her companion stealing masks from a dime store, and he even posed with a Halloween mask in hand for *Life* during a photo session in Kansas.

Halloween was approaching, so it was possible for guests to find a selection of masks in toy stores and novelty shops. A two-sided Batman and Robin mask was very popular that year, as were rubber masks of mutant monsters and plastic masks of cartoon characters and clowns. But women who had spent time and money on expensive gowns were unwilling to hide their faces under comical or horrific masks of molded plastic. They wanted to look beautiful, and that called for a visit to a professional who understood how to decorate a head—a talented and trusted hatmaker.

The ever boastful Mr. John insisted that he was the leading milliner in town, but the most exciting hats were coming from the workrooms of Adolfo and Halston. Adolfo Sardiña was born in Cuba and moved to New York in 1948. He started his millinery career as an assistant at Bergdorf Goodman and went on to become the head designer for the popular Emme line. A cultivated man with a keen appetite for literature and the arts, Adolfo produced hat collections that were often inspired by such artists as Toulouse-Lautrec, Gainsborough, and Watteau. Like a sculptor, he created hats with his hands and materials, skipping the sketching stage. The *New York Times* praised the fanciful Cuban's imaginative works.

Roy Halston Frowick, who shortened his name to the more distinctive Halston, won the first of what would turn out to be many prizes when he was voted Healthiest Baby at the Iowa State Fair. Even as a child, he enjoyed making hats. He moved to New York to pursue a career in millinery and landed a job at the salon of Lily Daché. His success there led to a new job as chief hatter at Bergdorf Goodman, where he found fame and a following after he designed Jacqueline Kennedy's much-admired pillbox hat for the

1961 inauguration. Halston's salon became one of Bergdorf's busiest principalities. It was so successful that he convinced Andrew Goodman to let him place his own label in his hats—a first, as house designers were usually anonymous. In 1966, Halston expanded his brand by introducing his first line of clothing.

Both Adolfo and Halston had started exciting new careers as fashion designers, but Truman's Black and White Ball forced them to concentrate on the role of maskmaker. Their best clients— including Babe Paley, Amanda Burden, C. Z. Guest, Dru Heinz, Mrs. Watson Blair, Jean Vanderbilt, Mrs. Thomas Schippers, Anne Ford, Brooke Astor, and Jayne Wrightsman—descended on them, pleading for help with Truman's challenging assignment. Even the most fashionable women had little experience with masks.

Adolfo was uniquely prepared to handle their requests because his 1965 fall collection featured a number of stunning masks and headdresses. He had been inspired by eighteenth-century Venetian masks because he loved the way they introduced mystery and fantasy to a woman's appearance. "In Venice," he pointed out, "a woman would wear a mask just to wear a mask." Adolfo hoped the same women who bought his fanciful hats would consider wearing a dressy mask for an evening out.

If there was not a big demand for Adolfo's masquerade masks before Truman announced his ball, there was a rush for them after the invitations arrived. Adolfo was besieged by about 125 excited clients who wanted custom masks in a hurry. He studied the designs of their dresses and made suggestions. He knew they would be happiest with a mask attached to a stick instead of one that rested on the face—false eyelashes were very popular then and anything that sat too close to the eye would disturb a woman's makeup. In addition to the masks he designed for specific clients, Adolfo sold more than a hundred masks at his Saks Fifth Avenue boutique. Rose Kennedy came in and paid forty dollars for a domino with tall egret feathers. She carried it out of the store in a special twenty-four-inch box that Adolfo had ordered to hold his delicate creations.

"A lot of birds donated their feathers to the cause," quipped Adolfo. It was the Spanish rooster, the bird that produced coq feathers, that sacrificed the most plumage. Coqs, the rooster's long, curved, and iridescent tail feathers, were plucked from the bird to trim hats or, in this case, masks. Adolfo preferred coq feathers because they were beautiful and dramatic and could be counted on to maintain their shape.

While Adolfo was reassuring nervous clients, turning other customers away, and staying up all night to fill the orders he had accepted, Halston was equally overwhelmed by his demanding followers. At Bergdorf's, ball-goers came straight to him after a fitting in the custom department. Babe Paley wanted a mask to match her white Castillo gown. She provided extra paste jewels to match the ones on the neckline of her dress so that he could work them into the design. Ever the perfectionist, Babe wanted not one but *three* different versions of the mask so that she would have a selection. Jayne Wrightsman needed a white feather mask for herself and a black one for her husband. A white, long-eared bunny mask would be just the thing to complement Marisa Berenson's black-and-white gown. Every time he met with a client, Halston tried to come up with a concept that was original. "Each mask is going to be different," he announced confidently to Eugenia Sheppard at the beginning of the siege. Yet as the ball drew closer and his workshop pulsated with activity, the exhausted designer complained, "The ladies have killed me."

Kay Graham met with Halston in October to discuss her mask. As he and Adolfo had suggested to all their clients, he recommended that she carry one on a stick. The idea worried her, she said in a letter, because she knew she would have to receive guests with Truman and needed to be in a position to shake hands. Her other concern was height. "I am already 5'9" without added height," she wrote, "so that I wish that whatever sticks up wouldn't stick up too far." Halston agreed to come up with a design that could be attached to her head without ruining her hair.

"The ladies vote for Halston, Adolfo, Mr. John, Archie Eason, Robert Mackintosh, and Menichetti for their masks," wrote *Women's Wear Daily*. Some ball guests wanted to avoid the crowds at Adolfo's and Halston's, and they turned to alternative designers. Mr. John took care of the singer Kitty Carlisle Hart. Lee Menichetti, an Italian American designer who was the Gepetto-like creator of whimsical accessories (such as a purse that could be worn as a hat and "Shu-masks" that magically changed the appearance of unadorned pumps), made a sequin-studded peacock feather mask for *Life* magazine's Jane Howard. The costume designer Robert Mackintosh made a mask for Pat Kennedy Lawford, despite the fact he was having a busy season designing Angela Lansbury's outfits for the musical *Mame* and launching a new clothing line. Archie Eason, an up-and-coming milliner, concocted a frothy mask and an oversized headdress for Mrs. Irving Lazar. Milliners and maskmakers all over town were experiencing unprecedented prosperity. The African American photographer Gordon Parks, who claimed he was invited "to make it a real black and white ball," said that he and his wife couldn't afford to eat for two weeks because she had spent so much money on a rhinestone mask.

Several women bought their masks in Europe: Countess Brandolini, Gianni Agnelli's sister, ordered a cat's-eye mask from Mme. Grès in Paris, and the designer Valentina's mask came from Venice, where she had it molded from her own face. Some guests—men and women—enlisted artists for one-of-a-kind creations. The interior decorator Billy Baldwin asked Gene Moore, the mastermind behind Tiffany's famous window displays, to conceive something spectacular for him. Kenneth Jay Lane agreed to create something fun and flamboyant for Pamela Hayward. The actor Henry Fonda spent two weeks making a mask for his wife, Shirlee. The resourceful Lydia Katzenbach whipped up a mask to go with her homemade dress. And the clever ladies in Kansas planned on decorating masks they'd bought to complement their gowns. Marie

Dewey added a whimsical touch to her mask by gluing false eye-lashes around the eyes.

In an article entitled "A Brush with Truman Capote," illustrated by two photographs, the *World Journal Tribune* reported that some women had come up with a daring idea for the ball: they would have their faces painted. The story went on to say that Joe Eula, a multitalented artist best known for his fashion illustrations, had been retained to decorate the faces of several international beau-ties, including Marisa Berenson and Benedetta Barzini. Eula said that he planned on painting Berenson's eyes with his version of the "I'd rather fight than switch" look made popular by the Tareyton cig-arette campaign.

Suzy Knickerbocker, Eugenia Sheppard, and Carole Bjorkman reported the details of mask fever in their columns, and these items were often accompanied by beautiful illustrations of masks and gowns, usually sketched by Kenneth Paul Block. "That's the Way the Ball Bounces" was the headline in a pre-ball piece in *Women's Wear Daily*. "He calls it a dance," the article went on to say, "others call it the decadent party of the decade."

Suzy told her readers, "Capote's next bestseller is his caper,'" and predicted that the Plaza Hotel would jump six feet in the air the night of the party because the guest list was so exciting. Though a seasoned social observer, even Suzy was surprised to hear that some of the ladies were paying as much as $500 for their masks. Yet that amount seemed like a bargain compared to the cost of two masks that could be seen in the window at Cartier. Called "Mephistopheles," the masks consisted of black velvet acanthus leaves with baguette, pear, and marquise diamonds, and they ranged in price from $35,000 to $38,000. The more expensive mask had an ostrich-feather trim. Truman followed these stories with amuse-ment. He found *his* mask, an ordinary black domino, at F.A.O. Schwarz, and it cost him all of thirty-nine cents. He bought a sup-ply to hand out to men who might come to the ball without masks.

In this case, he underestimated the efforts of his male guests.

"*Lots* of men have taken as much trouble as the women for Truman Capote's masked ball tonight," reported Eugenia Sheppard. Adolph Green had his son's nanny working on a special creation. Richard Avedon turned to Halston, Henry Ford to Adolfo, and Darryl F. Zanuck was depending on a Venetian craftsman to design a mask that could accommodate his glasses and his cigar.

Actually, Truman's party was not the only *bal masqué* in town. The socialite Mrs. Watson (Josie) Blair announced—after Truman—that she would host a "Come as your favorite dream" party on November 10 at her home in the East Sixties, and two hundred of her friends were invited to don masks and costumes to fete her daughter, Mary McFadden. Halston, who was called upon to make masks for this event, too, claimed, "I think masked balls are wonderful. It is like going to a strange city, where you don't know the people, when people wear masks. . . . look how beautiful a woman looks with a bit of black lace on her face." Commenting on the sudden popularity of masked balls, *Women's Wear Daily* asked, "Will the mask replace the frug?"

The Blair party came and went, but requests for invitations to Truman's ball poured in at the rate of twenty a day. Suzy raised the point that an event this hot was bound to attract crashers. When Charles de Beistegui had hosted his famous ball in Venice, the canals were filled with costumed imposters who hoped to sneak in without an invitation. How, Suzy wondered in her column, would Truman handle uninvited guests who showed up at his door?

He had left nothing to chance, he told Suzy when he called from San Francisco to reveal his carefully laid plans for party security. Guests would enter the hotel via the main door opposite Grand Army Plaza. Cameras would be permitted to capture the arrivals, and there were bound to be plenty of them, so anyone who wanted to avoid photographers was encouraged to use a secret entrance that had been set up on the side of the hotel.

Inside the Plaza, guests had the choice of walking up the stairs or taking the elevator. There would be two separate checkpoints on the way to the Grand Ballroom: one manned by the able Elizabeth Davies, who knew the guest list by heart; the other presided over by a male secretary. Guests would present their admittance cards, and their names would be matched to the list. Finally, they would arrive at the receiving line, consisting of an announcer, Truman, and Kay Graham.

As for those nasty intruders, Truman said that he had secured the services of ten burly bouncers to deal with gate-crashers and jewel thieves. The security guards would be disguised in dinner jackets and masks, and one would stand close to Truman in the receiving line. One signal from the host and any interlopers would be forcibly removed, "a hideous way of committing social suicide," Suzy warned potential intruders.

Nightmarish was the word Truman used to describe the last few days before the ball. He was bombarded with attention during the countdown. Every network wanted to send a crew to televise the evening, although bulky cameras and cables had practically ruined a recent charity ball. Newspapers and magazines, domestic and international, argued that their reporters had to be present, despite Truman's insistence that only a few select members of the press would be admitted to his ballroom. "No, repeat no, photographers will be allowed inside, and only three, repeat three, reporters have been invited—Charlotte Curtis of the *New York Times* and Eugenia Sheppard and Suzy Knickerbocker of the New York *World Journal Tribune*," insisted Aileen Mehle.

❧

As for those requests for invitations—they were amusing at first, because Truman did not take them seriously. Now, with time running out, the daily solicitations from the uninvited exhibited a marked change of tone. Politesse was replaced by desperation and anger as would-be guests *demanded* that Truman send an invitation immediately. He was mystified by their behavior and said, "They're nice people that you'd never expect to do a thing like that. I don't understand it."

The ball was not the only source of anxiety in his life. The paperback release of *In Cold Blood*, with the largest first printing of any in history, was scheduled for December, as was the telecast of ABC's dramatization of "A Christmas Memory," starring Geraldine Page. David Merrick's *Breakfast at Tiffany's*, now titled *Holly Golightly*, was set to open on December 26. And the upcoming movie version of *In Cold Blood* was in the news with reports that unknowns would play the killers, and the production would shoot inside the house where the actual murders took place in Kansas.

Truman loved being in the limelight—in the case of the ball, he had actually turned the high beams in his own direction—but the pressure of unremitting exposure was beginning to take its toll on him. In November, Truman canceled a public reading in Dallas and a private dinner planned by Stanley Marcus. He was sorry, he said, but with his hectic schedule, he "was about to crack up if something didn't give."

By the end of the month, Truman was a wreck. Friends who were invited to the ball descended upon him from various locations in America, Europe, and South America, and every day brought new distractions. Complaining, "My nerves were jangling, and so were all my telephones," Truman decided he had to withdraw from the circus. He disconnected his telephone and dropped out of sight for a few days, fleeing to his house in the Hamptons. His location was a mystery, and only Babe knew how to get in touch with him.

"The Capote ball will not only be his biggest, it will be his last," predicted a reporter who interviewed Truman during his pre-party slump. "After the last drink has been downed, he vows he is retiring forever from the social circuit." The exhausted host was already looking ahead to life after the ball, but his excited guests could think of one thing only: the night of Monday, November 28.

As Truman's guests jumped through hoops to prepare for the upcoming evening, Truman tried to stay calm. Yet there was one late-breaking development on the morning of the party that left him cackling with excitement. Truman called Elizabeth Davies—something he had done too many times that day—pulling her out of the shower to hear his news. The maharajah and the maharani of Jaipur were coming to the ball! They were flying in from India tonight. Winston Guest had agreed to meet them at the airport and rush them over to the Plaza. No time for their highnesses to dress in black or white, of course. But just this once, for these very important and titled guests, Truman would make an exception.

16

The Clock Ticks

"I HOPE YOUR MASK—YOUR SATIN TRACK SHOES AND YOUR VITAMIN injections are ready," warned Carol Bjorkman in *Women's Wear Daily* on the morning of the ball. Everyone in New York, from cabdrivers to CEOs, knew what was going to happen that night. The mere sight of a mask prompted onlookers to ask, "Going to Truman's ball?" Monday's madness had begun on Sunday, when the city braced itself for the onslaught of incoming out-of-town guests. So many private jets were expected to land at LaGuardia's Butler Airport that its runways were closed to commercial traffic. Among the arrivals were Frank Sinatra and his new wife, Mia Farrow, as well as Gloria Guinness (her husband, Loel, though a friend of Truman's, had called the party "childish" and said he would stay home). As jet-setters, they could jet into town one day and out the next. Suzy said, "The compulsion of this crowd is to keep moving because when they sit down they have to think."

On November 28, Truman's horoscope in the *Daily News* urged him to "clear the decks for action" and "don't be caught napping." The advice was unnecessary. Sleep was the last thing on his mind that day. He was too busy attending to last-minute details and putting out fires. Two of the ten security guards he had hired were unable to work that night, and Truman had to find replacements in a hurry. Fortunately, there were a couple of burly elevator operators at U.N. Plaza who were willing to take the job.

In another part of town, the West Coast literary agent Maria Theresa Caen sat in her hotel room waiting anxiously for a telephone call. The unthinkable had happened: she and her husband, the San Francisco columnist Herb Caen, had flown in for the ball and, upon landing, discovered that the airline had lost the bag containing her gown. Would she have to wear a bath towel that night, she wondered? Her friend Geraldine Stutz solved the problem by sending over a dress from Henri Bendel, but Caen wanted her own gown and hoped for the best.

Halston also found himself at the center of an unanticipated wardrobe drama. Marisa Berenson had never shown up for her final fitting, so the designer assumed that she had changed her mind about attending the ball. When Candice Bergen contacted him, looking for an outfit, Halston gave her Berenson's gown. No sooner had he done so than Berenson came calling. Her dress was gone, and Halston had been picked clean of anything black or white except for the wedding dress from his first collection. He convinced Berenson that the hooded white satin robe would be fabulous on her and promised to deliver it personally later that day.

Peter Duchin received a last-minute call from the columnist Earl Wilson, who was determined to find a way into the Plaza ballroom. He had a bold and improbable plan that required Duchin's help: would the bandleader consider smuggling him into the party as one of his musicians, perhaps as a trombonist? Duchin was amused and politely promised to consider the idea but never gave it another thought.

There were bound to be more dramas and disasters as the day progressed, but Truman, for one, was ready to start partying. He threw himself into the role of jaunty man-about-town and headed for the Colony to lunch with Lee Radziwill. Eager photographers snapped their picture as they posed outside, looking calm and happy.

All the best restaurants were packed with the "Chosen People," as *Women's Wear Daily* called the ball guests. La Grenouille had Gloria Guinness, C. Z. Guest, and Princess Luciana Pignatelli tête-à-têting with Eugenia Sheppard, Oscar de la Renta, and the *Washington Post*'s Ben Bradlee. The subject of conversation at these choice tables could have been the foul weather—it was rainy and windy, and the forecast for the rest of the day was bleak. If the diners had read their newspapers carefully that morning, they might have been prompted to discuss the Aransan quintuplets (three had already died and two were fighting for their lives in a Pittsburgh hospital); the bombing of Cambodia (B-52 planes had saturated a jungle area 250 miles northwest of Saigon); or the tragic floods in Florence (the city had no water, no light, no gas, and no heat, and there were threats of rats and typhoid). But it was far more likely that the buzz in these fancy watering holes was about little other than Truman's party. In analyzing the upcoming evening, one morning newspaper asked, "What will Mrs. Paley say to William Styron? What will Al Dewey say to Bennett Cerf?" *This* was news.

Most of the women who indulged in lunchtime trysts had to scurry off to hairdresser appointments. Cursing the rain, they headed to Kenneth's in their limousines, creating traffic jams on the streets surrounding the salon. There was pandemonium inside Kenneth's normally serene townhouse as one client after another—Slim Keith, Marella Agnelli, Pamela Hayward, Amanda Burden, Carol Bjorkman, Dru Heinz, Isabella Eberstadt, Jayne Wrightsman, Anne Ford, Kitty Carlisle Hart, and the Camelot contingent of Lee Radziwill, Rose Kennedy, Pat Lawford, and Jean Smith—presented their heads for more than a customary styling. (Babe Paley decided to skip the chaotic scene at the salon and have her hair done at home.) Today, the challenge for Kenneth and his top stylists Mary Farr and

Norbert was to create coiffures that could accommodate a stunning array of masks and headdresses. More important, each woman had to look different.

Denise Bouche, the widow of the artist Rene Bouche, had planned the most ambitious hairstyle of the evening. She envisioned a complicated Madame de Pompadour confection constructed of black and white hair and feathers. Some of her hair would be dyed black, while the rest would be dusted with white powder. The fantasy look would take a long time to achieve—hours, in fact—but Bouche was confident she would get what she wanted. "At Kenneth's they're never surprised by what I ask for," she said.

Wanting to look her best, Kay Graham had made an appointment to have her hair done at the salon. When she set out to see her stylist (neither Kenneth nor one of his young superstars), she was surprised to find that the street in front of the building was blocked with limousines, and inside the salon was a madhouse. The assistant who escorted Kay to her stylist apologized for the pandemonium. "We're all so busy preparing for the ball," she explained.

Not well known in New York and rather mousy, Kay shocked the woman by responding that she was going to be Truman's guest of honor that night. Instantly, plain Kay became the focus of all attention. Kenneth himself would do her hair, the assistant pronounced, as she hustled her suddenly V.I.P. client to the salon's most important chair.

Kay waited patiently while Kenneth put thousands of ringlets in Marisa Berenson's hair, then took her turn with the master. Kenneth studied her face and wisely fashioned a sleek bouffant for the unassuming woman who had never worn makeup before this occasion. Kay's hair was so simple and classic that Denise Bouche, who was sitting next to her, suddenly felt a little silly about the elaborate topiary that was being sculpted atop her head.

A short distance away at the Plaza Hotel, the ladies from Kansas admired their freshly coiffed hair. They had been styled at Edward of the Plaza earlier that morning. A *New York Times* photographer was there to take their picture as they sat in a chorus line–like row under the salon's hair dryers. Lee Masoner, Marie Dewey, Kay Wells, and Vi Tate were good sports about the shoot (Jonell Williams and Margaret Maxfield declined), although they suspected that the *Times* viewed them as country mice who had come to gawk at the big city. New York papers had a tendency to portray the Kansas visitors with condescension. Margaret Maxfield bemoaned the fact that the Kansans were treated "as if we had arrived in a wagon train pursued by Indians." Reporters liked to call Odd Williams a farmer because it seemed so colorful to think that Truman had befriended an authentic Kansas yokel. In reality, Williams was a successful banker and businessman who managed a vast network of farm properties spanning three states.

The Kansans were a smart and resourceful crew even when they were not on their home turf. On Sunday, Bob Wells and Paul Masoner wanted to see the Kansas City Chiefs play the Jets at Shea Stadium, but there were no tickets. They talked their way into the game by persuading the Kansas City radio announcer Tom Hedrick to let them provide color commentary during his play-by-play broadcast. Wells and Masoner got their seats—an accomplishment that was probably more meaningful to them than their invitations to the Black and White Ball—and they celebrated when the Chiefs won, 32–24.

In Washington, another one of Truman's out-of-town friends started getting ready for the ball. Liz Hylton was very excited about the trip. She had made grown-up appointments for herself and was having her hair done and getting a facial before boarding the train to New York City. She was unhappy about the weather and worried that the rain would wilt her coiffure and wrinkle her gown. Then, at the beauty salon, she had further cause for concern upon discovering that out of inexperience, she had booked a facial rather than a makeup session. Having a technician poke and prod at her face was the last thing she wanted on a day when she hoped to look beautiful, but Liz was not one to dwell on small setbacks. She headed into her glamorous New York evening with high spirits and great expectations.

Don Bachardy, who had flown in from Los Angeles on Sunday, was a man on a mission. He needed a mask in a hurry, and, unlike Truman and some of the other male guests, he was not willing to settle for a dime-store domino. Bachardy was unprepared for the big night because he hadn't been sure he would attend until the very last minute. Truman had told Bachardy and his companion Christopher Isherwood that it was going to be the "most fabulous ball you've ever seen." Isherwood decided to stay home in Los Angeles because the musical version of *Cabaret*, based on his short story collection, *Goodbye to Berlin*, had just opened in New York, and he did not want to be anywhere near it. Bachardy was reluctant to go alone but forced himself. If Truman's ball promised to be the party of the century, he wanted to be there.

Bachardy decided that the most expedient solution to his mask problem would be to rent one from a theatrical costume house. He located a place on the West Side of Manhattan and looked for a mask that was as glamorous as the occasion. He found something sleek, shiny, dashing, and a little mysterious that fit his face perfectly. His preparations complete, he relaxed and looked forward to Glenway Westcott's dinner before the ball.

Mark Goodson, the principled extra man who had declined Truman's invitation because he wanted to bring a date, was in the throes of an eleventh-hour dilemma. Even though he felt completely justified in not going to the ball, the last thing he wanted was for people to think he hadn't been invited in the first place. To save face at the office, he called a special meeting of his executives. Most of them feared they were going to be fired, given the volatility of the television business. Instead, when they assembled in the conference room, Goodson announced solemnly that he wanted his staff to know that he had been asked to the Black and White Ball but had declined the invitation.

In the late afternoon, the ballroom at the Plaza was slowly coming to life. Truman's guests were expected at ten, and preparations were already well under way. Joe Evangelista, one of the waiters assigned to work the ball, had traveled to the hotel from his home in Astoria, Queens. He loved his commute because his train went directly to the Plaza, so he rarely had to walk above ground. Joe had started at the hotel as a busboy in 1964. He was a handsome and capable young man who quickly worked his way up to the position of waiter in the banquet department. Because he was so likable, his manager depended on him to take care of high-profile guests, such as Queen Sikrit of Thailand. Joe knew all about the celebrity crowd expected that night, but as far as he was concerned, there was only one real star in his firmament—Frank Sinatra, the idol of waiters, bartenders, and working-class people everywhere. Sinatra treated them as if they were somebodies and had a reputation for dispensing generous tips. Tonight would be Joe's first time serving Sinatra. He was anxious to meet the big man and promised himself he would remember all the details so that he could share them with his friends.

Right now, there was work to be done. Joe and his partner, Peter, were responsible for setting up four of the fifty-three tables in the ballroom. Later, they would have a quick dinner in the kitchen, don their red jackets, and position themselves by their assigned tables. They joked about the assistant director of catering, a man they called the Prince because he always came in late. He took care of the society people and liked to behave as if he were one of them, even though they were worlds apart.

While Joe was busy covering his tables with red cloths, another Sinatra fan entered the ballroom. Gedall Kovalsky, a piano tuner from Odessa in Soviet Ukraine, had been summoned at the last minute to check Peter Duchin's piano. Kovalsky was excited to be there because he was under the impression that Sinatra might sing that night. As far as he was concerned, every note that piano would produce had to be perfect.

Elsewhere in the Plaza, Truman was checking into suite 437. His corner rooms overlooked Fifth Avenue and 58th Street, so he could see the growing crowds of photographers and onlookers below. Later, he dressed in a leisurely fashion and called for Kay Graham, the Deweys, and his other friends who were staying at the hotel. Kay had asked him repeatedly what *she* could do. Finally, Truman told her to arrange a light supper in her suite—a bird and a bottle would be just right. They would make a brief appearance at the Paleys' dinner party—just a quick drink—because Truman wanted to return to the hotel early. Thrilled to have an assignment, Kay ordered roasted chicken and some caviar from "21." This was her first time buying caviar, and she found the price to be so high that she decided a quarter pound would be sufficient, not realizing that was a relatively small amount.

Dining rooms all over Manhattan (although predominantly on the Upper East Side) were being prepared for the private dinner parties Truman had organized. "16 hosts and hostesses who had volunteered to give preball dinners simmered on the verge of hysteria," *Time* reported. Yet Kay Meehan was an experienced Park Avenue hostess who was unruffled by the activity in her apartment. She had given many dinners and knew the formula for a successful evening. The chef was the key person—if you didn't have your own, the next best thing was to maintain a relationship with one who could be retained regularly for parties. Cocktails, always champagne for the ladies, were served in the living room, followed by a three-course meal in the dining room—a cheese soufflé, meat with an interesting sauce, and a dessert selected by the chef. Tonight, guests would dine at three tables of eight. Even Meehan's husband, Joe, was looking forward to the evening: he adored Truman—most of the husbands did when they got to know him—and he was a great dancer.

At 820 Fifth Avenue, John, the doorman, watched impassively as decorators and caterers headed for the Paleys' eighth-floor apartment. Miss Kagan, Babe's secretary, was tight with any information but told reporters there would be lots of flowers, "in the English style," including white chrysanthemums. John, who did some snooping when he had visited the Paley kitchen earlier in the day, was happy to talk about what he saw—quantities of ham, oysters, and extra staff, hired by the Paleys for the occasion. Norbert, Babe's hairdresser, made a quick stop at her apartment to create a simple evening hairdo for his client. As usual, Babe would apply her own makeup.

At approximately 7:30 p.m., the curtain rose, the guests scurried to take their places, and the pre-ball overture began. Behind the scenes, Halston dropped off Marisa Berenson's gown, then hastened to get himself ready. Carol Bjorkman persuaded him to slip into the ball as her second escort, and he planned on covering his face with a mask designed by Gene Moore. Maria Theresa Caen's wayward gown showed up at the hotel at the last minute, and she was surrounded by excited maids exclaiming, "Oh, your dress is here! Your dress is here!"

In a townhouse on East 79th Street, Penelope Tree descended the stairs to join her father and mother, Sir Ronald and Marietta Tree; her older sister, the writer Frances Fitzgerald; a family friend, Susan Mary Alsop; and Patrick Litchfield, a friend and a photographer who had been invited to the ball. Everyone witnessed her entrance and her father's shocked response. "I thought her father was going to have a fit when he saw what she was wearing," Litchfield recalled. Her spaghetti-strapped tunic was very revealing, and she wore black triangles around her eyes as a mask. Even Tree's governess was in tears because her young charge's clothing was so extreme. But Tree confidently topped her outfit with a belted maxicoat and headed out into the rain for the Burdens' dinner party.

Many people were late because of the weather. There were no taxis to be had, and limousine companies were so overbooked that they turned off their telephones. An eager photographer stationed at the Dakota snapped a picture of Lauren Bacall as she hurried into the building, not realizing that she was going to her own apartment instead of to the Burdens'. Her arms were filled with shopping bags and her gown. In fact, she and her husband, Jason Robards, were expected at the Paleys, and they were probably going to be late.

While scores of guests scurried off to their pre-ball festivities, Mark Goodson forged ahead with his plans for the evening. He still felt justified in turning down Truman's invitation and was looking forward to dining with his girlfriend, the woman he was not permitted to bring to the ball. They had a reservation at "21," one of the city's most insider restaurants. When they arrived, Goodson and his date were shocked to see that the place was virtually empty. Everybody who was anybody was either en route to the ball or hidden out of sight so that it would not be apparent that they had not been invited. For the first time, he had second thoughts about missing the party.

At the Plaza, Truman made one quick stop before he left to go to Babe's. He popped into the ballroom for a peek, with the Deweys and Vi Tate in tow (they had met the Paleys during their previous visit to New York and had been invited to the pre-ball dinner). Everything was in place, he was happy to note, including the vine-entwined centerpieces and the large bouquet of iridescent balloons he had ordered to hang from the ceiling. The ladies were very impressed. "Truman, you've done just a lovely job—it looks absolutely marvelous," said Vi.

Outside the ballroom, the Plaza was besieged by photographers and camera crews jockeying for the best place to set up their equipment. "The Battle of the Communications has already begun," reported *Women's Wear Daily* at 8:30 p.m. The Plaza banquet manager, who controlled access to the best spots inside the hotel, was playing ball with CBS because the network had planned a live broadcast at 11 p.m. Jean Parr, who was working on the segment, was dressed in a gown and a mask ("I look like a devil with horns," she complained to one of her cameramen). The *Newsday* photographer called foul and tried to rally the other print journalists, but any protest was futile. The people at the Plaza understood that a live broadcast trumped all newspaper coverage, and they behaved accordingly. No matter where they were positioned, some two hundred members of the press braved bad weather outdoors and tight spaces indoors as they awaited the much-anticipated arrivals.

Guests would not be coming anytime soon, because they were dallying at their dinner parties. At Dru Heinz's riverside triplex, diners feasted on pheasant, scalloped potatoes, and tiny cream puffs. Greta Garbo was supposed to join them but never arrived. The atmosphere was more charged than polite at Piedy Gimbel's gathering. Norman Mailer, in a pugnacious mood, was seated between his hostess and Pat Lawford. He bewildered Gimbel by telling her, "You ought to be an elevator operator. You just go up and down." Then he sparred with Lawford, who said she'd heard he was "awful" and didn't understand why she had to sit next to him. As the dinner progressed, Mailer and Lawford developed a grudging respect for each other, and their insults gave way to playful barbs.

In Greenwich Village, Eleanor Friede and her guests were listening to music on the radio while they dined. They were surprised when an announcer interrupted the broadcast to describe the crowds assembling outside the Plaza. The spectators had read so much newspaper coverage about the party that they had come to see the celebrities in their gowns and masks. Expectations were so high—for onlookers and participants alike—that some of Truman's friends worried (or hoped, if they were the jealous type) that the evening would be a disappointment. "Frankly," said Pamela Hayward, "we were afraid that with all this publicity . . . it might have flopped."

Truman and Kay left the Paleys' apartment behind schedule and returned to the Plaza a little after nine. There was such a crush of photographers waiting for them that they had to abandon their plan to dine in Kay's suite. Kay found the attention "exciting and terrifying." With barely enough time to sample the caviar, they donned their masks, posed for photographers, and positioned themselves outside the ballroom. They were joined by the announcer the hotel provided for the evening. Joe Evangelista and the other members of the Plaza staff were well acquainted with the imposing man dressed in white tie and tails—he was actually a judge from New Jersey who moonlighted at receptions to make extra money, but with his strong and impressive voice, he added a touch of formality to the proceedings.

Ten o' clock—the appointed hour—came. Peter Duchin watched from the stage for the maître d's signal to begin playing. Usually, Duchin waited until the guests outnumbered the band before he started his first set, a selection of upbeat numbers that would set the tone for the night. With no masked revelers in sight, however, the ballroom was quiet, the atmosphere hushed and even a little strained. Outside, the spectators were becoming impatient. It was rainy and chilly—and so far there was nothing worth seeing. *This* was the party of the century? they wondered.

Diana Vreeland had a secret. The night of the ball, she dressed in black, posed for photographers in the lobby of the Paleys' apartment building, and attended Babe and Bill's celebrity-studded dinner party. Yet when it was time to go to the Plaza, she quietly stepped back and headed home instead. Vreeland's husband had died recently, and she was not in the mood for an evening of revelry. The next morning, when she spoke to Truman, she acted as if she had been there and seemed to know all about the evening— from Penelope Tree's gown to Billy Baldwin's mask—and he was never the wiser.

17

Night of Nights

THE STRAINED SILENCE INSIDE THE PLAZA WAS BROKEN WHEN THE first guests, Mr. and Mrs. Alexander Lieberman of Condé Nast, walked up the stairs and made their way to the receiving line. After being announced, they were greeted enthusiastically by Truman and Kay. The host and his guest of honor were flanked by a lace-clad Eugenia Sheppard and a masked Charlotte Curtis, their pencils poised to document every detail. Later, they were joined by a miniskirted Suzy Knickerbocker, who told a gleeful Truman that there were parties all over town, including at "21," staged by the people who *hadn't* been invited to the ball.

The legendary beauty Mrs. William Rhinelander Stewart was the next arrival. Then the procession began. A seemingly never-ending line of limousines inched their way to the entrance of the Plaza. George, the doorman on duty, had been working at the hotel for twenty years, so he was blasé about the evening. "I've seen a thousand just as exciting," he muttered. But the crowd standing behind the police barricades—mostly young, fresh-faced women with stars in their eyes—seemed awed and excited. One ingenue had worn a boldly striped black-and-white rain hat in honor of the occasion.

"They rolled off the assembly line like dolls," Enid Nemy wrote of the guests in the *New York Times*, "newly painted and freshly coiffed, packaged in silk, satin and jewels and addressed to Truman Capote, the Plaza Hotel." Ball-goers who had attended dinner parties came in small congenial groups. As Truman had hoped, they were in excellent spirits because the earlier part of the evening served as a warm-up, priming them for the festivities to come.

Many of the guests were surprised by the banks of cameras awaiting them at the hotel. "I didn't know it would be like this," said one guest when faced with the flashbulbs. After all, it was supposed to be a *private* party. Experienced celebrities and socialites knew how to make a red carpet entrance—to effortlessly strike a pose that was natural and flattering. Earlier in the century, master choreographers had staged entrances for important ball guests. Now the famous were left to their own devices, and there were mishaps. Tongues were still wagging over a recent incident, when a pilot-fish social climber had aggressively attached herself to a stunning It girl who was about to enter a party, and she refused to let go. The socialite's grand entrance—a grand entrance was always made alone, or with a semi-invisible male escort—was ruined by her appendage as photographers were forced to snap both women.

The crowd was not content to watch silently as the guests paraded past the flashing cameras. They were a lively group, quick to applaud and just as quick to make barbed comments. "Oh, dear, what a catastrophe," remarked one critic (who turned out to be a maskmaker who was eager to belittle the handiwork of his competitors). "They should have made the masks bigger to cover their entire faces," he whined. When one effeminate young man called a masked Jacob Javits "the Lone Ranger," the senator replied by saying sarcastically, "Thank you, *ladies*." The actress Joan Fontaine, draped in an elegant fishnet gown and a matching mask, overheard a woman say, "The only people I can't recognize are those with their masks off." Frank Sinatra remarked to Suzy, "I don't know how anyone can recognize Mia with her mask on," Suzy responded, "I think it has something to do with her haircut, Frank, honestly I do," referring to the boyish new style Mia Farrow Sinatra had gotten for *Rosemary's Baby*. Those who did recognize her speculated incorrectly that her white Directoire dress might be concealing a little secret. Somehow, famous faces remained identifiable underneath their disguises and commanded a great deal of attention.

People who were not famous were ignored by the media. Truman's writer friends had to tell reporters their names—"Gunther, you know, I'm a writer," insisted John, the acclaimed author of *Death Be Not Proud*. John Knowles, the author of *A Separate Peace*

Truman and the party honoree Katharine Graham.

said, "They turned on the [Klieg] lights and looked at us. Nobody. The lights went off again." The literary bad boy Norman Mailer was an exception. Because he was well known, there was all the more reason to criticize him for wearing a rumpled trench coat that even he described as "dirty gabardine." Reporters tried to bait him about *In Cold Blood* outselling his books, but Mailer refused to bite and good-naturedly retorted, "It just shows that I'm no longer the biggest thief in America." When a photographer asked Darryl F. Zanuck to identify himself, the producer complained, "If you don't know, you shouldn't be here."

Famous or nameless, most of the guests wanted an opportunity to promenade in their finery. "The action is on the staircase," said Carol Bjorkman, "no one's using the elevator—they want to be seen—up where the photogs are, baby." Up they walked, past the CBS cameras and cables, past the coatroom, until they reached the marble stairs leading to the ballroom. Some people—Candice Bergen, Penelope Tree, and Ashton Hawkins (fresh from the dinner party at the Burdens), along with Don Bachardy and other masked guests—did use the mirror-lined elevator to take them to the ballroom. Pat Lawford made a point of avoiding the photographers by rushing to the elevator and holding her large white mask like a shield to block her face from their cameras.

There was a crush at the check-in desk, where guests presented their red and white admission cards. Working with Elizabeth Davies to keep the in in and the out out was the doorman from the U. N. Plaza, outfitted in a tuxedo thoughtfully provided by Truman. Davies had been unnerved earlier in the evening—she had slipped and fallen on her way into the hotel, dropping her lists and spilling the contents of her bag. Now she was composed, though, and graciously greeted Truman's guests at the same time that she guarded the all-important list from prying eyes. Her date, Robert Launey, waited for her, circling the ballroom and watching the steady stream of arrivals. When he saw lovely Amanda Burden, he wished he had the nerve to ask her to dance.

Several guests made last-minute adjustments to their masks and gowns inside the Plaza. Ann Birstein, radiant in her beautiful dress, stopped in front of a mirror to don her mask and headdress, then posed for photographers. Mary Lazar hoped that her stunning over-sized headdress of black velvet and net looked right, because she had to pull it this way and that to squeeze it into her Rolls Royce on the way over. Lee Radziwill, outfitted in cool metallic, glanced at her reflection and with a quick "There we are" positioned her "dia-mond" mask over her eyes and moved on. Marion Javits, the wife of the New York senator, did not have to fuss with her mask at all because it was painted artfully in gold onto her face.

Ladies who had lost sleep trying to figure out how to wear a mask without looking like a refugee from Halloween were exasper-ated by the sight of stunning Princess Luciana Pignatelli. They wished they had been as clever as the Roman beauty, who was so reluctant to cover her pretty face that she had asked the jeweler Harry Winston if she could borrow a large gem to wear on her fore-head instead of a conventional mask.

He had agreed and selected the Schwab Diamond, a spectacular sixty-carat, pear-shaped stone, to adorn her graceful forehead. Unlike some stones, the Schwab Diamond did not have a long, dramatic history—the pear shape was a relatively new twentieth-century cut—but its story was colorful nonetheless. The brilliant gem came from South Africa and had been purchased by the Bethlehem Steel founder, Charles M. Schwab, a self-made man who became so rich that he spent six million pre-income-tax dollars building Riverside, a seventy-five-room French château that once occupied an entire city block on New York's Upper West Side. The robber baron Andrew Carnegie had said that the Schwab mansion made his house "look like a shack."

Schwab suffered a reversal of fortune in the late 1920s and died penniless in 1939. The $600,000 diamond that bore his name had been purchased by Harry Winston, who planned to sell it when the right buyer came along. Until then, Winston was delighted to lend it to the beautiful princess so that she could suspend it from her feather headdress and wear it to Truman Capote's masked ball.

For the most part, women seemed to enjoy wearing their masks. Some dutiful ladies even complied with Truman's request to carry fans, although it was difficult to hold a mask and a fan at the same time. Predictably, most of the men were not as keen on covering their faces. Like disobedient children, they guiltily dispensed with their masks as soon as possible. "It itches and I can't see," grumbled Alfred Gwynne Vanderbilt about his cat mask. George Plimpton, the author of the recently published book *Paper Tiger*, had a different complaint. The inside of his mask was covered with cheap glue that gave off intoxicating fumes, and he was dizzy until it finally occurred to him to take it off before he passed out. The artist Andy Warhol outsmarted everyone with his ingenious solution to the mask problem: he simply didn't wear one.

The CBS crew scrambled to film the guests as they arrived. Truman asked them to leave the coat-check area—he had strong feelings about uninvited press intruding on his evening—but he did not persist when they refused to move. Charles Kuralt, a young, folksy CBS newsman, stood in the hallway leading to the coat check, microphone in hand. As the Beautiful People walked by him, he told his viewers, "This is how the other half lives. . . . we know you were not rich, social, or beautiful enough to be invited, or you wouldn't be up watching the news." He added, "The 'Henrys' are here, Ford and Fonda . . . but not the 'Edwards,'" meaning the duke of Windsor and Kennedy, both of whom declined.

Kuralt made a point of saying that he was filming the ball in color, but the footage appeared to be in black and white because of the guests' attire. Occasionally, there was a splash of red or brown from a coat or a mink stole. Late-night viewers—the show was on at eleven—observed that it was a night of high hair. Women wore multiple hairpieces, teased, tamed, and twisted by Kenneth's expert hands to create fantasy coiffures. None of it was supposed to look real. On the quick flashes of film, the women were young and beautiful. Leo Lerman told the *Life* photographer Henry Grossman that he "had never seen so many beautiful women in one place at one time." Ironically, some of the loveliest ladies—Babe Paley and Marion Javits, for example—were escorted by husbands who appeared prosperous, powerful, and significantly older. Both men and women were awkward and self-conscious in front of the cameras, unused to being on live television, distracted by tuxedo-clad photographers and polite female reporters who competed for their attention. Many sailed right past the press, while a few mugged for the cameras.

CBS missed the arrival of Lynda Bird Johnson, who came with her *McCall's* editor, Robert Stein, and a dozen somber Secret Service men, all wearing black masks. When asked by a *Washington Post* reporter to name the designer of her checkerboard-patterned gown, the president's daughter coyly retorted, "That's the last thing I'll tell you. I'm just here to have fun." Yet they did catch Tallulah Bankhead, Henry and Shirlee Fonda, Joan Fontaine, Babe and Bill Paley, Gloria Guinness, and Carol Bjorkman in her feathery Halston gown and headdress.

Truman and Kay stood at the entrance to the ballroom for two hours, shaking hands, air-kissing, and embracing the people who stopped to greet them. Since Kay did not know many of the guests, Truman had to make introductions. According to Eugenia Sheppard, at eleven o'clock he mopped his brow and said, "Whew, we're working hard." Truman was delighted to see his characters, the names he had inscribed on his list with such care—come to life. Spectacular masks, such as the golden-curled unicorn head that Gene Moore created for the interior designer Billy Baldwin, received special praise from the appreciative host. "Oh, Billy, that's fantastic," Truman congratulated. Isabella Eberstadt's fanciful black and white entwined swans, fashioned by the multitalented milliner, writer, and photographer Bill Cunningham, created a sensation, as did the cartoonist Charles Addams's grim executioner's mask.

The smash hit of the evening, though, was the ingenue Penelope Tree. More naked than dressed in her flowing black tunic and form-fitting tights, Tree caught the eye of every person in the room. Even the CBS camera lingered on her narrow, exposed midriff, as if entranced. Jean Harvey Vanderbilt, the wife of Alfred Gwynne Vanderbilt, described Tree's ensemble as "stark, like a Halloween ballet costume." Her entrance signaled the presence of a new generation at the ball. Tree was discovered by the fashion world that night. Cecil Beaton and Richard Avedon were so enchanted by her unspoiled beauty that they conspired on the spot to turn her into a cover girl—which is what she soon became.

Truman's guests looked beautiful as they filed past on their way to the ballroom, and he was impressed that they had gone to so much trouble to please him. As he had imagined, they looked like exquisite black and white chess pieces set against a red, white, and gold background. "Oh, it's very pretty, isn't it!" he said excitedly, happy with the scene unfolding before him.

At one point, Truman halted the receiving line to introduce a very special guest to Kay. "Here's Jack," he said, presenting his longtime companion, Jack Dunphy. A few of Truman's society friends, the Paleys and the Guinnesses among them, knew Jack, but Dunphy was a cantankerous and reclusive figure who preferred to be on his own in Switzerland or in the Hamptons, where Truman had given him a little house on his property. Never one to appreciate high society, which he thought was a bad influence on Truman, Jack had his doubts about the entire evening but appeared nonetheless.

Upon entering the ballroom, Truman's guests were escorted to tables. Frank Sinatra told his friends, "I'll get the table for us 'cause I know all the waiters," and he commandeered one of the best tables in the room right by the stage. A happy Joe Evangelista was his waiter for the night. The Sinatras were joined by Pamela and Leland Hayward, Bennett and Phyllis Cerf, Claudette Colbert, Steven and Jean Kennedy Smith, and the playwright Harry Kurnitz.

Mia did not spend much time sitting—she danced with energetic young partners such as Christopher Cerf, while her husband ("Frank *never* dances," said Pamela Hayward) talked and table-hopped. Joe Evangelista saw to it that there was always a bottle of Wild Turkey, Frank's favorite drink, within reach.

The evening was off to a fabulous start, although the historian Arthur Schlesinger commented knowingly, "History begins *after* midnight." The room "was always shimmering," said the producer David Merrick, who thought the ball deserved "a rave review." Jean Harvey Vanderbilt compared the party to the court of Louis XV because "people promenaded around the perimeter of the room in their finery, looking at each other." One guest commented, "It's weird, there are only black and white and red in this room, and yet everything's so . . . so *colorful*." Everyone was in constant motion, walking around and around to the strains of Peter Duchin's intoxicating music. Songs like "Put on a Happy Face" had guests whirling on the dance floor, where they showed off those fancy steps they had learned from William de Rahm and Miss. Bloss and other society dance teachers.

Throughout the night, Duchin paid homage to guests who were composers and performers by playing their signature songs, such as Alan Jay Lerner's "On a Clear Day You Can See Forever," and Harold Arlen's "A Sleepin' Bee" and "Can I Leave Off Wearing My Shoes?" from Truman's *House of Flowers*. While he played, Duchin nodded to his relatives and friends on the dance floor, including his wife, Cheray (who sat at a lively young table with Charlotte Ford, Wendy Vanderbilt, and Lynda Bird Johnson), and his godparents, Averill and Marie Harriman.

The idea behind the masks was that any guest could ask any other guest to dance. The masks were supposed to make everyone equal and anonymous, until the official unmasking at midnight. Yet the masks did little to promote egalitarianism. Most people took them off because they were awkward or uncomfortable and then went back to being exactly who they were. Lynda Bird lost hers and had to enlist the help of her Secret Service men to find it. Fortunately, being without a mask did not prevent anyone from having a good time on the dance floor.

Vogue reported that the newspaper editor Clifton Daniel "jitterbugged with an expertise that increased one's respect for the *New York Times*," and Norman Mailer and his wife, Beverly, made up a dance that mimicked walking on a tightrope. Ann Birstein danced all night with various partners, once memorably with Al Dewey, while Kansas's dashing banker Odd Williams proved himself to be an indefatigable hoofer. The U.N. Plaza doorman twirled Kay Graham around the floor and thanked her for "the happiest evening of my life." McGeorge Bundy showed off his famous waltz. And the former professional dancer Jack Dunphy dazzled even world-weary Gloria Guinness with his fancy footwork. "You certainly cut a mean rug," she told him admiringly.

The economist John Kenneth Galbraith was a sensation on the floor, mainly because he was tall (six feet eight and a half inches) and fiercely independent in his moves. He even danced alone. At one point in the evening, he and the athletically inclined writer George Plimpton tossed napkins and cradled candelabra in a game of musical football.

The actress Lauren Bacall rarely had a moment to sit. When she danced with the choreographer Jerome Robbins "in a fashion that Fred Astaire and Ginger Rogers might have envied," Truman said admiringly, all eyes were upon them. Arthur Schlesinger tried to cut in, but Bacall refused, saying, "Don't you see whom I'm dancing with?" She was more gracious to Truman's Kansas friend Dr. Russell Maxfield when he approached her. Yet Bacall's graceful turns around the floor with Robbins had left her exhausted, so a gentlemanly Maxfield quickly escorted his tired partner back to her seat.

Don Bachardy did not dance, because he was alone and felt a little shy about finding a partner. An artist, he appreciated the beautifully lit room and was "happy to observe rather than participate." He sat off to the side with Jack Dunphy and Glenway Westcott in one of the ballroom's arched balconies. His only problem was his perfect mask. Bachardy had no idea how painful a mask could be until he had worn his for an hour. He wanted to rip it off his face but dutifully kept it on until the proper moment.

Photographers shot Truman dancing with Kay Graham; Gloria Guinness; Lee Radziwill (who gave up because the beads from her gown showered the dance floor every time she moved too vigorously); Kay's daughter, Lally Weymouth; and Kay Wells. But Truman was too busy being the host to spend a lot of time on the dance floor. Instead, Truman hopped, skipped, and jumped from table to table, saying, "Aren't we having the most wonderful time? I love this party." When the midnight supper was served, including the Plaza's famous Chicken Hash, Truman was not one of the appreciative diners. There were too many people to admire and too many stories to tell. He was his usual impish self, whispering to Joan Axelrod, the wife of the playwright and screenwriter George Axelrod, the name of the woman whose husband had wangled an invitation by telling Truman his spouse had threatened to commit suicide if she didn't get one.

When the Soul Brothers had their turn at the bandstand (for which they were paid $750), the dancers proved they knew their stuff. The leader Benny Gordon said that the party was "out of sight" and was "surprised there were so many hip people (especially the oldsters) in society." Songs like "Twist and Shout" and "Up and Down" had everybody on their feet boogalooing. One of the Brothers had a single appreciative word for Babe Paley: "Wow!"

As predicted, crashers stormed the gates. One pleasant, well-dressed couple was caught and politely turned away before reaching the ballroom. A not-so-well-dressed woman in a black street dress managed to intrude and spoke to Truman. "I'm sorry. . . . I just wanted so much to see what it would look like," she explained. Truman softened at her words and invited her to enjoy a glass of champagne, at which point she became surly and lashed out at him. "Spending all this money," she criticized, "when there are people all over the world starving to death." He called over a security guard and instructed him to ask the interloper to dance and then to waltz her out of the room.

Despite Truman's eagle eyes and tight security, two trespassers eluded him. Susan Payson, a beautiful young public relations executive at Bergdorf Goodman, and her shy and proper date, Jerry Jones, an up-and-coming staffer at McKinsey, sat by the Plaza fountain after having left an unexciting party—the Ski Ball, or some such tired affair—at a nearby hotel. A plucky young woman who excelled at athletics and loved a challenge, Susan mentioned to Jones that she'd love to go to Truman Capote's party at the Plaza, and he said, "You'll never get in"—words guaranteed to spark mischief. "Watch," said Susan.

Following her lead, Jones walked into the lobby of the Plaza, where they attached themselves to a group of latecomers who were on their way to the ball. Susan thought they would drift into the dance with the others—she was dressed appropriately in a black scoop-necked gown and Jones was wearing a tuxedo—never imagining that Truman himself would be standing guard at the door. He saw them, and for a moment it appeared they would be the couple committing social suicide by getting publicly removed from the ballroom.

Instead, Truman greeted them warmly. He feigned familiarity, asking to be reminded who they were, then ushered them to a nearby table. Payson and Jones were astonished that they had engineered such a coup—they had actually *crashed* the Black and White Ball. Truman seated them with the personable Kansas contingent. Susan did not make the connection that the tall man next to her was Al Dewey of *In Cold Blood* fame until she asked his profession and he answered, "Detective." In fact, the guests from Kansas did not look any different from Truman's other friends. *Time* described them as "chic, bright, attractive people of quick humor and engaging charm" and said that "only their regional accents . . . certainly not their clothes or manners, set them apart from the New Yorkers." One thing they had in common was that they were Truman's greatest fans.

Vi Tate told *Time*, "You know, I think there's nothing Truman can't do. He writes like an angel, he's the dearest and most understanding friend—and now this party, the most superb thing I've ever seen."

Noteworthy scenes occurred throughout the ballroom. The daughters of three presidents, Lynda Bird Johnson, Margaret Truman Daniel, and Alice Roosevelt Longworth, traded White House stories at one of the tables. Longworth, who called Truman "one of the most agreeable men I know," was delighted to learn that her domino mask, which she had attached to her face with Band-Aids, cost four cents less than her host's thirty-nine-cent bargain. Gloria Guinness, who wore only pricey accessories, complained that her entwined diamond and ruby necklaces were so heavy, she would have to stay in bed the next day, a comment so elitist that it made Truman laugh out loud.

Truman had taken the time to introduce Rose Kennedy to Brendan Gill, the editor of the *New Yorker*. Gill politely led the seventy-six-year-old Kennedy matriarch to the dance floor. When the number was over, they sat together and found common ground in their lives, specifically discussing large families: Gill and his wife, Catholics like the Kennedys, had seven children. Mrs. Kennedy marveled that all of Gill's children were alive and talked about her own sad experiences with death, a poignant conversation in the midst of the gaiety all around them.

Elsewhere, Norman Mailer, who was still feeling a little belligerent, exchanged harsh words about Vietnam with McGeorge Bundy. Mailer was offended because Bundy, who had worked in government until recently taking charge of the Ford Foundation, implied condescendingly that the writer didn't know much about the war. Those were fighting words to Mailer, who wanted to take their conversation outside to the street. Good manners prevailed, and Mailer managed to control his temper.

Beautiful Benedetta Barzini, who was wearing a Kenneth Jay Lane necklace as a mask, had an uncomfortable moment when Lane attempted to introduce her to the producer Sam Spiegel. Both men were surprised when she rudely snubbed the man responsible for the Oscar-winning *Lawrence of Arabia* and *Bridge on the River Kwai*. Later, she explained to Lane that Spiegel had been one of the first people she visited when she moved to America at age seventeen. Even though she had presented a letter of introduction to Spiegel from her father, an old friend, he attempted to seduce her. Benedetta was not planning on talking to him that night or any other.

One famous actress, whom Truman refused to name, danced the night away with a tuxedoed young man, mesmerized by his brawny good looks. Truman did not have the heart to tell her she had fallen under the spell of his elevator man from the U.N. Plaza. But Cupid refrained from shooting an arrow at the young filmmaker Al Maysles. Al circled the room, enjoying the spectacle with his brother David (Al's eating while David picks up girls, his family joked), not knowing that his future wife, Gillian Walker, was one of the lovely young women at the ball.

At about 2:45, Sinatra asked the people at his table if anyone wanted to join him at Jilly's, a hole-in-the-wall that was his favorite bar. Truman begged him not to leave the party, knowing that its high wattage would be diminished by the superstar's absence, but Sinatra was ready to move on. He tipped Joe Evangelista with a hundred-dollar bill, called on the Secret Service men for help ("They're all my friends," he told Pamela Hayward), and made a speedy escape, leading Mia, the Haywards, and Herb and Theresa Caen through back passageways to the street below. As Joe cleared Sinatra's table, he vowed that he would save the bill to commemorate the wonderful night.

By 3:00 a.m., the ball was winding down, but Truman's guests were reluctant for the long-anticipated event to be over. They lingered in the ballroom even as their host resumed his position at the entrance. He and Kay said good evening to each departing guest. For some, the night was just beginning. Gianni Agnelli and "the friends of Gianni," as his cronies were called, proceeded to one of their favorite haunts, Elaine's restaurant, for a game of poker. The fun-loving Kansans, who had been among the first to arrive, were the last to leave. They helped a forlorn woman find a large pearl that had fallen off her shoe and decided to continue their festivities by going to a nightclub in Greenwich Village. The women in their group were a little more enthusiastic about the excursion than the weary men were. Peter Duchin, a veteran of many late nights, headed home, too wired to even think about sleep. Outside the Plaza, a few spectators lingered, hoping to see celebrities on their way out.

When Truman finally closed his eyes that morning in his Plaza suite, memories of the ball "whirled like a flurry of snowflakes" inside his head. Random images stood out in his mind: the maharani of Jaipur dressed in gold and emeralds; John Kenneth Galbraith, "tall as a crane but not as graceful"; Babe Paley, "floating in a dress of the sheerest white chiffon"; a "galaxy of masked black and white guests" having the best time in the most beautiful room in the city.

"It was just what it set out to be," a contented Truman had told reporters at the end of the evening; "I just wanted to give a party for my friends."

Before the ball, friends and security experts had told Truman that he had to provide a secret entrance at the hotel so that his celebrity guests could evade the photographers and the reporters who were expected to congregate en masse outside the Plaza. Truman obligingly made the arrangements. At the end of the evening, after the last camera had been packed away and all the guests and the paparazzi had gone home, Truman realized that not a single person, famous or unknown, had made any attempt to use this entrance to avoid the press.

18

Publicity

NORMAN MAILER WAS SURE IT WAS ONE OF THE BEST PARTIES HE HAD ever attended. Katharine Graham had such a good time, she could not bear to think that the ball was over and would never happen again. Lynda Bird Johnson didn't show up for work on Tuesday morning. Mrs. Gordon Parks was so overwhelmed by the beauty of the evening that she could go back to wearing her blue jeans because she had experienced a "Cinderella night." Alice Roosevelt Longworth told the *Times* that the ball was "the most exquisite of spectator sports" and may have had more to say on the subject but was distracted by the fact that her Washington home had been robbed while she was at the party. (When she was told by the police that her house had been ransacked, she wondered how they could tell—it always looked that way.) Appreciative guests deluged Truman with effusive thank-you notes, flowers, and expensive bottles of champagne.

"He did it. He did it. He always said he'd do it—and indeed he did." With these words from an Alan Jay Lerner and Frederick Loewe song from *My Fair Lady*, Suzy Knickerbocker announced to the world that Truman Capote's Black and White Ball had been a

smash hit. She and the other journalists Truman had invited, Eugenia Sheppard (*World Journal Tribune*), Carol Bjorkman (*Women's
Wear Daily*), Charlotte Curtis (*New York Times*), Gloria Steinem
(*Vogue*), Jean Howard (*Life*), Jean Sprain Wilson (*Chicago Tribune*), and Jim Broadhead (*Time*), their heads filled with the sights,
the sounds, and the sensations of the night before, filed stories with
their respective publications. Unlike the reporters who had been
forced to huddle in groups outside the hotel or stake out spots in
the hallway near the cloakroom, these privileged insiders were at
the center of the action, masked and in the ballroom, the ones with
the inside scoop.

On Tuesday morning, the *World Journal Tribune* devoted more
than a page to the ball. The headline read, "The Capote Caper,
Starring the Five Hundred." Suzy Knickerbocker and Eugenia
Sheppard shared the space, and their columns were surrounded by
whimsical drawings of ball guests—including Billy Baldwin, Gloria
Vanderbilt, and Penelope Tree—dressed in their finery. The figures
had been sketched by the artist Joe Eula, who also drew two tiny
Trumans, one balancing on a leg and juggling balls in the air, the
other with his arms open wide, as if welcoming his guests.

In her column, Suzy Knickerbocker proclaimed Truman Capote
"the host of the year, the decade, the era." She reminded readers
that she attended parties every night of the week, but in all her
years of socializing, she had "never seen so many really magnificent
looking women . . . as were on display last night." Her fellow guests
felt the same way and expressed their opinions of the ball in a succession of superlatives. "Marvelous!" "Sensational!" "Glorious!"
"Fantastic!" "This is the party of all parties," and from an ecstatic
Frenchwoman, "*Formidable!*"

Eugenia Sheppard's coverage was equally enthusiastic. She
praised the masks, especially the marabou cat faces worn by the
designer Oscar de la Renta and the French fashion editor Françoise
de Langlade, and Pamela Hayward's "wood nymph mask of black
velvet leaves and flowers," designed by Kenneth Jay Lane. She

AMANDA BURDEN

THE CHOSEN PEOPLE

The front page of Women's Wear Daily
*the day after the ball, sketched by
Kenneth Paul Block.*

singled out Dru Heinz, one of the "few hardy souls" in evening pants, for her black Irene Galitzine "pajamas." But she was completely captivated by Penelope Tree, whom she described as "a coming-up beauty with big eyes and lots of hair," wearing "the dress of the evening." The dress caused such a sensation that the designer Betsey Johnson made it available at Paraphernalia in black and in neon colors.

Sheppard ended her account of the ball's fashion highlights with a prediction. She doubted that any party at any time in the future would cause such a commotion. Having spent weeks speculating about the details of Truman's big night, she wondered what on earth she would find to write about now that the ball was over.

A sketch of Amanda Burden in her Ascot dress, drawn by Kenneth Paul Block, was the eye-catching front page of *Women's Wear Daily*. The daily "Eye" column, titled "The Chosen People," opened with a rhyme about "the Elected and the Selected—plus some of the Dejected—a gathering of the Jet Set that looked more like the Wet Set," and continued with more details about the evening. Inside, Carol Bjorkman offered a blow-by-blow account of her Black and White Ball experiences, beginning with her afternoon at Kenneth's. There were a few photographs of ball guests on their way to dinner parties, but most of the guests were shown in illustrations sketched by Block because the ball had started after *WWD* went to press at 8 p.m.

On Wednesday, *Women's Wear Daily* exploded with extensive ball coverage. An illustration entitled "The Morning After" showed Truman and his friends Marella Agnelli, Bunny Mellon, and Babe, lunching at Lafayette, looking "fresh as a daisy" after the "big ball of the century." Elsewhere on the front page, a writer using the nom de plume "Pierre Porte-Parole" penned a satirical piece about the ball, offering a disgruntled Frenchman's point of view about the American bastardization of the classic *bal masqué*. Yet the story that readers were most curious to see was inside, three pages of photographs entitled, "In Cold Blood—The Ratings." The guests were shown wearing their masks and gowns and were rated from good to great. Gloria Guinness and Marella Agnelli led the pack, with four and a half stars each. Truman rated four stars. Lee Radziwill, Kay Graham, and C. Z. Guest were awarded two stars. The accompanying text posed the unusual question, "Now that it's all over . . . what did it all mean?" suggesting that there was some larger significance to the party or that there should have been.

In the *New York Times*, Charlotte Curtis reported the story in her usual cool and analytical way. She tallied the champagne bottles, described the guests, and retraced Truman's steps in planning the party. The *Times* demonstrated its excitement by dedicating a generous amount of space to the story in each of its editions that day. The early *Times* ran two pages on the ball, featuring the photograph of Truman's Kansas friends sitting under the hairdryers at the Plaza beauty shop and an article about how guests prepared for the evening, written by the veteran staffer Enid Nemy. The story was illustrated with whimsical drawings of masks, including Marietta Tree's over-the-top feather concoction and Henry Ford's understated black satin sunglasses, sketched by the artist Maning, who was making a name for himself in fashion circles. The Late City Edition carried Curtis's article "Capote's Black and White Ball: The Most Exquisite of Spectator Sports," a shorter version of Nemy's piece about the Kansans, and the scoop to end all scoops, a copy of the "List of Those Who Were Invited to the Party at the Plaza Hotel."

The list of Truman's invitees, in alphabetical order for handy reference, sparked several storms. First of all, which list was it? The people to whom Truman sent invitations or the roster of guests expected to attend? More important, how did the *New York Times* get hold of this heretofore top-secret document? Intrigued by these questions, *Time* asked a reporter to investigate.

He examined the list with great enthusiasm, noting that it was odd that the maharaja and the maharani of Jaipur were on it, because they had been last-minute additions the very afternoon of the ball. They were friends of C. Z. and Winston Guest, who had asked Truman if they could come. Furthermore, many of the most famous names on the list, Jacqueline Kennedy, Elizabeth Taylor and Richard Burton, and the duke and duchess of Windsor, for example, had sent their regrets long before a door list was compiled. So it was not strictly a list of the invited, nor was it a list of acceptances. In fact, the only purpose the published list seemed to serve was to impress the people who read it. As Charlotte Curtis said subsequently, "It made the party look more fabulous than it really was."

Truman was famous for being a publicity hound, so most people assumed that he had given the list to Charlotte Curtis. There was a precedent. In 1892, Ward McAllister had given his list of the four hundred people worth inviting into a ballroom to the *New York Times*. An earnest Elizabeth Davies denied that Truman had anything to do with leaking the list to the press, but *Time* disagreed and said as much in its December 9 coverage of the ball. "In a moment of almost understandable weakness," reported *Time*, "he (Truman) gave the *New York Times* his guest list, not bothering to cross off those who had regretted or who had not come." *Time* believed that the published list transformed the party from a private affair to a public event. Truman's motives became suspect, as observers wondered whether the Black and White Ball had been nothing more than a publicity stunt or an elaborate exercise in self-promotion.

Truman was infuriated by the suggestion that he was guilty of giving the list to Charlotte Curtis and fired off a letter to *Time*, insisting that "the list was not obtained from me nor was it published with my knowledge or permission." He maintained that Curtis "cleverly contrived to acquire" the list, although a rumor persists in *New York Times* circles that Truman looked the other way or deliberately left Curtis alone so that she could swipe it from his apartment.

The published list spelled doom for the uninvited. Those who had assumed that they could bluff their way out of social ignominy by taking that "important" trip to Nassau, feigning illness, or even dressing in black and white and pretending they were going to the ball had a rude awakening when they opened their *New York Times* and found the list staring back at them on Tuesday. The Chosen, Truman's handpicked selection of prospective guests, were there for all to see. "It was awful, really awful," said Truman. "Who I felt most sorry for was [*sic*] the people who had left town. 'I do wish we could stay and go to Truman's party, but it's the only time Richard can get away for that little holiday we've been planning in Nassau.'... Then there was another category of people I'm sorriest for of all. They were invited, but for some reason I'll never know, their names weren't on the list Charlotte picked up!"

Curtis was concerned that her first story about the ball had been sketchy, so she ran another one in early December. The hook was that the producer David Merrick had such a good time at Truman's party that he wanted to host his own extravaganza. What's more, he planned on getting his friend Truman to help him. Curtis wrote in depth about the dinner parties, the antics on the dance floor, and the guests who were unable to attend. She ended the piece with a quote from Truman, who talked about an upcoming trip to an oasis in the Sahara where he planned to start working on his new book. "You can't write with people around you," he said.

Newspapers all over the country followed New York's lead by running articles and photographs. The reporter Jean Sprain Wilson, who had been one of Truman's guests at the ball, filed a story with the Associated Press that appeared in locations as disparate as upstate New York, Maryland, and Wisconsin. Frederick Winship's story "Capote's Party Is a Real Ball" went out on the United Press International wire and landed in a number of unlikely places, most notably an Ohio newspaper, where it appeared next to the Grange News about upcoming 4-H meetings. Coahocton, Ohio, the site of these farming get-togethers, could not have been farther away from the beaux arts ballroom where the party took place, but people everywhere were eager to hear details about the event. There was even a story in the *Asahi Evening News* in Japan.

Magazines such as *Vogue, Life, Newsweek*, and *Time* ran extensive party coverage, most of it laudatory and heavily illustrated
(*Vogue* had sent the photographer Elliot Erwitt to the ball to shoot
in color and Lawrence Fried to take pictures in black and white).
Readers were bombarded by images of Truman and his masked
guests, echoing the frenzy that had occurred when *In Cold Blood*
was published. *Vogue* was so enchanted by Kay Graham's fairy-tale
transformation that the editor in chief Diana Vreeland arranged for
a special photo shoot to commemorate the moment. Kay was persuaded to have herself redone by Kenneth and photographed by
Cecil Beaton. Her friend Arthur Schlesinger wrote the accompanying text, calling Katharine Graham the "New Power in the American
Press." "No one has been more astonished by her own emergence as
a personality in Washington, New York, and London than Katharine
Meyer Graham," observed Schlesinger. With Truman's help, Kay
had become a bona fide celebrity.

Kay's son-in-law, Yann Weymouth, a talented artist and designer,
created the most original coverage of the ball. With pen and ink, he
sketched a full-page drawing of a newspaper called *Women Wears
Gaily, Who Wears What Where*. There were articles and illustrations,
all dedicated to the family's experiences at the ball the night before.
"Kay Staggers Fashion World," announced one headline. "Lally Super
in Black," by Charlotte Curtis, said another. "Paraphernalia Proudly
Announces New Shop Dedicated to the KAY-KAY Look," proclaimed
a third. The illustrations were clever and whimsical, perfectly mim-
icking the tone, the look, and the format of *Women's Wear Daily* and
other newspapers that covered society and fashion news.

While various guests and members of the press were debating
whether Truman's bash had been the party of the year, the decade,
or the century, there were several voices of dissent. Not everyone
who attended the ball was complimentary. That night, Candice
Bergen had complained to Lael Scott of the *New York Post* that
she was bored and would be leaving the party as soon as possible. A

succession of eyewitnesses, Bergen among them, shared their negative feelings about the evening with the writer and fellow ball-goer George Plimpton, who included them in his book about Truman Capote. Bergen said that other people, especially some reporters, tried to make her feel guilty for doing something as decadent as dressing in bunny ears and attending a ball when there was war and deprivation in the world.

The producer Harold Prince also felt uncomfortable with the raging elitism of the evening. When he and his wife approached the Plaza and saw the crowds standing outside, the French Revolution was the first thought that came to his mind. The writer Alan Pryce-Jones said flat-out that he thought it was "one of the more terrible parties I'd ever seen. . . . It never got off the ground at all." The columnist Herb Caen made a similar observation and said that Truman practically begged Frank Sinatra not to leave because he was afraid the evening would come to an abrupt end without him.

The most candid assessment came from the outspoken Jack Dunphy, who contradicted the most common assertion about the ball. Many people who were in the ballroom that night, including Peter Duchin, praised Truman for assembling people from disparate worlds—high society, show business, politics, literature, art, and others—and enabling them to have a good time together despite their differences. But Dunphy maintained that guests stayed within their own established groups that night. "I've never seen such ghettoizing in all my life," he complained to Plimpton. "No group mixed with another group." Dunphy sat on the sidelines with Don Bachardy and some of Truman's other friends who could be categorized as artists and intellectuals, as the wealthy, jet-setting Agnellis sat with the wealthy, jet-setting Paleys, Brandolinis, and Gloria Guinness.

One guest recalled that the Agnellis and the Brandolinis had not been impressed by Truman's party. The photographer Frederick Eberstadt had overheard the Italians talking outside the Plaza ballroom. "Is this what we flew over for?" they asked. They were accustomed to extravaganzas like the Beistegui ball in Venice, and found the Black and White Ball to be a little low on spectacle and opulence.

Thanks to his network of spies, Truman was well aware of any negative comments. He had a specific form of punishment in mind for the guests who voiced them. "Any derogatory remarks automatically put the transgressor on probation," he warned. That person would not be invited the next time around, implying that there would be a next time.

Truman must have felt the same animosity toward members of the press who panned his ball. He never forgot—or forgave—a bad review of one of his books, and his party was just as important to him. Drew Pearson, a columnist and Kay Graham's close friend, promised her that he would not write about the party; she had been afraid he would condemn the event as being superficial and excessive. Promise notwithstanding, Pearson's ire got the best of him. He dashed off an account of the "Garden Citians'" experiences at the ball for a Kansas newspaper, combining innocuous facts about Margaret Maxfield's wardrobe with a sobering suggestion: a party that celebrated *In Cold Blood* was a party that exploited the Clutter murders. Truman's success had been built on their blood. Pearson speculated that only the guests from Kansas gave a moment's thought to Herb Clutter, his wife, and their two children, but another guest expressed a similar weighty thought. Cecil Beaton wondered whether anyone would think of Perry Smith and Dick Hickock. "While the two bands are blaring and the champagne drunk, who will remember the two murderers but for whose garrulous cooperation . . . the book could not have been written."

Pete Hamill, a columnist for the *New York Post*, composed a provocative exercise in contrasts, to counter the media's extensive coverage of masks, gowns, and bon mots. His article "The Party" alternated satirical, sycophantic descriptions of the evening ("Party of the year—bull, this was the party of the *century* . . . party of the entire century . . . there were some *Negroes* there, too") with news reports of battles and casualties in Vietnam ("A jeep pulled up and they brought in a girl about eight years old. Her face, arms, chest, and back were burnt away by napalm."). He made his point that Truman's party had been a frivolous undertaking at a time when young men were risking their lives in Vietnam.

Soldiers voiced their opinions regarding the ball. Private R——from Fort Jackson, South Carolina, wrote a letter to *Time*, saying that he couldn't "bear to think of my country's future at the hands of this fat, lethargic, useless intelligentsia." Another soldier, however, responded that one of the reasons he was fighting in Vietnam was to preserve the American way, which included the right to host a party.

Editorial pages weighed in with their perceptions of the ball. The *Valley Independent*, a newspaper in Pennsylvania, published a scathing editorial entitled "Who's Beautiful?" "For an example of sheer bad taste, high society will have to wait a while to match the well-publicized 'ball of the decade' given in New York City by the newly rich author, Truman Capote," the writer blasted. Like Pearson, he was offended by the fact that Truman's good fortune was born of a mass murder. He also wondered how anyone with a conscience could participate in such a ridiculous evening, knowing that the country was fighting a war in Asia and a war on poverty. "If this is what it takes to be 'in' in 1966 America," the editorial concluded, "let us pray."

On a lighter note, the humorist Russell Baker wrote an "Observer" column about Truman's party for the *New York Times*. It appeared on the editorial page alongside serious commentary on student riots in Berkeley and political unrest in Rhodesia. In the past, Baker pointed out, writers had enjoyed dubious social standing. Now, "with a single fling, Mr. Capote has given the writer the right to social dignity." Not only did Truman include writers on his famous guest list, the host himself was one. With tongue in cheek, Baker lauded Truman for his "noble" efforts on this front. As for the people who had been left out, Baker wrote, "If he has ruined a few lives among the uninvited, so much the better. You have to break a few egos to make an omelet."

In December, a reference to the ball even appeared on a Christmas list. The columnist Ward Cannel suggested gifts for the person who has everything. For Truman Capote, he recommended "a trial membership in the Public Relations Society of America and 540 friendship rings." For Baby Jane Holzer, he thought, "a belated invitation to Truman Capote's party" would be appreciated.

19

❦

Hangover

ONE YEAR LATER, IN DECEMBER OF 1967, *ESQUIRE* RAN A COVER that proved Truman's party was still a hot topic. Eight celebrities representing different worlds—Jimmy Brown, Kim Novak, Tony Curtis, Pat Brown, Ed Sullivan, Pierre Salinger, Lynn Redgrave, and Casey Stengel—stared into the camera, their faces grim and angry. "We wouldn't have come even if you *had* invited us, Truman Capote!" the cover line read. Inside the magazine, William F. Buckley, who had been a guest at the ball, dissected the party's politics, questioning whether the guest list had any larger social meaning. He came to the conclusion that Truman's party was all about Truman. "The politics of Capote's ball," wrote Buckley, "were that there were no politics." The cartoonist David Levine drew caricatures of the ball guests to illustrate the article.

The issue also featured an article entitled "Why Your Parties Will Never Be as Good as Truman Capote's," written by *Esquire's* resident hipsters David Newman and Robert Benton. "When it comes to throwing a party, old Tru makes you look like a bum,"

scoffed the duo. They offered some helpful hints to improve the *Esquire* reader's future efforts at entertaining, suggesting that would-be hosts should never serve onion cheese dip, toss coats on the bed, or show slides of that vacation in Yosemite.

๛

Ultimately, it didn't matter what people were saying about the ball, whether they were for it or against it, singing its praises, or uttering words of condemnation. The point was, they were still talking about it. Truman became known as the man with the best friends and the best headlines. Instead of retreating into isolation to concentrate on his work, as he usually did after a burst of socializing, Truman lingered in society. In addition to being a famous author, he was the most desirable guest in the world. "Mr. Capote is considered by many to be a 64 inch, 136 pound magnet particularly attractive to the gilded people who count when it comes to fashionable fundraising," wrote Enid Nemy in the *New York Times*. His presence added luster to any event, and he was generous with his company. He attended premieres in Manhattan and benefits in the Hamptons. He traveled with his friends, visited the sets of *In Cold Blood* in Kansas and *The Thanksgiving Visitor* in Alabama, and talked about writing *Answered Prayers*, which was supposed to be well in the works. Whenever he wanted to relive the stunning success of the Black and White Ball, he leafed through three oversized black albums he had filled with newspaper clippings and photographs.

During one of his visits to the Cerfs' country house, Truman made a surprising discovery about the ball. Susan Payson, the spirited young crasher, had married the publishing executive Bill Fine and was also a guest of the Cerfs. Teasingly called Joe Active by her hosts because of her inability to sit still, Susan was contemplating swimming laps when a high-pitched voice asked, "Are you a little bored? Let me tell you a story." When he finished, she said, "Now *I* have a story for you," and proceeded to tell him about the young couple who boldly walked right into his party. Truman jumped up, grabbed her hand in a champion salute, and announced, "*This* is the woman who crashed the Black and White Ball!" He was delighted and continued to affectionately introduce Susan as his crasher whenever they met.

After the success of *In Cold Blood* and the Black and White Ball, people believed that Truman had the magic touch: he could turn anything into gold. He started to believe in his own powers and decided that he could transform Lee Radziwill into an actress. In 1967, Truman convinced the producer David Susskind to gamble on the princess's untapped dramatic skills by casting her in a television adaptation of Otto Preminger's classic romantic mystery *Laura*. Truman wrote the script and coached his friend through the arduous process of filming. In the end, he was not a magician. Lee's performance—or what was left of it, after extensive cutting—was mediocre. She wisely went back to being a socialite, while Truman tried to write.

❧

Truman had begun to lack discipline. The Truman who rewarded himself with a social life after periods of productivity had been replaced by a party monster. He seemed to have forgotten that "gregariousness is the enemy of art," or that he needed to go into training "like a prizefighter" to accomplish his best work. The harder it was for him to concentrate, the more he avoided isolation. Jack, who had never had much patience for Truman's forays into society, observed, "There's something terribly wrong with his life."

Truman's poor judgment extended to all aspects of his life. He decided to make his long-standing relationship with Jack Dunphy platonic and took up with a succession of inappropriate men, Rick Brown and John O'Shea among them. Truman turned to drugs and alcohol to distract himself from his slow disintegration. Even his choice of residence—a home in Palm Springs, California, of all places—suggested that he was not his former self. Young Truman had arrogantly decreed that a person lost a point of I.Q. for every year spent in California. In his current state, he was no longer troubled by the thought of intellectual deterioration.

In November of 1971, Kay Graham wrote to Bob Wells in Kansas, saying, "I'm worried about our friend, Truman." She had good reason to be concerned. Truman was drifting. His relationship with John O'Shea was destructive and excessively dramatic; insults were exchanged, drinks were tossed, and ultimatums delivered. Truman's old friends were horrified by his rapid decline.

Truman rallied in 1975 when he completed "Mojave," a short story about Sarah Whitelaw, a beautiful society woman and her compromised marriage. He envisioned it as a segment of *Answered Prayers* but decided to publish it first as a freestanding piece in *Esquire*. Readers were fascinated by Truman's depiction of his heroine but seemed to overlook the inescapable conclusion that Sarah and Babe Paley were one and the same. There were too many similarities between Truman's fictional socialite and Babe for the parallels to be coincidental.

Truman seemed to be intimately acquainted with Sarah (which means "princess") and her bird-in-a-gilded-cage situation. Sarah looked like Babe—her hair is described as "fluffy and tobacco-colored, like a childish aureole around her deceptively naïve and youthful face." She dressed like Babe, posing by her fireplace in an opulent "grey silk caftan and grey silk slippers with pearl buckles." They both used the services of the exercise trainer Joseph Pilates. And Sarah and her husband (separated in age by fifteen years, while Bill Paley was fourteen years older than Babe) had stopped having a sexual relationship after the birth of their second child, an intimate detail that Truman knew and shared with other friends in gossip fests about the Paleys' troubled marriage.

Finally, Sarah's dedication to her husband's comfort was so extreme, just like Babe's, that she even helped him to select his mistresses. Truman's suggestion to Gloria Vanderbilt and Carol Marcus that they have an affair with Bill Paley—for Babe's sake—implies that Babe helped to discreetly orchestrate her husband's liaisons. As for Sarah's affair with Dr. Benson in the story, there were rumors that Babe had also had the occasional affair—she was spotted lunching with a gentleman in an out-of-the-way restaurant. She was the kind of dutiful wife who would have been tortured by her own infidelity, feelings she could confess to Truman, her closest friend.

Yet for Truman, all secrets were becoming fair game. Any confession, observation, or choice piece of gossip was likely to be repeated at today's lunch and to turn up in tomorrow's story.

When people asked whether they were in *Answered Prayers*, Truman often quipped, "Not yet, but like Forest Lawn cemetery, I've reserved a plot for you." The friends he mined for material, though, never thought of themselves as sources. They may have missed the real-life parallels in "Mojave," but they were shocked by the blatant references they encountered in "La Côte Basque," the next installment from *Answered Prayers*. They were shocked by the publication of "La Côte Basque," the next installment from *Answered Prayers*. Like "Mojave," "La Côte Basque" debuted in *Esquire*. Truman was merciless in his depiction of friends and acquaintances enjoying lunch and the latest gossip at the famous restaurant. Gloria Vanderbilt, Slim Keith, Carol Matthau, and the Paleys were savaged by his pen. One story, ostensibly about the media tycoon Sydney Dillon and his beautiful wife, Cleo, told the embarrassing tale of Dillon's one-night stand with the wife of a former governor. It was a more obvious roman à clef than "Mojave" was and more disparaging because it focused on Bill Paley instead of on Babe. Ann Woodward, a socialite who literally got away with murder (she shot her husband because she thought he was an intruder, or so she said), killed herself after she read Truman's portrayal of her as social climber and a ruthless killer.

One of Truman's friends warned him that his society buddies would not appreciate his betrayal of their confidences, but he maintained that they were too dumb to recognize themselves. He had underestimated them. Not only were they not dumb, they were smart enough to know that Truman was someone who could not be trusted. All the doors that once opened wide to welcome the famous author, host, and bon vivant now closed in his face. "Capote Bites the Hands That Fed Him," declared the cover of *New York* magazine. All of his swans, with the exception of the good-natured C. Z. Guest, abandoned him. Babe never forgave him. Explanations were dismissed. Calls were not returned. Invitations were ignored. *Esquire*'s publication of "Unspoiled Monsters," another installment from *Answered Prayers*, in December of 1976, alienated more people, Tennessee Williams and Katherine Anne Porter among them.

Truman had become a caricature of himself. In 1976, he played a Truman Capote–like writer, fat and vitriolic, in the movie *Murder by Death*. Yet even in his diminished state, Truman knew he had to pull himself together. He began on the outside, taking years off his appearance with cosmetic surgery. Andy Warhol, impressed by Truman's physical renovation, told him that he looked like "a new same old you." During this time, Truman revived his *In Cold Blood* self by writing *Handcarved Coffins*, a nonfiction novella about a series of unusual murders in Nebraska. But for most people, Truman was the court jester of television talk shows. Truman was the odd little man who exaggerated his already high voice and squandered his savage wit on senseless, who-said-what-first feuds with the writers Jacqueline Susann and Gore Vidal.

His prolonged tussle with Vidal (Truman embellished a story about Vidal having been thrown out of the Kennedy White House) cost him his friendship with Lee Radziwill. She could have come to Truman's defense by testifying that there was some truth to the reckless anti-Vidal statements that he had communicated to *Playgirl* in a drunken, tell-all state, but she refused to do so. Lee's betrayal was shocking, considering Truman's longtime devotion to her. Gradually stripped of his friends and social connections, the man who had led the list of in's in the 1960s was now officially and irrevocably out.

As his stock went down, the cost of his party went up. In 1966, Truman was proud of the fact that he had paid a mere $16,000 for the ball. In the years that followed, he periodically inflated the sum. He told one journalist that he had spent $75,000 and another, $155,000.

His reduced social status gave Truman more time to work on *Music for Chameleons*, a collection of short pieces that included the previously published "Mojave." The book appeared on the *New York Times* nonfiction best-seller list on August 31, 1980, and stayed there for sixteen weeks. Critics were encouraged by this unexpected manifestation of Truman's former talent and enthusiastically awaited the finished version of *Answered Prayers*.

The 1980s, however, were not kind to Truman. In the 1980s, Truman was not kind to himself. He surrendered to drugs and alcohol because, as Gerald Clarke wrote so eloquently, "to his tired eyes, everything now looked stale. He had, as he often said, used up the world." Truman spent time in Los Angeles with his loyal friend and former U.N. Plaza neighbor Joanne Carson, the ex-wife of Johnny Carson. She was kind and patient and listened attentively as he spun fantasies about the stories he would write, the trips he would take, and the parties he would host.

There would be a sequel to the Black and White Ball, he announced, better than the first. At first, Truman thought he might host it in Los Angeles. But, no—he needed a more exotic locale; guests would fly to faraway Paraguay for the festivities. Joe Petrocik, a friend from the Hamptons, saw him draft an invitation, one far more casual than the engraved card he used in 1966. It read, "Don Señor Truman Capote requests your company for a masked ball— in Asunción, Paraguay."

Had Truman purchased another black-and-white composition book, labeled it *Dance*, and attempted to fill its pages with the names of his fabulous friends, he would have realized that the ball in Paraguay was an impossible dream. That 1966 moment—when glamour was the rule instead of the exception, when celebrity was earned, and when Truman Capote was the man of the hour—was gone forever. His friends were gone, too. Evie Backer, his chief consultant for the Black and White Ball, had died in 1971. Babe, his adviser on all matters of taste, had died of cancer in 1978, without reconciling with him. Many of the people who were still alive would not have crossed the room to speak to Truman, let alone fly to South America to attend his party.

Fortunately, Truman did not have to confront these unpleasant truths because he never had a chance to host the ball. He suffered one physical breakdown after another, until he died in Joanne Carson's guest room on August 25, 1984, at the age of fifty-nine.

In an observation that was unkind but accurate, Gore Vidal called his rival's demise "a good career move."

Truman's memorial service at the Shubert Theater on September 25, 1984, complete with a printed invitation, an admittance card, and a tasteful program provided by Tiffany's, was the closest he would ever again come to being the star attraction at an event like the Black and White Ball.

Afterword

T HERE WERE MANY CHANGES IN THE MONTHS, YEARS, AND DECADES that followed the ball. Harry Winston paired the brilliant Schwab Diamond with a sixty-two-carat mate to form a set of fabulous earrings for an Iranian princess. In a more romantic coupling, the shy, sweet filmmaker Al Maysles met and married a fellow ball guest, Gillian Walker, without either of them realizing that they had been at Truman's party at the same time.

Bill Berkson, the young poet who had escorted his widowed mother to the ball, set out for another iconic event of the 1960s, Woodstock. Jerry Jones, the gentleman who had reluctantly crashed the ball with Susan Payson, moved to Washington, D.C., where he worked for the Committee to Re-Elect President Nixon. His name came up on a list of Nixon staffers who could have been the infamous Deep Throat, but he was ultimately dismissed as a possibility. Princess Luciana Pignatelli became famous in the early 1970s when she wrote the best-selling style guide *The Beautiful People's Beauty Book* and appeared in commercials advertising Camay soap.

The Plaza's Joe Evangelista worked as a banquet waiter for the next thirty-nine years and, at some point during that time, lost the prized hundred-dollar bill he had received from Frank Sinatra.

Bergdorf Goodman discontinued its custom department and discarded the mannequins that had served as body doubles for generations of beautifully dressed women. Kenneth Battalle's salon burned to the ground in 1985 and reopened at the Waldorf Hotel. Today, developers are converting many rooms at the Plaza Hotel into private apartments, similar to the way it was in 1907 when Alfred Gwynn Vanderbilt lived there. Most newspaper articles about the Plaza conversion have described the endangered hotel as the site of Truman Capote's legendary Black and White Ball.

Many of the guests have died—Katharine Graham; swans such as C. Z. Guest, Gloria Guinness, Slim Keith, and Babe Paley; George Plimpton; the Irving Lazars; David Merrick; Richard Avedon; Cecil Beaton; Alvin and Marie Dewey; Pamela Hayward Harriman; Andy Warhol; Carol Bjorkman; and dozens, possibly hundreds, of others. Of the surviving attendees, most use superlatives to describe the evening and still remember the relief they had felt when they received their invitations. Kitty Carlisle Hart, who was invited everywhere, recalled, "The build-up was extraordinary. I knew an awful lot of people who were left out and I was very pleased to have been included."

Some guests saved their masks and dresses. Hart was able to pull her headdress, designed by Mr. John, from its original hatbox. The black and white gowns that made Ann Birstein and Elizabeth Hylton feel special remain in their closets, reminders of that magical night. Joanne Carson, who had missed the ball because she had the flu, saved the dress she had purchased for the occasion—a striking black Pierre Cardin with chrome inserts. Billy Baldwin's fantastic unicorn head, so admired by Truman; the gowns that Halston had designed for Carol Bjorkman and Candice Bergen; and the magnificent swan headdress that Bill Cunningham had created for Isabella Eberstadt reside at the Museum of the City of New York, while Katharine Graham's white Balmain is a few blocks away at the Metropolitan Museum.

A few guests are dismissive when they discuss Truman's party. One veteran ball-goer imperiously asked, "What's to remember?" implying that it was just another night at the Plaza. Another guest, a prominent author who looked as if he'd had fun at the time—a photograph shows him smiling broadly for the camera—reversed his opinion, calling the ball "silly and vulgarly publicized."

Whatever the guests thought, the ball had been a pivotal moment in social history. Peter Duchin, who has observed society both from the vantage point of his piano and as a privileged insider, remarked that the ball "closed an era of elegant exclusiveness and ushered in another of media madness—the one in which we still live." It triggered an insatiable thirst in readers for the very who-what-when-and-where prose that is so popular today.

⊛

Other would-be hosts, including Sean "Puffy" Combs, have tried to recreate Capote's stunning social victory. Combs hosted a New Year's Eve party in 2001 that was supposed to surpass the original evening but didn't. Hosts and hostesses all over the country stage black and white balls as charity events, anniversary parties, and even as Bar Mitzvahs.

The Young Lions of the New York Public Library, an enthusiastic group of young supporters of that institution, paid homage to the Black and White Ball by making it the theme of their annual benefit in April 2004. One of the reasons they selected this theme was that the library houses thirty-two boxes of Capote's papers, including the original planning notebook, the guest list, and the invitation for the ball. Yet a more compelling reason seemed to be that these young people felt an intense nostalgia, almost an "era envy," for a party that took place before they were born. They may not have read anything written by Capote, but they know all about his fabulous party because it has been kept alive in articles and fashion layouts in magazines such as *Vanity Fair*, *Vogue*, *Esquire*, and *GQ*.

The spectacular *bal masqué*, complete with cast, costumes, lavish sets, high drama, and divine comedy, may have been Truman Capote's most famous and enduring creation. In the four decades that have ensued, much of Capote's writing is still considered good, some of it even great. Yet it has never been questioned that his Black and White Ball was the party of the century.

Appendix
The Guest List

List of those who were invited to the party at the Plaza Hotel

Leroy Aarons
Charles Addams
Richard Adler
Count Adlerberg
Mr. and Mrs. Gianni Agnelli
Count Umberto Agnelli
Edward Albee
Mr. and Mrs. Archibald Albright
Nelson Aldrich
Shana Alexander
Mr. and Mrs. Charles Allen
Mr. and Mrs. Joseph Alsop
Mr. and Mrs. Stewart Alsop
Mr. and Mrs. Cleveland Amory
Princess Charles d'Arenberg
Mr. and Mrs. Harold Arlen
Odette Arnaud
Mrs. W. Vincent Astor
Mary Louise Aswell
Mr. and Mrs. William Attwood
Mr. and Mrs. Louis Auchincloss
Mr. and Mrs. Richard Avedon
Mr. and Mrs. George Axelrod

Don Bachardy
Mr. and Mrs. George Backer
James Baldwin
William Baldwin
Miss Tallulah Bankhead
Samuel Barber
Trumbull Barton
Benedetta Barzini
Charles Baskerville

Mr. and Mrs. Theodore Bassett
Cecil Beaton
Mr. and Mrs. Frederick S. Beebe
S. N. Behrman
Mr. and Mrs. Harry Belafonte
Marisa Berenson
Candice Bergen
Mrs. Seymour Berkson
William Berkson
Mr. and Mrs. Irving Berlin
Sir Isaiah and Lady Berlin
Mr. and Mrs. Leonard Bernstein
Mr. and Mrs. Robert Bernstein
Lemoyne Billings
Mrs. Pierre Billotte
Carol Bjorkman
Mr. and Mrs. Watson Blair
Mr. and Mrs. Charles Bohlen
Mr. and Mrs. Anthony di Bonaventura
Mrs. Rene Bouche
Anthony Bower
Mr. and Mrs. Thomas Braden
Mr. and Mrs. Benjamin Bradlee
Count and Countess Brando Brandolini
Henry Brandon
Mr. and Mrs. Frederick Brisson
James E. Broadhead
Donald Brooks
Mr. and Mrs. Richard Brooks
Eve Brown
Mr. and Mrs. John Mason Brown
Mr. and Mrs. David K. E. Bruce
Mrs. Mellon Bruce

Mr. and Mrs. William Buckley
Dr. and Mrs. Ralph Bunche
Mr. and Mrs. McGeorge Bundy
Susan Burden
Mr. and Mrs. S. Carter Burden Jr.
Mr. and Mrs. Abe Burrows
Robert Burtis
Mr. and Mrs. Richard Burton
Mrs. Robin Butler
Mr. and Mrs. J. F. Byers 3rd

Paul Cadmus
Mr. and Mrs. Herb Caen
Mrs. William M. Campbell
Mr. and Mrs. Cass Canfield
Prince Carlo Caracciollo
Prince and Princess Nicola Caracciollo
Leslie Caron
Margaret Case
Mr. and Mrs. Dan Platt Caulkins
Mr. and Mrs. Bennett Cerf
Christopher Cerf
Lord Chalfont
Mr. and Mrs. Hugh J. Chisholm Jr.
Blair Clark
Mr. and Mrs. Richard Clurman
Harold Cole
Dr. and Mrs. John Converse
Senator and Mrs. John Sherman
    Cooper
Mr. and Mrs. Wyatt Cooper
General John Coulter
Noel Coward
Chandler Cowles
Mr. and Mrs. Gardner Cowles
Count and Countess Rudolfo Crespi
Mr. and Mrs. Walter Cronkite
Bessie de Cuevas
Charlotte Curtis
Thomas Quinn Curtiss
Mr. and Mrs. Frederick Cushing
Minnie Cushing

Mr. and Mrs. John Daly
Mr. and Mrs. Clifton Daniel
Mr. and Mrs. Sammy Davis Jr.
Oscar de la Renta
Françoise de Langlade
Arnaud de Renée

Mr. and Mrs. Robert Delheim
Alan Delynn
Mr. and Mrs. Armand Deutsch
Mr. and Mrs. Alvin Dewey
Marlene Dietrich
Mr. and Mrs. Douglas Dillon
Ainslie Dinwiddie
Mrs. Kingman Douglass
Sharman Douglas
Mrs. Peter Duchin
Drew Dudley
Marquis and Marchioness of Dufferin
Jack Dunphy
Mr. and Mrs. Robert Dunphy
Mr. and Mrs. F. W. Dupree

Mr. and Mrs. Frederick Eberstadt
Mr. and Mrs. Osborn Elliott
Mr. and Mrs. Ralph Ellison
Mr. and Mrs. Charles Engelhard
Jean Ennis
Mr. and Mrs. Jason Epstein
Elliott Erwitt
Mr. and Mrs. Rowland Evans Jr.

Douglas Fairbanks Jr.
William Farenga
Mrs. John R. Fell
Mr. and Mrs. Mel Ferrer
Mrs. Marshall Field
Jason Biddle Fishbein
Frances Fitzgerald
Janet Flanner
Mr. and Mrs. Henry Fonda
Joan Fontaine
Mr. and Mrs. Henry Ford 2nd
Mrs. McDonnell Ford
Michael Forrestal
Mr. and Mrs. James Fosburgh
Gray Foy
Mrs. Jared French
Lawrence Fried
Mrs. Donald Friede
Clayton Fritchey
Mr. and Mrs. Winston Frost

Mr. and Mrs. Martin Gabel
Mr. and Mrs. John Kenneth Galbraith
John Galliher

Greta Garbo
Geoffrey Gates
Henry Geldzhaller
Mr. and Mrs. Brendan Gill
Genevieve Gillaizeau
Mr. and Mrs. Roswell Gilpatric
Mrs. Bailey Gimbel
Peter Gimbel
Bernard Giquel
Peter Glenville
Tony Godwin
Mr. and Mrs. William Goetz
Ambassador and Mrs. Arthur J.
    Goldberg
Mr. and Mrs. Samuel Goldwyn
Henry Golightly
Mr. and Mrs. Richard Goodwin
Mark Goodson
Mrs. Philip Graham
Mr. and Mrs. Adolph Green
Mr. and Mrs. Stefan Groueff
Lauder Greenway
Mrs. Polk Guest
Mr. and Mrs. Winston F. C. Guest
Mrs. Loel Guinness
Thomas Guinzburg
Mr. and Mrs. John Gunther
Baron de Gunzberg
David Guthrie

Mr. and Mrs. William Haddad
Mr. and Mrs. Richard Halliday
Hamish Hamilton
Jean Hannon
Lord Hardwicke
Ambassador and Mrs. W. Averell
    Harriman
Mrs. Moss Hart
Ashton Hawkins
Kitty Hawks
Mr. and Mrs. Harold Hayes
Mr. and Mrs. Lennie Hayton
Mr. and Mrs. Leland Hayward
Mr. and Mrs. William Randolph
    Hearst Jr.
Mr. and Mrs. Henry J. Heinz 2nd
Miss Lillian Hellman
John H. Hemingway
Princess Domiella Herculani

Mr. and Mrs. John Hersey
Helene Hersent
Mr. and Mrs. Andrew Heiskell
Elizabeth Hilton
Horst P. Horst
Jane Howard
Milton Holden
Mr. and Mrs. Arthur Hornblow
Emmett John Hughes

Christopher Isherwood

Maharajah and Maharanee of Jaipur
Senator and Mrs. Jacob K. Javits
Lynda Bird Johnson
Philip Johnson

Mr. and Mrs. Garson Kanin
Mr. and Mrs. Warren Kask
Mr. and Mrs. Nicholas deB.
    Katzenbach
Mr. and Mrs. Alfred Kazin
Dr. Benjamin Kean
Mrs. Kenneth Keith
Horace Kelland
Senator and Mrs. Edward M. Kennedy
Mrs. John F. Kennedy
Mrs. Joseph P. Kennedy
Senator and Mrs. Robert F. Kennedy
Mr. and Mrs. Walter Kerr
Prince Amyn Khan
David King
Mr. and Mrs. Donald Klopfer
Alfred Knopf
John Knowles
Mr. and Mrs. Joseph Kraft
Jack Kroll
Harry Kurnitz
Mr. and Mrs. Steven Kyle

Melissa Laird
Baron Leon Lambert
Kenneth Lane
Mr. and Mrs. Kermit Langner
Lewis Lapham
Marquis Raimundo de Larrain
Mrs. Mary Lasker
Robert Launey
Mrs. Patricia Lawford

Valentine Lawford
Barbara Lawrence
Mr. and Mrs. Irving Lazar
Harper Lee
Vivien Leigh
Mrs. Oates Leiter
Mr. and Mrs. Jack Lemmon
Leo Lerman
Mr. and Mrs. Alan Jay Lerner
Herman Levin
Mr. and Mrs. Alexander Lieberman
Mr. and Mrs. Goddard Lieberson
Mayor and Mrs. John V. Lindsay
Mr. and Mrs. Walter Lippmann
Mr. and Mrs. Joshua Logan
Mrs. Nicholas Longworth
Anita Loos
Mr. and Mrs. Robert Lowell
Mr. and Mrs. Henry Luce
Andrew Lyndon

Shirley MacLaine
Mr. and Mrs. Norman Mailer
Mr. and Mrs. Joseph Mankiewicz
Marya Mannes
Mr. and Mrs. Stanley Marcus
Mr. and Mrs. William Marshall
Mr. and Mrs. Paul Masoner
Mr. and Mrs. Walter Matthau
Paul Matthias
Mr. and Mrs. Peter Matthieseon
Mr. and Mrs. Graham Mattison
Dr. and Mrs. Russell Maxfield
Albert Maysles
Ken McCormick
Roddy McDowall
John McHugh
Mr. and Mrs. Robert McNamara
Mr. and Mrs. Joseph A. Meehan
Marcia Meehan
Aileen Mehle
Frederick Melhado
Mr. and Mrs. Paul Mellon
Gian Carlo Menotti
David Merrick
Robert Merrill
David Metcalfe
Mrs. Agnes E. Meyer
André Meyer

Mr. and Mrs. James Michener
Catherine Milinaire
Mr. and Mrs. Arthur Miller
Mr. and Mrs. Gilbert Miller
Mrs. Walter Millis
Mr. and Mrs. Vincent Minnelli
John Moore
Marianne Moore
Mr. and Mrs. Thomas Moore
Mr. and Mrs. William S. Moorhead
Mr. and Mrs. Walthes Moreira-Salles
Edward P. Morgan
Stanley Mortimer
Ann Mudge
Mrs. Natalia Murray

Mr. and Mrs. Samuel I. Newhouse Sr.
Mrs. Stavros Niarchos
Mike Nichols
Eric Nielsen
Norman Norell

Serge Obolensky
Lord and Lady David Ogilvy
John O'Hara
Patrick O'Higgins

Mr. and Mrs. Bruno Pagliai
Mr. and Mrs. William S. Paley
Mr. and Mrs. Gordon Parks
Mr. and Mrs. Iva S. V. Patcévitch
Mr. and Mrs. Samuel Peabody
Mr. and Mrs. Drew Pearson
Mr. and Mrs. Gregory Peck
William Pennington
Mr. and Mrs. Frank Perry
Mr. and Mrs. Michael Phipps
Mr. and Mrs. Ogden Phipps
Mr. and Mrs. Thomas W. Phipps
Princess Luciana Pignatelli
Duarte Coehlo Pinto
George Plimpton
Mr. and Mrs. Norman Podhoretz
Katherine Anne Porter
Dr. and Mrs. Joel Pressman
Mr. and Mrs. Harold Prince
Alan Pryce-Jones

Prince and Princess Stanislas Radziwill

Count Vega del Ren
Mr. and Mrs. James Reston
Vicomtesse Jacqueline de Ribes
Mr. and Mrs. Larry Rivers
Mr. and Mrs. Jason Robards Jr.
Jerome Robbins
Governor and Mrs. Nelson A.
   Rockefeller
Mr. and Mrs. Richard Rodgers
Mr. and Mrs. William P. Rogers
Philip Roth
Baroness Cecile de Rothschild
Baron and Baroness Guy de Rothschild
Theodore Rousseau
Mr. and Mrs. John Barry Ryan 3rd
Mrs. John Barry Ryan Jr.

Arnold Saint-Subber
Herbert Sargent
John Sargent
Mr. and Mrs. Robert Sarnoff Jr.
Mr. and Mrs. Frank Schiff
Mr. and Mrs. Thomas Schippers
Mrs. George Schlee
Mr. and Mrs. Arthur Schlesinger Jr.
Jean Schlumberger
Mr. and Mrs. Mark Schorer
Mrs. Zachary Scott
Peggy Scott Duff
Nelson Seabra
Daniel Selznick
Mrs. David O. Selznick
Mrs. Irene Selznick
Mr. and Mrs. Irwin Shaw
Mrs. Robert E. Sherwood
Mr. and Mrs. Sargent Shriver
Robert Silvers
Agnes Sims
Mr. and Mrs. Frank Sinatra
Richard Sircre
Earl E. T. Smith
Oliver Smith
Preston Smith
Mr. and Mrs. Stephen Smith
Daivd Somerset
Steve Sondheim
Theodore Sorensen
Charles F. Spalding
Sam Spiegel

Mr. and Mrs. Jules Stein
Mr. and Mrs. Robert Stein
Susan Stein
Mr. and Mrs. John Steinbeck
Gloria Steinem
Mr. and Mrs. George C. Stevens Jr.
Marli Stevens
Mrs. William Rhinelander Stewart
Monica Stirling
Mr. and Mrs. William Styron
Mr. and Mrs. Arthur Ochs Sulzberger

Harold E. Talbott
Mrs. Roland Tate
Mr. and Mrs. Walter Thayer
Ambassador and Mrs. Llewellyn E.
   Thompson
Virgil Thomson
Alfredo Todisco
Alvin Topping
Mr. and Mrs. Warren Topping
Mr. and Mrs. Michael Tree
Penelope Tree
Mr. and Mrs. Ronald Tree
Mr. and Mrs. Lionel Trilling
Van Day Truex

Mr. and Mrs. Giancarlo Uzielli

Mr. and Mrs. Jack Valenti
Baron and Baroness Van Zuylen
Mr. and Mrs. William vanden Heuvel
Mr. and Mrs. Alfred Gwynne Vanderbilt
Mrs. Murray Vanderbilt
Wendy Vanderbilt
Duke di Verdura
Mrs. Doris Vidor
Marquis and Marquesa Cristobal
   Villaverde
Mrs. T. Reed Vreeland

Gillian Walker
Mr. and Mrs. John Walker 3rd
William Walton
Walter Wanger
Mr. and Mrs. Edward Warburg
Andy Warhol
Mr. and Mrs. Robert Penn Warren
Whitney Warren

David Webb
Mr. and Mrs. Robert Wells
Glenway Wescott
Mr. and Mrs. Anthony West
Mr. and Mrs. Yann Weymouth
Monroe Wheeler
Robert Whitehead
Mr. and Mrs. John Hay Whitney
Mr. and Mrs. Billy Wilder
Thornton Wilder
Edward Bennett Williams
Mr. and Mrs. Odd Williams
Tennessee Williams

Mr. and Mrs. Edmund Wilson
Jean Sprain Wilson
Donald Windham
Duke and Duchess of Windsor
Frederick M. Winship
Mr. and Mrs. Norman K. Winston
Mrs. Frank Wisner
Mrs. William Woodward
Alfred Wright, Jr.
Mr. and Mrs. Charles Wrightsman

Darryl Zanuck

Notes

Introduction

4   *"about as tall as a shotgun"* and *"the most wonderful party"*   Quoted in Lerman, "The Tiny Terror," 820.

Chapter 1. A Lonely Boy

10   *By midday, when the heat was unbearable*   Lee, *To Kill a Mockingbird*, p. 5.

11   *Breakfast, lunch, and dinner*   Clarke, *Capote*, p. 18.

11   *On Sundays, the intimate family circle*   Rudisill, *The Southern Haunting of Truman Capote* p. 54.

11   *Gossip was not merely an exchange of information*   Clarke, *Capote*, p. 19.

12   *"Don't you look"*   Rudisill, *The Southern Haunting of Truman Capote*, p. 85.

12   *"Other people inhabit the house"*   Capote, *A Christmas Memory*, p. 213.

12   *"a bird of paradise in a flock of crows"*   *Monroeville*, p. 26.

12   *"curiosity"* and *"stuck to his head like duckfluff"*   Lee, *To Kill a Mockingbird*, p. 8.

12   *"a pocket Merlin"*   Ibid. p. 10.

14   *"According to his cousin"*   Moates, *A Bridge of Childhood*, p. 51. (Note: A similar account of the party Truman hosted in Monroeville can be found in George Plimpton's *Truman Capote*.)

16   *Leo Lerman had no use*   Lerman, "The Tiny Terror," 820.

Chapter 2. Small Man, Big Dreams

19   *Yet Truman charmed her*   Saroyan, *Trio*, p. 19.

19   *They wore their hair long*   Capote, *Answered Prayers*, p. 146.

20   *Truman loved to impress*   Clarke, *Capote*, p. 71.

21   *In his tiny handwriting*   *Summer Crossing*, Truman Capote Papers.

23   *Readers came out of the war*   1945: Magazines. Encarta Online http://encarta .msn.com/encnet/refpages/search.aspx?q=magazines+during+1945 (accessed 8 August 2005).

25   *McCullers arranged for him to join her at Yaddo*   Clarke, *Capote*, p. 99.

26   *Truman's tower room*   Werth, *The Scarlet Professor*, p. 101.

26   *"Newton was my Harvard"*   Ibid., p. 119.

26   *"reads Greek at the breakfast table"*   Clarke, *Capote*, p. 18.

26   *"Now Spooky"*   Newton Arvin letter to Truman Capote. Truman Capote Papers.

26   *"I always felt he was a kind of secret friend"*   Grobel, *Conversations with Capote*, p. 96.

27   *"the best-known unpublished novelist in America"*   Werth, *The Scarlet Professor*, p. 108.

27   *the writer Edna Ferber thought*   Clarke, *Capote*, p. 134.

28   *"the love of my life"*   Jeff Heim, "Oona O'Neil Chaplin," *Point Pleasant Historical Society*, http://home.att.net/~ppbhist/time_ooneill.ht (accessed 10 October 2005).

28   *He visited Joan Crawford*   Clarke, *Capote*, p. 148.

29   *"This is Truman Capote"*   *New York Times*, p. 26.

29   *"The most discussed writer in New York literary circles today"*   "People Who Read and Write," BR8.

29   *"The most exciting first novel"*   Grobel, *Conversations with Capote*, p. 82.

29   *"the hope of modern literature"*   "People Who Read and Write," BR8.

29   *"the author who was really his main influence hadn't been singled out"*   "Books—Authors," p. 21.

30   *he implied that he had quit his job"*   "People Who Read and Write," BR8.

30   *In an item that ran in April*   "Books—Authors," p. 21.

31   *"everybody from Marlene Dietrich to Walter Winchell"*   Clarke, *Capote*, p. 137.

31   *She had firsthand recollections of "sad-eyed"*   Proust: Ibid., p. 168.

32   *"a satisfying conclusion"*   Capote, *Music for Chameleons*, p. xiii.

Truman's Swans

33-34 *"a gathering of swans"*   Avedon and Capote, *Observations*, p. 26.

34   *"Of first importance"*   Ibid., p. 28.

34   *"dumbness seldom diminishes"*   Ibid.

34   *"Authentic swans"*   Ibid.

35   *"waters of liquefied lucre"*   Ibid., p. 29.

Chapter 3. Romance and Sadness

36   *"hectic, nerve-wracking influences"*   Clarke, *Too Brief a Treat*, p. 39.

37   *He thought that Dunphy*   Plimpton, *Truman Capote,* p. 94.

37   *"a remarkable first novel"*   *New York Times*, "John Fury's Crescendo of Wrath" 27 October 1946.

38   *"If you want something badly enough"*   Clarke, *Capote*, p. 189.

38   *"was like a carefully planned military campaign"*   Plimpton, *Truman Capote*, p. 105.

38   *"The works he described"*   Clarke, *Capote*, p. 202.

39   *The evening was a feast for the senses*   Ibid., p. 201.

39   *Like Six Degrees of Kevin Bacon*   Clarke, *Too Brief a Treat*, p. 169.

40   *"easy to work with"*   Clarke, *Capote*, p. 237.

40   *Bogart dubbed him "Caposey"*   Ibid., p. 240.

44   *Doris Lilly*   Plimpton, *Truman Capote*, p. 41.

Chapter 4. Babe Paley and High Society

45   *After one leisurely automobile ride*   Grafton, *The Sisters*, p. 54.

45   *Like so many of his contemporaries*   Ibid., p. 62.

46   *"a willowy socialite eyeful from Boston"*   Lehrer, *Explorers of the Body.*

46   *"were married to a combined fortune"*   "The Cushing Sisters," 41–44.

47   *Babe would rise early*   Smith, *In All His Glory*, p. 338.

47   *"Truman Capote, our great American writer"*   Clarke, *Capote*, p. 281.

48   *"Babe looked at him"*   Ibid.

48   *"one of the two or three great obsessions"*   Ibid., p. 283.

49   *"Truman credited Paley with giving him marvelous advice"*   Ibid., p. 285.

49   *"Marilyn Monroe, a sexy broad"*   Ibid., p. 286.

49   *"He'll take good care of you, honey"*   Saroyan, *Trio*, p. 114.

49   *A few years later*   Vanderbilt, *It Seemed Important at the Time*, pp. 59–60.

50   *Being Mrs. William Paley, he advised*   Clarke, *Capote*, p. 287.

50   *"Now Babe knows"*   Vanderbilt, *It Seemed Important at the Time*, pp. 59–60.

51   *"the most perfect writer"* and *"changed two words"*   Clarke, *Capote*, pp. 314–15.

51   *"The novel is called"*   Clarke, *Too Brief a Treat*, p. 258.

Gloria

55   *When Hitler came into power*   Tappert and Edkins, *The Power of Style*, p. 176.

55   *Fakhri did not have much money*   Ibid.

55   *"It is such a bore to me"*   Fairchild, *The Fashionable Savages*, p. 150.

56   *"arrogant elegance"*   Bender, *The Beautiful People*, p. 143.

56-57 *One of her many tricks*   Tappert and Edkins, *The Power of Style*, p. 180.

58   *When particularly annoyed*   Clarke, *Capote*, p. 280.

Chapter 5. In Cold Blood

60   *"A psychopathic personality"* and *"Psychopathic Ills Are Emotional, Not Due to a Lack of Intelligence."*   *New York Times*, 24.

60   *"fiction with the added knowledge that it was true"*   "In Cold Blood . . . An American Tragedy," 59.

61   *Truman thought he was taking the easy way out*   Plimpton, *Truman Capote*, p. 166.

61   *When Lyndon declined*   Clarke, *Capote*, p. 319.

61   *He dressed in odd little outfits*   Plimpton, *Truman Capote*, p. 169.

61   *"I do something so outrageous"*   Ibid., p. 157.

62   *He told Al Dewey*   Plimpton, *Truman Capote*, p. 174.

63   *"Big Work"*   Clarke, *Capote*, p. 331.

63-64 *He kept a list of words*   Capote, *In Cold Blood*, p. 146.

64   *"Truman saw himself in Perry Smith"*   Plimpton, *Truman Capote*, p. 173.

64   *According to Nye*   Plimpton, *Truman Capote*, p. 188.

64   *An impersonal dedication*   Clarke, *Capote*, p. 327.

65   *"Will H & S live to a ripe and happy old age?"*   Clarke, *Too Brief a Treat*, p. 363.

65   *"Gregariousness is the enemy of art"*   Howard, "A Six-Year Literary Vigil," 70–76.

65   *Only Kansas, and the people there*   Clarke, *Too Brief a Treat*, p. 340.

67   *"In a tentful of famous people"*   Dunne, *The Way We Lived Then*, p. 124.

67   *When he walked onstage*   Clarke, *Capote*, p. 352.

68   *"Adios, amigo"*   "In Cold Blood . . . An American Tragedy," 55.

68   *"For the entire three days"*   Howard, "A Six-Year Literary Vigil," 70–76.

Marella

70   *He crashed into a truck*   Smith, *Reflected Glory*, p. 160.

72   *"More Caroline, less Agnelli"*   Bachrach, "La Vita Agnelli," 211.

72   *"If they were both in Tiffany's window"*   Graham, *Personal History*, p. 393.

Chapter 6. Truman and Kay

74   *"When I'm flying my flag in town"*   Howard, "A Six-Year Literary Vigil," 70–76.

75   *"luxury liner"*   "In Cold Blood . . . An American Tragedy," 59.

75   *"because it's so glamorous"*   Warren, "Home Up to $166,000 Sweet Home," 38.

75   *"very cozy"* and *"huge enormous view"*   Ibid.

75   *"It's like writing a book"*   "In Cold Blood . . . An American Tragedy," 59.

76   *"somehow remind you"*   "Ibid., p. 63.

76   *"expensive without looking"* and *"is the new world"*   Vickers, *Beaton in the Sixties*, p. 138.

77   *The boat was crowded*   Graham, *Personal History*, p. 379.

77   *"in four big gulps"*   "People are Talking About," 94–95.

78   *"a tour de force of reporting"*   Stanton, *Truman Capote*, p. 130.

78   *"the first non-fiction novel"*   "People Are Talking About," 94-95.

79   *When he was a young writer*   Capote, *Summer Crossing*. Truman Capote Papers.

80   *They were so concerned*   Lerner, personal interview.

82   *"weren't treated any more royally"*   The Distaff Side, December 1965. "Kansas Lawman"   "Kansas Lawman, Wife Give NY Elite Excuse for Party."

82   *The parties were so fashionable*   Ibid.

83   *"as if their feet hurt them"*   Dougherty, "Vanity on the Potomac," 19.

83   *"Any connection between entertaining"*   Graham, *Katharine Graham's Washington*, p. 157.

83   *In 1945, she had bravely*   Graham, *Personal History*, p. 156.

84   *Typically, Graham set*   All party details are from materials in the Katharine Graham Collection.

85   *Joe Fox, Truman's editor*   Joe Fox to Katharine Graham. 11/22/1965. Private Collection.

85   *For Marie Dewey, the party was the highlight of the whole week*   Marie Dewey to Katharine Graham. 11/28/1965. Private Collection.

85   *"the most beautiful and delightful one"*   Vi Tate to Katharine Graham. 11/29/1965. Private Collection.

85   *"I've never gotten"*   Katharine Graham to Joe Fox. 12/6/1965. Katharine Graham Collection.

85   *"Precious Kay-Kay"*   Truman Capote to Katharine Graham. 11/23/1965. Katharine Graham Collection.

86   *"Marie Dewey's conversation"*   Mary McGory to Katharine Graham. 11/21/1965. Katharine Graham Collection.

86   *"the whole party took off like a rocket"*   Kay Evans to Katharine Graham. 11/21/1965. Katharine Graham Collection.

86   *"any small time Wall Street operator"*   Gilroy, "A Book in a New Form Earns $2-Million for Truman Capote," 23.

Slim

89   *"scrubbed clean, healthy"*   Quoted in Tappert and Edkins, *The Power of Style*, p. 171.

91-92 *There were rumors*   Smith, *Reflected Glory*, p. 203.

92   *Truman saw them together*   Clarke, *Capote*, p. 315.

92   *"nobody marries Pam Churchill"*   Tappert, with Keith, *SLIM*, p. 251.

92   *"tout New York"*   Clarke, *Capote*, p. 316.

93   *"a Slimite to the death"*   Ibid.

Chapter 7. Riding a Wave

94   *"a contemporary equivalent"*   Fox, Introduction, Capote, *Answered Prayers*, p. xi.

95   *"a liar, a cheat, and a crook"*   Kriendler, *"21,"* pp. 219–20.
97   *"Talk about cold blood!"*   "Cutting Room," 54.
97   *Cornelius Ryan's* The Longest Day   "The Country below the Surface," 83.
97   *"the longest interview in its history"*   Fremont-Smith, "Literature-by-Consensus," 28.
97   *When Marie Dewey*   Marie Dewey to Katharine Graham. Private Collection.
98   *"the Svengali primarily responsible"*   Smith, "Advertising: A Success Money Didn't Buy." 16.
98   *The publicity department*   Ibid.
99   *"vast, self-generating promotional mill"*   Fremont-Smith, "Literature-by-Consensus," 28.
99   *"Macy's Thanksgiving Day balloon"*   Ibid.
99   *"leading the grape-stomp"* and *"Why . . . couldn't Capote"*   Alexander, *Life*, 22.
99   *"the hottest property"*   Nichols, "In and Out of Books," 268.
100   *"he looks like a tycoon"*   Vickers, *Beaton in the Sixties*, p. 138–39.
100   *"Truman is happy"*   *Newsweek*, "In Cold Blood . . . An American Tragedy," 63.
101   *"great, big, all-time spectacular present"*   Lerman, "The Tiny Terror," 820.
101   *Instead, it would be written about*   Ibid.
101   *Charity balls*   Curtis, "They Keep the Charity Ball Rolling," 88.
102   *but it was postponed*   Ibid.
102   *"Without them"*   Ibid.

C. Z.
104-105 *Her high spirits*   "Open End."
106   *The Guests maintained*   "Caught Short."
106   *"Either she's there"*   "Open End."

Chapter 8. Dreaming of Masquerades
107   *"nearly all the 'memorable balls'"*   Quoted in Laver, ed., *Memorable Balls*, p. v.
108   *"enslave true Englishmen"*   "The Anti-Masquerade Movement." http://www.umich.edu/~ece/student_projects/masquerade/anti.html (accessed 7 August 2005).
108   *The government was reluctant*   Ibid.

Chapter 9. Guest of Honor
114   *"Had lunch one day"*   Clarke, *Too Brief a Treat*, p. 337.
115   *But Lee enjoyed the freedom*   Radziwill, *Happy Times*, p. 134.
115   *Rumor has it that she proposed to him*   DuBois, *In Her Sister's Shadow*, p. 61.
115   *According to Diana DuBois*   Ibid., p. 89.
116   *"I really think your wife"*   Ibid., p. 96.
116   *"with an enormous heart"*   Radziwill, *Happy Times*, p. 72.
116-117 *"Unwilling to settle"*   Walters, "Jackie Kennedy's Perplexing Sister," 30.
117   *For the sake of appearances*   Peters, *Nemesis*, p. 72.
117   *"What I am seeking"*   DuBois, *In Her Sister's Shadow*, p. 161.
117-118 *That December,* Time *dubbed*   *The Sixties Chronicles*, p. 290.
118   *Vitamins and solid nutrition*   Marwick, *The Sixties Cultural Revolution*, p. 410.
118   *Marylin Bender of the* New York Times   Bender, "The New Society, Young and Daring, Swings into Style," 47.

119   *"understated clothes"*   Wolfe, *The Kandy-Kolored Tangerine-Flake Streamline Baby*, p. 206.

119   *"There is no class anymore"*   Bender, "The New Society, Young and Daring, Swings into Style," p. 47.

119   *"The press watches Jane Holzer"*   Wolfe, *The Kandy-Kolored Tangerine-Flake Streamline Baby*, p. 205.

120   *"the greatest pair of starring sweethearts"*   Bender, *The Beautiful People*, p. 143.

120   *"Switched on has had it"*   Ibid., p. 147.

121   *"Honey, I just decided"*   Clarke, *Capote*, p. 373.

121   *"the nicest party, darling"*   Graham, *Personal History*, p. 391.

Chapter 10. The In Crowd

123   *"I'm here to tell you"*   Lerman, "The Tiny Terror," p. 820.

123   *One couple*   Clarke, *Capote*, p. 276.

124   *"A ball that any one"*   Homberger, *Mrs. Astor's New York*, p. 211.

125   *The names in the debut edition*   Amory, *Who Killed Society?* p. 125.

126   *"Down here, we know"*   Ibid.

126   *"use your own judgment"*   Ibid., p. 7.

127   *"full Christian and maiden name"*   Ibid., p. 128.

127   *"anti-American"*   Grafton, *The Sisters*, p. 116.

127   *"If you willingly go along"*   "A Millionaire's Mission," 51.

127-128 *"the greatest anachronism"*   Bender, *The Beautiful People*, p. 148.

128   *"I don't think anyone"*   Amory, *Who Killed Society?* p. 7.

128   *"the decibel ring of the name"*   "The Noisemakers."

128   *"fame recognized beyond"*   Amory, ed., *Celebrity Register*, p. v.

129   *"Nobody looks at Mrs. Vanderbilt's"*   "The Noisemakers."

130   *"the most beautiful girl going"*   Bender, *The Beautiful People*, p. 145.

131   *"the 'In' Crowd would love"*   Classified Advertisements.

131   *"You could be living it up"*   Classified Advertisements.

131   *"emphatically replaced the Four Hundred"*   Morrow, "The In Crowd and the Out Crowd," 12.

132   *"a teeny tiny dance"*   Ibid., p. 18.

132   *"a part of a horde"*   Ibid.

133   *"original without being beginners"*   Guinness, "Who's Chic, Who's with It?" 52.

133   *"rootless, bouillabaisse society"*   Winship, "New Callers Rule Old '400,'" 24.

133   *"these people are on the move so much"*   Ibid.

134   *"Honey, maybe I'll invite you"*   Lerman, "The Tiny Terror," 820.

134   *"an international list for the guillotine"*   Clarke, *Capote*, p. 371.

Chapter 11. Making the List

135   *"I had that list with me"*   Curtis, *The Rich and Other Atrocities*, p. 96.

136   *"I thought he was inventing the ball"*   Plimpton, *Truman Capote*, p. 249.

137   *He wanted to know*   Plimpton, *Truman Capote*, pp. 250–51.

137   *"in 90% of the cases"*   "Lawman, Capote Cut Interrogation Ruling," 7.

137   *During that visit*   Details about Katharine Graham's menus and guest lists can be found in the Katharine Graham Collection.

138   *Even television crews were there*   Clarke, *Too Brief a Treat*, p. 426.

142   *His recent play*   Elyse Summer, "Tiny Alice." *Curtain Up*, 1 November 2000, http://www.curtainup.com/tinyalice.html (accessed 11 October 2005).

142   *Advance sales were very strong*   Ibid.

142   *"I don't like the score or the leading lady"*   Ibid.

145   *"kicky, not stuffy"*   Morris, "The Kicky Look in Couture Clothes," 68.

145   *"a gauzy black gown"*   Curtis, "Gala Throng of Notables Attends Benefit Premiere," 41.

146   *"major agony"*   Plimpton, *Truman Capote*, p. 253.

147   *"Finding one hundred presentable"*   Capote, "Guests," 214.

147   *"You can keep your hundred extra men"*   Clarke, *Capote*, p. 370.

147   *"Apparently, many of these ladies"*   Capote, "Guests," 152.

149   *"I filled all the right-hand pages"*   Curtis, *The Rich and Other Atrocities*, p. 96.

150   *"What is Truman trying to prove?"*   Vickers, *Beaton in the Sixties*, p. 171.

Chapter 12. The Place to Be

152   *"Nobody gives a damn"*   Amory, *Who Killed Society?* p. 133.

152   *It was whispered*   Fairchild, *The Fashionable Savages*, p. 139.

152-153   *"He'd lined up things to tell you"*   Plimpton, *Truman Capote*, p. 231.

154   *Evie advised that a few duchesses never hurt*   Evie Backer to Truman Capote. Truman Capote Papers.

154   *"it's the only beautiful ballroom"*   Curtis, *The Rich and Other Atrocities*, p. 93.

154   *But his longtime friend Phyllis Cerf believed*   Plimpton, *Truman Capote*, p. 248.

155   *In fact, ninety percent of the hotel was reserved*   Brown, *The Plaza*, p. 32.

155   *Built by the Otis Elevator Company*   Ibid., p. 31.

156   *"the battle of the ballrooms"*   Curtis, "N.Y. Hilton Scoring in Battle of the Ballrooms," 40.

156   *The newly opened New York Hilton*   Curtis, "Gala Throng of Notables Attends Benefit Premiere," 41.

158   *"Peter," he said*   Duchin, personal interview.

160   *"Be cheerful"*   Lehman, *Dancing for All Occasions*, p. 186.

160   *"just force you to dance"* and *"knock you right out of your seat"*   "Slipping the Disque."

161   *In her classic book*   Post, *Etiquette in Society, in Business, in Politics, and at Home*, http://www.gutenberg.org/etext/14314 (accessed 8 August 2005).

162   *"If you haven't received"*   "The Eye." *Women's Wear Daily*, 18 September 1966.

Chapter 13. "Have You Heard?"

166   *"She would arrive at a fashion show"*   Bender, *The Beautiful People*, p. 97.

167   *but Bjorkman recognized*   Brady, "Halston In and Out of Fashion."

167   *"the beginning of modern fashion reportage"*   Schiro, "Eugenia Sheppard, Fashion Columnist, Dies," 15.

167   *"a dear little girl"*   Bender, *The Beautiful People*, p. 83.

168   *Sometimes, she had to depend*   Schiro, "Eugenia Sheppard, Fashion Columnist, Dies," 15.

168-169   *Cassini incurred the wrath*   Walls, *Dish*, p. 59.

169   *"walk into a room"* "No. 1 Society Snooper," 59.

169   *"Society Snippet"*   "People." *Time*, 1 November 1963.

169   *"refreshing irreverence"*   "Trilling from a New Tree," *Time*, 30 June 1967.

169   *"I adore Aileen Mehle"*   Kelly, *The Wonderful World of Women's Wear Daily*, p. 217.

170   *"I have the fastest eye in the house"*   "Kidding the Social Setup."

171   *Why not observe*   Greenwald, *A Woman of the Times*, p. 75.

171   *"Something has happened"*   Ibid.

171-172   *Curtis also noted*   Curtis, "Social Register Keeps Rockefeller," 43.

172   *"I bone up"* and *"third largest Jewish population"*   "Sociologist on the Society Beat."

172   *"caustic asides"* and *"quotations to let her subjects hang themselves"*   Greenwald, *A Woman of the Times*, p. 65.

172   *"He admits he is a genius"*   Ibid.

173   *His drawings were so stunning*   Norwich, "Fashion Illustrator Gets Show of His Own."

174   *"I started doing something"*   Ibid.

Chapter 14. How to Be Lovely

177   *"I don't go to parties"*   Wilson, "It Happened Last Night," 10.

177   *Lena Horne didn't want to go alone*   *Jet*, 15 December 1966.

177   *The writers Peter Matthiessen and William Styron*   Plimpton, *Truman Capote*, p. 255.

178   *"Almost all I invited accepted"*   Capote, "Guests," 214.

178   *"I feel like I fell"*   "Truman's Compote."

179   *"I'd love to have you come to my party"*   Plimpton, *Truman Capote*, p. 251.

179   *Truman's aunt, Marie Rudisall*   Clark, *Capote*, 374.

180   *"the only ball in 25 years"*   "In Cold Focus."

180   *"door prizes and table favors"*   Capote, "Guests," 214.

180   *As much as she wanted to attend the party*   Plimpton, *Truman Capote*, p. 253.

181   *"teen-age Garbo"*   "The Cockney Kid."

182   *"Eat, Eat, Eat Your Pounds Away"*   Trotta, "Eat, Eat, Eat Your Pounds Away," 72.

182   *"Craigie tones me up"*   "What to Do When Your Looks Go Wrong," 131.

183   *"Can't travel without the machine"*   "Vogue's Ready Beauty," 148.

183   *"tan all over"*   "Beauty Bulletin," Ibid., p. 103.

185   *When the moment came*   Bender, *The Beautiful People*, p. 275.

185   *"Are there things you love or hate about your hair?"*   Ibid.

185   *"Mr. Cool of the haute coiffure"*   Ibid.

186   *"That's enough!"*   "People and Their Hairpieces."

186   *Apparently, 1966 was a very good year*   Bender, *The Beautiful People*, p. 258.

186   *"The most important men"*   Ibid., p. 257.

186   *"rhinestones to diamonds"*   Lane, *Faking It*, p. 7.

187   *at in-set parties as often as his jewelry*   "They Bug Me."

Chapter 15. Plumage

189   *"In most women's lives"*   Proust, *The Guermantes Way*, p. x.

189   *Eugenia Sheppard suspected*   Sheppard, "Capote Has a Hot Idea."

189   *"I've never seen women"*   Ibid.

191   *Headed by the fashion director Ethel Frankau*   Herndon, *Bergdorf's on the Plaza*, p. 159.

193   *"They are walking out of the store"*   "Suits That Suit."

195   *"long, slim 'far-out' mysterious cool self"*   Betsey Johnson in an e-mail to Deborah Davis.

195   *"a prodigiously large dollop of joy"*   Birstein, *What I Saw at the Fair*, p. 206.

197   *"best dress this winter"*   Nemy, "Behind the Masks at Truman Capote's Party."

199   *"In Venice," he pointed out*   Adolfo personal interview with Deborah Davis.

200   *"A lot of birds donated"*   Collins, "A Night to Remember," 130.

200   *"Each mask is going to be different"*   Sheppard, "Capote Has a Hot Idea."

200   *"The ladies have killed me"*   Collins, "A Night to Remember," 130.

200   *"I am already 5'9" without added height"*   From the Katharine Graham Collection.

201   *"The ladies vote for Halston"*   *Women's Wear Daily*, 22 November 1966.

201   *"to make it a real black and white ball"* and *said that he and his wife*   Plimpton, *Truman Capote*, p. 263.

202   *Eula said that he planned*   "A Brush with Truman Capote."

203   *"lots of men"*   Sheppard, *World Journal Tribune*, 28 November 1966.

203   *"I think masked balls are wonderful"*   *Women's Wear Daily*, 11 November 1966.

203   *"Will the mask replace the frug?"*   Ibid.

204   *"No, repeat no, photographers"*   Mehle, "Capote at the Gate."

204-205 *"They're nice people"*   Ibid.

205   *"was about to crack"*   Robertson, "In Cold Focus," *Women's Wear Daily*, 11 November 1966, 1.

205   *"My nerves were jangling"*   Capote, "Guests," 214.

Chapter 16. The Clock Ticks

207   *"Going to Truman's ball?"*   Plimpton, *Truman Capote*, p. 256.

207   *her husband, Loel*   Ibid.

207   *"The compulsion of this crowd"*   "No. 1 Society Snooper," 59.

208   *but Caen wanted her own gown*   Plimpton, *Truman Capote*, p. 255.

209   *"What will Mrs. Paley say"*   "Eye." *Women's Wear Daily*, 28 November 1966.

211   *"as if we had arrived in a wagon"*   *Time* Archives.

212   *If Truman's ball*   Don Bacardy personal interview with Deborah Davis.

214   *"16 hosts and hostesses"*   *Time* Archives.

214-215 *"in the English style"*   "Eye." *Women's Wear Daily*, 29 November 1966.

215   *Maria Theresa Caen's wayward gown*   Plimpton, *Truman Capote*, p. 256.

215   *"I thought her father"*   Dwight, *Diana Vreeland*, p. 162.

216   *"Truman, you've done just a lovely job"*   "The Chosen People."

217   *"You ought to be an elevator operator"*   Plimpton, *Truman Capote*, p. 258.

217   *Then he sparred with Lawford*   Ibid.

217   *"'Frankly," said Pamela Hayward*   *Time* Archives.

217   *"exciting and terrifying"*   Graham, *Personal History*, p. 392.

Chapter 17. Night of Nights

220   *"I've seen a thousand just as exciting"*   Scott, "Capote Party: A Novel Affair," 3.

221   *"They rolled off the assembly line like dolls"*   Nemy, "Behind the Masks at Truman Capote's Party."

221   *"I didn't know it would be like this"*   Preston, "What They Wore with Their Masks," 48.

221   *"Oh, dear, what a catastrophe"*   Scott, "Capote Party: A Novel Affair," 3.

222   *Suzy responded*   Sheppard, "The Capote Caper."

223   *"They turned on the (Klieg) lights"*   Plimpton, *Truman Capote*, p. 259.

223   *"dirty gabardine"*   Ibid., p. 276.

223   *"It just shows"*   Scott, "Capote Party: A Novel Affair," 3.

223   *"If you don't know"*   Wilson, *Bucks County Courier Times*.

223   *"The action is on the staircase"*   Bjorkman, "The Chosen People."

225   *"It itches and I can't see"*   "Truman's Compote."

225   *but he did not persist*   *Time* Archives.

226   *"That's the last thing I'll tell you"*   Aarons, "Society of the Sixties."

226   *"Whew, we're working hard"*   Sheppard, "The Capote Caper."

227   *"stark"*   Jean Harvey Vanderbilt, personal interview with Deborah Davis.

228   *"a rave review"*   Curtis, "David Merrick, Taking a Cue from Capote, Considers a Party of His Own," 90.

228   *"It's weird"*   *Time* Archives.

228   *"While he played, Duchin nodded"*   Curtis, *The Rich and Other Atrocities*, p. 88.

229   *"You certainly cut a mean rug"*   Plimpton, *Truman Capote*, p. 263.

229   *"in a fashion that Fred Astaire"*   Capote, "Guests," 214.

230   *He wanted to rip it off*   Bachardy personal interview.

230   *"Aren't we having the most wonderful time?"*   Plimpton, *Truman Capote*, p. 270.

230-231 *He called over a security guard*   Capote, "Guests," 214.

231   *Time described them*   *Time* Archives.

232   *"You know, I think there's nothing Truman can't do"*   *Time* Archives.

232   *Mrs. Kennedy marveled*   Gill, "Rose Kennedy, Remembering a New York Night," 28.

233   *Gianni Agnelli and the "friends of Gianni"*   Plimpton, *Truman Capote*, p. 273.

234   *"whirled like a flurry of snowflakes"*   Capote, "Guests," 214.

234   *"It was just what it set out to be"*   "Evening at the Plaza," *Newsweek*, 12 December 1966: 66–67.

234   *"I just wanted to give a party for my friends"*   "Truman's Compote," 88–89.

Chapter 18. Publicity

236   *"Cinderella night"*   *Jet* Chicago, 15 December 1966.

237   *"never seen so many really magnificent women"*   Mehle, "The Capote Caper."

237   *"Marvelous!" "Sensational!"*   Ibid.

241   *"It made the party look more fabulous"*   *Time* Archives.

241   *"he (Truman) gave the New York Times his guest list"*   "Truman's Compote," 88–89.

241   *"the list was not obtained from me"*   "Letter to the Editor." *Time*, 12 December 1966.

241   *"cleverly contrived to acquire"*   Capote, "Guests," 214.

242   *"It was awful, really awful"*   Buckley, "The Politics of Truman Capote's Ball," *Esquire*, 12 December 1967.

242   *"You can't write with people around you"*   Curtis, "David Merrick, Taking a Cue from Capote, Considers a Party of His Own," 90.

243   *"No one has been more astonished"*   Schlesinger, "Katharine Graham: New Power in the American Press," *Vogue*, 1 January 1967: 108.

243   *Kay's son-in-law*   Katharine Graham Collection.

243   *That night*   Plimpton, *Truman Capote*, p. 268.

244   *"one of the more terrible parties"*   Ibid., p. 270.

244   *"I've never seen such ghettoizing"*   Ibid., p. 263.

244   *"Is this what we flew over for?"*   La Ferla, "Unearthing the Notebook That Unnerved Society."

245   *"While the two bands are blaring"*   Vickers, *Beaton in the Sixties*, p. 171.

245   *His article, "The Party"*   Hamill, "The Party," 45.

246   *"bear to think of my country's future"*   Private Charles Rosner, letter to editor, *Time*, 23 December 1966.

246   *"If this is what it takes"*   "Who's Beautiful."

246   *"with a single fling"*   Baker, "Observer: Truman Capote's Gift to Literature," *New York Times*, 8 December 1966.

247   *"a trial membership"*   Cannel, "Cannel at Bay: Possible Gifts Suggested for Man 'with Everything'" a-11.

Chapter 19. Hangover

251   *"There's something terribly wrong"*   Clarke, *Capote*, p. 408.

252   *"I'm worried about our friend, Truman"*   Katharine Graham letter to Bob Wells. Katharine Graham Collection.

255   *The book appeared*   Clarke, *Capote*, p. 527.

255   *"Don Señor Truman Capote"*   Collins, "A Night to Remember," 139.

Bibliography

Original Documents

The Katharine Graham Collection

Truman Capote Papers, Manuscripts and Archives Division, the New York Public Library, Astor, Lenox, and Tilden Foundations

Andrew Lyndon's Letters to Elizabeth Hylton

Articles and Periodicals

Numerous issues of the *New York Times*, *Women's Wear Daily*, *Vogue*, and *Harper's Bazaar* provided valuable information about Truman Capote, the Black and White Ball, the party guests, and the history and culture of the 1960s. Specific editions and issues of these and other periodicals consulted include:

Esquire. December 1967.

Jet. 15 December 1966.

Life. 7 January 1966.

Life. 8 December 1966.

Aarons, Leroy. "Society of the Sixties." *Washington Post*. 29 November 1966.

Alexander, Shana. *Life*. 18 February 1966.

Bachrach, Judy. "La Vita Agnelli." *Vanity Fair*. May 2003: 200.

Bender, Marylin. "The New Society, Young and Daring, Swings into Style." *New York Times*. 14 December 1964: 47.

"Books . . . Authors." *New York Times*. 30 April 1948: 21.

Brady, James. "Halston In and Out of Fashion." *Chronicle-Telegram*. 19 April 1990.

"A Brush with Truman Capote." *World Journal Tribune*. 25 November 1966.

Cannell, Ward. "Cannell at Bay: Possible Gifts Suggested for Man 'with Everything.'" *The Lima News*. 22 December 1966.

Capote, Truman. "Guests." *McCall's*. February 1977.

"Caught Short." *Time*. December 1967.

"The Chosen People." *Women's Wear Daily*. 29 November 1966.

"The Cockney Kid." *Time*. 11 November 1966.

Collins, Amy Fine. "A Night to Remember." *Vanity Fair*. July 1996.

"The Country below the Surface." *Time*. 21 January 1966: 83.

Curtis, Charlotte. "David Merrick, Taking a Cue from Capote, Considers Party of His Own." *New York Times*. December 1966: 90.

———. "Gala Throng of Notables Attends Benefits Premiere." *New York Times*. 22 October 1964: 41.

———. "N.Y. Hilton Scoring in Battle of the Ballrooms." *New York Times*. 25 June 1963: 40.

———. "Social Register Keeps Rockefeller." *New York Times*. 27 November 1963: 43.

———. "They Keep the Charity Balls Rolling." *New York Times*. 22 May 1966: 88.

"The Cushing Sisters." *Life*. 11 August 1947: 41-44.

"Cutting Room." *Newsweek*. 17 January 1966: 54.

Dougherty, Page. "Vanity on the Potomac." *New York Times*. 19 January 1947: 19.

"Eye." *Women's Wear Daily*. 29 November 1966.

Fremont-Smith, Elliot. "Literature-by-Consensus." *New York Times*. 26 January 1966: 28.

Gill, Brendan. "Rose Kennedy, Remembering a New York Night." *New Yorker*. 26 January 2005: 28.

Gilroy, Harry. "A Book in New Form Earns $2 Million for Truman Capote." *New York Times*. 31 January 1966.

Guinness, Gloria. "Who's Chic, Who's with It?" *Harper's Bazaar*. July 1965.

Hamill, Pete. "The Party." *New York Post*. 29 November 1966: 45.

Howard, Jane. "A Six-Year Literary Vigil." *Life*. 7 January 1966: 70–76.

"In Cold Blood . . . An American Tragedy." *Newsweek*. 24 January 1966: 59–63.

"Kansas Lawman, Wife, Give NY Elite an Excuse for Party." *Topeka State Journal*. 16 November 1965.

"Kidding the Social Set-Up." *Time*. 24 September 1965.

La Ferla, Ruth. "Unearthing the Notebook That Unnerved Society." *New York Times*. 25 November 2001.

"Lawman, Capote Cut Interrogation Ruling." *Chronicle-Telegram*. 22 July 1966.

Lerman, Leo. "The Tiny Terror: A Capote Memoir." *Vogue*. September 1967: 820.

Mehle, Aileen. "Capote at the Gate." *World Journal Tribune*. 10 November 1966.

———. "The Capote Caper." *World Journal Tribune*. 29 November 1966.

"A Millionaire's Mission." *Life*. February 1957: 51.

Morris, Bernadine. "The Kicky Look in Couture Clothes." *New York Times*. 9 November 1966: 68.

Morrow, Sherman L. "The In Crowd and the Out Crowd." *New York Times*. July 1965.

Nemy, Enid. "Behind the Masks at Truman Capote's Masked Ball." *New York Times*. 29 November 1966.

Nichols, Lewis. "In and Out of Books." *New York Times*. 22 February 1966: 268.

"No. 1 Society Snooper." *Life*. 11 November 1966: 59.

"The Noisemakers." *Time*. 14 December 1959.

Norwich, William. "Fashion Illustrator Gets Show of His Own." *New York Observer*. 15 November 2004.

"Open End." *Time*. 20 July 1962.

"People and Their Hairpieces." *Vogue*. June 1966.

"People Are Talking About." *Vogue*. 15 October 1965: 94–95.

"People Who Read and Write." *New York Times*. 15 February 1948: BR8.

Preston, Ruth. "What They Wore with Their Masks." *New York Post*. 29 November 1966: 48.

"Psychopathic Ills Are Emotional, Not Due to a Lack of Intelligence." *New York Times*. 3 April 1944: 24.

Schiro, Anne-Marie. "Eugenia Sheppard, Fashion Columnist, Dies." *New York Times*. 12 November 1984: 15.

Scott, Lael. "Capote Party: A Novel Affair." *New York Post*. 29 November 1966.

Sheppard, Eugenia. "Capote Has a Hot Idea." *World Journal Tribune*. 18 October 1966.

———. *World Journal Tribune*. 28 November 1966.

"Slipping the Disque." *Time*. 3 March 1964.

Smith, William D. "Advertising: A Success Money Didn't Buy." *New York Times*. 20 February 1966: 16.

"Sociologist on the Society Beat." *Time*. 19 February 1965.

"Suits That Suit." *Time*. 14 October 1966.

Summer, Elyse. "Tiny Alice." *Curtain Up*. 1 November 2000.

"They Bug Me." *Newsweek*. 28 November 1966.

Trotta, Gerri. "Eat, Eat, Eat Your Pounds Away." *Harper's Bazaar*. July 1965: 72.

"Truman's Compote." *Time*. 9 December 1966.

"Vogue." 15 January 1967.

"Vogue's Ready Beauty." *Vogue*. June 1966: 103.

Walters, Barbara. "Jackie Kennedy's Perplexing Sister." *Good Housekeeping*. March 1963: 30.

Warren, Virginia Lee. "Home Up to $166,000 Sweet Home." *New York Times*. 16 February 1966: 38.

"What to Do When Your Looks Go Wrong." *Vogue*. 15 April 1967: 131.

"Who's Beautiful." *The Valley Independent*. December 1966.

Wilson, Earl. *Bucks County Courier Times*. 2 December 1966.

———. "It Happened Last Night." *The Times Recorder*. December 1966: 10.

Winship, Frederick. "New Callers Rule Old 400." *The Lima News*. 3 December 1966.

Books

Amory, Cleveland. *The Last Resorts*. New York: Harper, 1948.

———. *Who Killed Society?* New York: Harper & Brothers, 1960.

Amory, Cleveland, ed. *Celebrity Register*. New York: Harper & Row, 1963.

Avedon, Richard, and Truman Capote. *Observations*. New York: Simon & Schuster, 1959.

Batterberry, Michael and Ariane. *On the Town in New York*. New York: Routledge, 1999.

Bender, Marylin. *The Beautiful People*. New York; Coward-McCann, 1967.

Birstein, Ann. *What I Saw at the Fair*. New York: Welcome Rain, 2003.

Blumenthal, Ralph. *Stork Club*. Boston: Little, Brown, 2001.

Brown, Eve. *The Plaza*. New York: Meredith Press, 1967.

———. *The Plaza Cookbook*. Englewood Cliffs, N.J.: Prentice Hall, 1972.

Broyard, Anatole. *Kafka Was the Rage*. New York: Vintage, 1993.

Capote, Truman. *Answered Prayers*. New York: Vintage, 1994.

———. *A Christmas Memory*. New York: Modern Library, 1996.

————. *Music for Chameleons*. New York: Vintage, 1994.

Clarke, Gerald. *Capote: A Biography*. New York: Carroll & Graff, 2001.

————. *Too Brief a Treat*. New York: Random House, 2004.

Curtis, Charlotte. *The Rich and Other Atrocities*. New York: Harper & Row, 1976.

DuBois, Diana. *In Her Sister's Shadow*. Boston: Little, Brown & Company, 1995.

Dunne, Dominick. *The Way We Lived Then: Recollections of a Well-Known Name Dropper*. New York: Crown, 1999.

Dwight, Eleanor. *Diana Vreeland*. New York: William Morrow, 2002.

Evans, Peter. *Nemesis: The True Story of Aristotle Onassis, Jackie O, and the Love Triangle That Brought Down the Kennedys*. New York: Regan, 2004.

Fairchild, John. *The Fashionable Savages*. New York: Doubleday, 1965.

Frommer, Myrna Katz, and Harvy Frommer. *It Happened in Manhattan*. New York: Berkley, 2001.

Gathje, Curtis. *At the Plaza*. New York: St. Martin's, 2000.

Grafton, David. *The Sisters*. New York: Villard Books, 1992.

Graham, Katharine. *Personal History*. New York: Vintage, 1998.

Graham, Katharine, ed. *Katharine Graham's Washington*. New York: Alfred A. Knopf, 2002.

Greenwald, Marylin S. *A Woman of the Times*. Athens: Ohio University Press, 1999.

Grobel, Lawrence. *Conversations with Capote*. New York: Da Capo, 2000.

Guest, C. Z. *First Garden*. New York: Rizzoli, 1976.

Herndon, Booton. *Bergdorf's on the Plaza*. New York: Alfred A. Knopf, 1956.

Heymann, C. David. *The Georgetown Ladies' Social Club*. New York: Atria Books, 2003.

Homberger, Eric. *Mrs. Astor's New York*. New Haven, Conn.: Yale University Press, 2002.

Kelly, Katie. *The Wonderful World of Women's Wear Daily*. New York: Saturday Review Press, 1972.

Kriendler, H. Peter. *"21."* Dallas: Taylor, 1999.

Kroessler, Jeffrey A. *New York Year by Year*. New York: New York University Press, 2002.

Lane, Kenneth Jay. *Faking It*. New York: Harry N. Abrams, 1995.

Laver, James, ed. *Memorable Balls*. London: Derek Verschoyle, 1954.

Lee, Harper. *To Kill a Mockingbird*. New York: Warner Books, 1988.

Lehman, Leona. *Dancing for All Occasions*. New York: Key, 1962.

Lehrer, Steven. *Explorers of the Body*. New York; Doubleday, 1979.

Lynes, Russell. *The Taste Makers*. New York: Harper & Brothers, 1955.

Marwick, Arthur. *The Sixties Cultural Revolution in Britain, France, Italy, and the United States*. Oxford: Oxford University Press, 1998.

Matthau, Carol. *Among the Porcupines*. New York: Ballantine, 1992.

Moates, Marianne. *A Bridge of Childhood*. New York: Henry Holt, 1999.

Monroeville: The Search for Harper Lee's Maycomb. Monroe County: Arcadia, 1999.

Moorhead, Lucy. *Entertaining in Washington*. New York: Putnam, 1978.

Plimpton, George. *Truman Capote: In Which Various Friends, Enemies., Acquaintances, and Detractors Recall His Turbulent Career*. New York: Doubleday, 1997.

Post, Emily. *Ettiquette in Society, in Business, in Politics, and at Home*. New York: Funk and Wagnalls, 1922.

Proust, Marcel. *The Guermantes Way*. New York: Viking, 2004.

Radziwill, Lee. *Happy Times*. New York: Assouline, 2000.

Rasponi, Lanfranco. *The International Nomads*. New York: Putnam, 1966.

Rudisill, Marie. *The Southern Haunting of Truman Capote*. Nashville: Cumberland House, 2000.

Saroyan, Aram. *Trio*. New York: Penguin Books, 1985.

The Sixties Chronicles. Lincolnwood, Ill.: Legacy Publishing, 2004.

Smith, Sally Bedell. *In All His Glory*. New York: Simon & Schuster, 1990.

———. *Reflected Glory: The Life of Pamela Churchill*. New York: Simon & Schuster, 1996.

Stanton, Robert J. *Truman Capote: A Primary and Secondary Bibliography*. Boston: G. K. Hall & Company, 1980.

Tappert, Annette, and Slim Keith. *Slim: Memories of a Rich and Imperfect Life*. New York: Simon & Schuster, 1990.

Tappert, Annette, and Diana Edkins. *The Power of Style*. New York: Crown, 1994.

Vanderbilt, Gloria. *It Seemed Important at the Time: A Romance Memoir*. New York: Simon & Schuster, 2004.

Vickers, Hugo, ed. *Beaton in the Sixties: The Cecil Beaton Diaries as He Wrote Them, 1965–1969*. New York: Alfred A. Knopf, 2004.

Waggoner, Susan. *Nightclub Nights*. New York: Rizzoli, 2001.

Walls, Jeanette. *Dish*. New York: Perennial, 2000.

Werth, Barry. *The Scarlet Professor*. New York: Anchor Books, 2001.

Wolfe, Tom. *The Kandy-Kolored Tangerine-Flake Streamline Baby*. New York: Bantam, 1999.

Zilkha, Bettina. *Ultimate Style*. New York: Assouline, 2004.

Credits

Quoted material

Grateful acknowledgment is made to Random House, Inc. for permission to quote from *Too Brief a Treat* by Gerald Clarke, copyright 2004, and for reprinting the New York Times advertisement for *Other Voices, Other Rooms*, copyright © 1948 by Random House, Inc. Used by permission of Random House. "Chicken Hash Truman Capote" reprinted with the permission of Simon & Schuster Adult Publishing Group, from *The Plaza Cookbook* by Eve Brown. Copyright © 1970 by Eve Brown. Grateful acknowledgment is made to the estate of Mary McGrory for permission to quote from her letter to Katharine Graham. Grateful acknowledgment is made to the estate of Katharine Graham for permission to use materials from the Katharine Graham Collection.

Text illustrations

Alfred Eisenstaedt/Getty Images: 45; Bert and Richard Morgan/Getty Images: 55; Bettmann/Corbis: 88 and 222; Carl T. Gossett Jr./New York Times: 96; Esquire Magazine: 249; Kenneth Paul Block/ WWD Archives: 238; Keystone/Getty Images: 71; Maning/New York Times: 109, 125, 166, and 188; Museum of the City of New York: ii and 191; Tony Palmieri/WWD Archives, Fairchild Publications, Inc.: 153; Truman Capote Papers, Manuscripts and Archives Division, The New York Public Library, Astor, Lenox and Tilden Foundation: i, 136, and 177. Permission to include several images from Truman Capote's black and white notebook has been kindly granted by the Truman Capote Literary Trust, Alan U. Schwartz, Trustee.

Insert illustrations

Truman and Arch Persons: Author's collection; Truman and costumed friends: Author's collection; Nina and Joe Capote: Truman Capote Papers, Manuscripts and Archives Division, The New York Public Library, Astor, Lenox and Tilden Foundation; Truman and Jaguar: Author's collection; Hickock and Smith: Copyright © by Bettmann/Corbis; Kay Graham: Katharine Graham Collection; Black and white notebook and page from notebook: Truman Capote Papers, Manuscripts and Archives Division, The New York Public Library, Astor, Lenox and Tilden Foundation. Permission to include several images from Truman Capote's black and white notebook has been kindly granted by the Truman Capote Literary Trust, Alan U. Schwartz, Trustee. Plaza Hotel: Author's collection; Adolfo drawing courtesy of

283

Index

NOTE: Page numbers in *italics* refer to illustrations and photos.